Sermons to Young Women

SERMONS

TO

YOUNG WOMEN.

382

SERMONS

TO

YOUNG WOMEN:

BY JAMES FORDYCE, D.D.

THE EIGHTH EDITION,

CORRECTED AND GREATLY ENLARGED.

DUBLIN.

Printed by Campbell and Shea,

FOR W GILBERT, P BYRNE, P WOGAN, W, JONES, AND
J MILLIKEN.

1796.

PREFACE.

THE corruption of the age is a complaint with many men who contribute to increafe it. In like manner, the inattention of the people is a complaint with many preachers who are themfelves to blame. A dull difcourfe naturally produces a liftlefs audience; there being few hearers who will attend to that by which their hearts are not engaged, or their imaginations entertained. To entertain the imagination principally, were a poor, and indeed a vicious aim in a preacher. To engage the heart, with a view to mend it, fhould be his grand ambition. Any farther than as it may prove fome way or other fubfervient to that, entertainment fhould never be admitted into a Sermon. There, to fay the truth, we feldom meet with too much of the latter. Would to God we often met there with more of the former!

The

The Author of the following Difcourfes was prompted to publifh them, from an unfeigned regard for the Female Sex; from a fervent zeal for the beft interefts of fociety, on which he believes their difpofitions and deportment will ever have a mighty influence; and, laftly, from a fecret defire long felt of trying whether that ftyle of preaching, which to him appears, upon the whole, adapted to an auditory above the vulgar rank, might fucceed on a fubject of this nature; nothing of the kind, that he knows of, having been endeavoured before, in any language. That the attempt was as difficult as it was new, and that this very difficulty was probably the caufe of its having been hitherto declined, he could not help confidering at the fame time; and the confideration created fuch a diffidence of fuccefs, as made him defirous of concealing himfelf. As to the candour of the public, he entertained no diftruft. On that he chearfully relied for every proper allowance, more efpecially refpecting fome fingularities in the mode of compofition, upon which we would not have ventured but for the uncommonnefs of the occafion. Nor has he been difappointed. But the public has not fhewn candour only; it

has

has even exercifed indulgence : perfons of both fexes, of various denominations, and of different taftes, have joined in expreffing the moft gene-rous approbation. The fears that attended the firft experiment being thus difpelled, there was no longer any reafon for fuppreffing the writer's name. And indeed it had been in vain, the majority of his readers having immediately dif-covered him.

Their very favourable opinion, fo far beyond his expectation, affords him peculiar pleafure, as it raifes his hopes, that what is here fuggefted may, by the bleffing of heaven, which he hum-bly implores, contribute to the improvement of the moft agreeable part of the creation, and by confequence both to their own felicity, and that of millions with whom they are now, or may be hereafter, connected. In this cafe, it will add to his happinefs to reflect, that he has rendered the plain voice of Truth acceptable amongft thofe who are daily tempted by the firen-fong of Flat-tery.

The preacher is willing to hope, that women of moft conditions, and at all ages, may meet with fome ufeful counfel, or fome falutary hint, should

should curiofity incite them to look into thefe difcourfes. Should any of thofe young perfons in
genteel life, to whom they are chiefly addreffed,
deem the reprehenfions they contain too fevere,
or too indifcriminate ; he can only fay, that as
all were dictated by friendfhip no lefs than by conviction, fo he wifhes it to be underftood, that
many were occafioned by a particular obfervation
of thofe characters and manners which are efteemed fafhionable amongft the YOUNG and the GAY
of this metropolis. In the Country (a denomina-
nation which, as matters are commonly conducted, he can by no means allow to the neighbourhood of London) the contagion of vice and folly,
it may be prefumed, is not fo epidemical. In
fhort, he is perfuaded, that women of worth and
fenfe are to be found every where, but moft frequently in the calm of retreat, and amidft the
coolnefs of recollection.

CONTENTS

CONTENTS.

x CONTENTS.

CONTENTS.

SERMON VIII.

On Female Virtue, with Intellectual Accomplishments

1. TIM II 8, 9.

I will——that women adorn themselves with Sobriety.

PROV IV 5, 6, 8, 9.

SERMON IX

On Female Piety.

1 TIM II 10.

—Which becometh women professing Godliness

PROV. XXXI 30.

SERMON X.

xii   C O N T E N T S.

SERMON I.

On the Importance of the Female Sex, especially the Younger Part.

I Tim. ii 8, 9, 10

I will—that women adorn themselves in modest apparel, with shamefacedness and sobriety, not with broidered hair, or gold or pearls, or costly array, but (which becometh women professing godliness) with good works.

"CAN a maid forget her ornaments, or a bride her " attire ?" is the Almighty's question by the mouth of a prophet Splendid attire and rich ornaments are in many places of scripture spoken of without censure, and in some with approbation "The king's daughter," says the psalmist, "is all glorious within " he adds, "her clothing "is of wrought gold, she shall be brought unto the king "in raiment of needle-work." The Virtuous Woman is in the Proverbs applauded for "clothing her houshold with " scarlet, and herself with silk and purple " The Creator has poured unbounded beauty over his works Witness the flowers of the field, celebrated by our Saviour himself, witness the gems of the mine, mentioned in the Revelation of St John, as employed to give additional lustre even

B

to

to the New Jerusalem, witnefs, in general, all that wonderful colouring, and thofe fair proportions, that pleafe the eye, and amufe the imagination, with endlefs variety. Who can refift, who indeed ought to refift, the agreeable effect. Surely the author of Nature does nothing in vain He furely meant, that by beholding her with delight we might be led to copy her with care, and from contemplating the inferior orders of beauty rife to the admiration of that which is fupreme

As he has furnifhed infinite materials for the exercife and entertainment, no lefs than for the provifion and accommodation of man, fo has he infpired that genius, and fupplied thofe powers, by which they are moulded into form, and heightened into fplendor In faying this we are warranted by revelation itfelf, where we are exprefsly told, that " the fpirit of the Lord filled Bezaleel, Aholiab," and others, " with wifdom, and underftanding, and know-
" ledge, to devife and work all manner of curious and cun-
" ning works of the carver of wood, the cutter of ftones,
" the jeweller, the engraver, the weaver, the embroiderer
" in blue and in purple, in fcarlet and in fine linen."
What multitudes are eafily employed and comfortably fupported by thefe and fuch like ornamental arts, hardly any one is ignorant

That works of ingenuity and elegance are particularly becoming in your fex, and that the ftudy of them ought to enter into female education as much as poffible, all, I think, are agreed In fine, none but the moft contracted, or the moft prejudiced, will deny that women may avail themfelves of every decent attraction, that can lead to a ftate for which they were manifeftly formed, and that, fhould they by any neglect of their perfons render themfelves lefs amiable than God has made them, they would fo far difappoint the defign of their creation

Thefe

These considerations will, I apprehend, be thought more than sufficient to prove, that the passage of St. Paul which I have selected for my text is not to be understood strictly and absolutely, where it seems to condemn female ornament in general It was common with the Hebrews to express comparative precepts in a positive manner, as might be shown from a number of texts But you are not disposed to doubt it What then is our apostle's meaning? ' I ' would exhort, and even enjoin christian women, always ' to dress with decency and moderation, never to go be- ' yond their circumstances, nor aspire above their station, ' so as to preclude or hinder works of mercy, not to value ' themselves on their dress, or despise others more mean- ' ly habited: in short, never to spend too much time or ' thought on the embellishment of the body, but always to ' prefer the graces of the mind, modesty, meekness, pru- ' dence, piety, with all virtuous and charitable occupations; ' all beautiful and useful accomplishments suited to ' their rank and condition These are the chief orna- ' ments of their sex, these will render them truly lovely as ' Women, and as Christians, these will more peculiarly ' become them ' Such, I conceive, is the doctrine of this divine writer, and of his fellow apostle St. Peter on the same subject; and such, in substance, was the doctrine of some of the wisest heathens Give me leave to quote one of them: " It is not gold, nor emeralds, nor purple, " but modesty, gravity, and decent deportment, that can " truly adorn a woman " Ah, my fair friends, how at- tractive and how happy might all of you be, were you ef- fectually persuaded to form yourselves on such maxims, and what singular pleasure would it afford the preacher, if by the blessing of GOD he might so persuade you!

Princes, it has been said, and young women, seldom hear truth It is a melancholy consideration Flattery you have often heard, and sometimes, I doubt not listened to,

May he hope for your attention, whofe character forbids him to flatter, and whofe principles are equally averfe to it? Nothing, I am convinced, can be more pernicious to your beft interefts, than the adulation with which you are fo early and fo generally entertained. You will not look for it here. But be not afraid, on the other hand, of the bitternefs of reproach, or the bluntnefs of incivility. If any thing fhould appear harfh, be affured it proceeds from real regard. We would not willingly offend, we are naturally folicitous to pleafe you, but we dare not promote your pleafure at the expence of your improvement. To tendernefs and refpect you are entitled; but certainly faithful and candid admronition is not incompatible with the latter, and of the former, if I be not miftaken, it is the trueft proof.

The Almighty has thrown you upon the protection of our fex. To yours we are indebted on many accounts. He that abufes you difhonours his mother. Virtuous women are the fweetners, the charm of human life. "A Vir-"tuous Woman—her price is far above rubies." This is not flattery, it is juft praife; and that every one of you may deferve fuch commendation, is my earneft prayer. Much, I am fure, depends on you. And this fhall be my Firft Point, to which I will devote the prefent difcourfe, as a proper foundation for what is to follow. That I thus addrefs you in particular is, principally owing to the idea I have formed of your confequence.

He that depreciates your fex is as unkind to fociety, as he is unjuft to you. Yet to do fo in your abfence is, I am forry to fay, too common with many men, with thofe very men that fcothe you to your faces, and are dupes to your fmiles. Is this either manly or fair? Becaufe there are foolifh and vicious women, does it follow that there are hardly any other? Were fuch an opinion to prevail
generally

generally, what would become of human kind? Were fo ungracious a fyftem once eftablifhed, is there not reafon to fear, it would foon grow to be too well founded? The world, we know, is mightily influenced by reputation Applaufe incites and animates, contempt has the contrary effect A concern for character is, from their conftitution, education, and circumftances, particularly ftrong in women; in all but thofe who, having loft their native honours, have with them loft their fenfe of fhame, an infamy to which they would have hardly defcended, had they not firft funk in their own eftimation.

That admired maxim of heathen antiquity, " Reverence thyfelf," feems to me peculiarly proper for a woman. She that does not reverence herfelf muft not hope to be refpected by others I would therefore remind you of your own value By encouraging you to entertain a juft efteem for yourfelves, I would on one hand guard you againft every thing degrading, and on the other awaken your ambition to act up to the beft ftandard of your fex, to afpire at every amiable, every noble quality that is adapted to your ftate, or that can infure the affection and preferve the importance to which you were born. Now this importance is very great, whether we confider you in your prefent fingle con-dition, or as afterwards connected in wedlock

Confidering you in your prefent fingle condition, I would begin where your duty in fociety begins, by putting you in mind how deeply your Parents are interefted in your beha-viour For the fake of the argument, I fuppofe your pa-rents to be alive Thofe that have had the misfortune to be early deprived of theirs, are commonly left to the care of fome friend or guardian, who is underftood to fupply their place; and to fuch my remarks on this head will not be altogether inapplicable. But I muft likewife fuppofe that your parents deferve the name, that they are really

concerned

concerned for your virtue and welfare ———Great God! are there then any of hy creatures so unnatural, as to neglect the culture and happiness of the children thou hast given them? Yes, and worse than to neglect it "Be asto-"nished, O ye heavens at this!" There are beings called Parents, and Christian parents, who are at pains to introduce their unexperienced offspring to folly, to vice, to every practice that can plunge them in misery!—What, Mothers too, and mothers "professing godliness!" Is it possible that they can train up the fruit of their womb, their own daughters, to dishonour and destruction? Alas! it is done every day, and passes unregarded There is not perhaps in the whole science of female vanity, female luxury, or female falshood, a single article that is not taught, and also exemplified, by those Christian Mothers, to the poor young creatures whom every dictate of nature, as well as every principle of the gospel, should engage their parents to bring up in modesty, sobriety, and simplicity of manners What words can paint the guilt of such a conduct?

Are you who now hear me blest with parents that even in these times, and in this metropolis, where all the corruption and futility of these times are concentred, discover a zeal for your improvement and salvation? How thankful should you be for the mighty blessing! Would you show that you are thankful? Do nothing to make them unhappy; Do all in your power to give them delight. Ah, did you but know how much it is in your power to give them! —But who can describe the transports of a breast truly parental, on beholding a daughter shoot up like some fair but modest flower, and acquire, day after day, fresh beauty and growing sweetness, so as to fill every eye with pleasure, and every heart with admiration, while, like that same flower, she appears unconscious of her opening charms, and only rejoices in the sun that clears, and the hand that shelters her?

her? In this manner, shall you, my lovely friend, repay most acceptably a part (you never can repay the whole) of that immense debt you owe for all the pains and fears formerly suffered, and for all the unutterable anxieties daily experienced, on your account,

Perhaps you are the only daughter, perhaps the only child of your mother, and her a widow. All her cares, all her sensations point to you. Of the tenderness of a much loved and much lamented husband you are the sole remaining pledge. On you she often fixes her earnest melting eye, with watchful attention she marks the progress of your rising virtues; in every softened feature she fondly traces your father's sense, your father's probity. Something within her whispers, you shall live to be the prop and comfort of her age, as you are now her companion and friend. Blessed Lord, what big emotions swell her labouring soul! But lest, by venting them in your company, she should affect you too much, she silently withdraws to pour them forth in tears of rapture, a rapture only augmented by the sweetly sad remembrance that mingles with it, while at the same time it is exalted and consecrated doubly by ardent vows to heaven for your preservation and prosperity. Is there a young women that can think of this with indifference? Is there a young woman that can reverse the discription, suppose herself the impious creature that could break a widowed mother's heart, and support the thought?

When a daughter, it may be a favourite daughter, turns out unruly, foolish, wanton, when she disobeys her parents, disgraces her education, dishonours her sex, disappoints the hopes she had raised, when she throws herself away on a man unworthy of her, or if disposed, yet by his

or

or her fituation unqualified, to make her happy, what her parents in any of thefe cafes muft neceffarily fuffer, we may conjecture, they alone can feel

The world, I know not how, overlooks in our fex a thoufand irregularities, which it never forgives in yours: fo that the honour and peace of a family are, in this view, much more dependant on the conduct of daughters than of fons, and one young lady going aftray fhall fubject her relations to fuch difcredit and diftrefs, as the united good conduct of all her brothers and fifters, fuppofing them numerous, fhall fcarce ever be able to repair   But I prefs not any farther an argument fo exceedingly plain. We can prognofticate nothing virtuous, nothing happy, concerning thofe wretched creatures of either fex, that do not feel for the fatisfaction, eafe, or honour of their parents

Another and a principal fource of your importance is the very great and extenfive influence which you, in general, have with our fex   There is in female youth an attraction, which every man of the leaft fenfibility muft perceive   If affifted by beauty, it becomes in the firft impreffion irrefiftible   Your power fo far we do not affect to conceal. That He who made us meant it thus, is manifeft from his having attempered our hearts to fuch emotions. Would to God you knew how to improve this power to its nobleft ends! We fhould then rejoice to fee it encreafed, then indeed it would be encreafed of courfe   Youth and beauty fet off with fweetnefs and virtue, capacity and difcretion— what have they not accomplifhed?

Far be it from me, my fair hearers, to damp your fpirits, or to wifh in the leaft to abridge your triumphs   on the contrary, by affifting you to direct, we would contribute to exalt and extend them   We are always forry when we fee them mifplaced or abufed, and—I was going to add, there

there is nothing more common To give them their juft direction, is truly a nice point Power, fiom whatever fource derived, is always in danger of turning the head It has turned many an old one What then fhall become of a young woman, placed on fuch a precipice? What can balance or preferve her, but fobriety and caution, a good providence, and good advice?

There are few young women who do not appear agreeable in the eyes of fome men And what might not be done by the greater part of you to fecure folid efteem, and to promote general reformation, among our fex? Are fuch objects unworthy of your purfuit? or will ye fay, that thofe which frequently engage it are of fuperior or equal importance?

If men difcover that you ftudy to captivate them by an outfide only, or by little frivolous arts, there are, it muft be confefled, many of them who will rejoice at the difcovery, and while they themfelves feem taken by the lure, they will endeavour in reality to make you their prey Some more fentimental fpirits, who might be dazzled in the beginning, will be foon difabufed; and a few more honourable characters will fcorn to take advantage of your folly Folly moft undoubtedly it is, by a wrong application of your force, to lofe the fubftance for the fhadow.

Now and then a giddy youth may be caught But what is the fhallow admiration of an hundred fuch, or the fmooth addrefs of artful deftroyers, to the heartfelt refpect of men of worth and difcernment, or the well-earned praife of reclaiming were it but one offender? I verily believe you might reclaim a multitude I can hardly conceive that any man would be able to withftand the foft perfuafion of your words, but chiefly of your looks and actions, habitually exerted on the fide of goodnefs

" Were

" Were Virtue,' said an ancient philofopher, " to ap-
" pear amongſt men in vifible fhape, what vehement de-
" fires fhe would enkindle!" Virtue exhibited without affectation by a lovely young perfon, of improved underſtanding and gentle manners, may be faid to appear with
the moſt alluring afpect, furrounded by the Graces, and
that breaſt muſt be cold indeed which does not take fire at
the fight!

The influence of the fexes is, no doubt, reciprocal, but
I muſt ever be of opinion, that yours is the greateſt. How
often have I feen a company of men who were difpofed to
be riotous, checked all at once into decency by the accidental entrance of an amiable woman. while her good
fenfe and obliging deportment charmed them into at leaſt a
temporary conviction, that there is nothing fo beautiful as
female excellence, nothing fo delightful as female converfation in its beſt form! Were fuch conviction frequently
repeated, (and it would be frequently repeated, if fuch excellence and fuch converfation were more general) what
might we not expect from it at laſt? In the mean time, it
were eaſy to point out inſtances of the moſt evident reformation wrought on particular men, by their having happily conceived a paſſion for virtuous women, but among the
leaſt valuable of your fex, when have you known any that
were amended by the fociety or example of the better part
of ours?

To form the manners of men various caufes contribute;
but nothing, I apprehend, fo much as the turn of the women with whom they converfe. Thofe who are moſt con-
verſant with women of virtue and underſtanding will be always found the moſt amiable characters, other circumſtances being fuppofed alike. Such fociety, beyond every
thing elfe, rubs off the corners that give many of our fex

an

an ungracious roughnefs It produces a polifh more perfect, and more pleafing, than that which is received from
a general commerce with the world This laft is often fpe-
cious, but commonly fuperficial. The other is the refult
of gentler feelings, and a more elegant humanity, the
heart itfelf is moulded, habits of undiffembled courtefy are
formed, a certain flowing urbanity is acquired; violent
paffions, rafh oaths, coarfe jefts, indelicate language of
every kind, are precluded and difrelifhed Underftanding
and virtue, by being often contemplated in the moft engaging lights, have a fort of affimilating power I do not
mean, that the men I fpeak of will become feminine; but
their fentiments and deportment will contract a grace.
Their principles will have nothing ferocious or forbidding,
their affections will be chafte and foothing at the fame inftant In their cafe the Gentleman, the Man of worth,
the Chriftian, will all melt infenfibly and fweetly into one
another How agreeable the compofition! In the fame
way too, honourable love is infpired and cherifhed —Honourable love! that great prefervative of purity, that powerful foftener of the fierceft fpirit, that mighty improver of
the rudeft carriage, that all-fubduing, yet all-exalting principle of the human breaft, which humbles the proud, and
bends the ftubborn, yet fills with lofty conceptions, and
animates with a fortitude that nothing can conquer—what
fhall I fay more?—which converts the favage into a man,
and lifts the man into a hero! What a happy change fhould
we behold in the minds, the morals, and the demeanour of
our youth, were this charming paffion to take place of that
falfe and vicious gallantry which gains ground amongft us
every day, to the difgrace of our country, to the difcou-
ragement of holy wedlock, to the deftruction of health,
fortune, decency, refinement, rectitude of mind, and dignity of manners! For my part I defpair of feeing the effeminate, trifling, and diffolute character of the age reformed, fo long as this kind of gallantry is the mode But

it will be the mode, fo long as the prefent fafhionable fyftem of Female Education continues

Parents now a days almoft univerfally, down to the loweft tradefman, or mechanic, who to ape his fuperiors
ftrains himfelf beyond his circumftances, fend their daughters to Boarding-fchools   And what do they moftly learn
there? I fay, Moftly, for there are exceptions, and
fuch as do the Miftreffes real honour   Need I mention that,
making allowance for thofe exceptions, they learn chiefly
to drefs, to dance, to fpeak bad French, to prattle much
nonfenfe, to practife I know not how many pert conceited
airs, and in confequence of all to conclude themfelves Accomplifhed Women? I fay nothing here of the alarming
fuggeftions I have heard as to the corruption of their morals   Thus prepared they come forth into the world
Their parents, naturally partial, fancy them to be every
thing that is fine, and are impatient to fhew them, or, according to the fafhionable phrafe, to let them fee Company, by which is chiefly meant exhibiting them in public
places   Tnither at leaft many of them are conducted
The cafe is youth, and perhaps beauty   The effect of
both is heightened by all poffible means, at an expence frequently felt for a long time after   They are intoxicated
by fo many things concurring to deprive them of their little
fenfes   Gazers and flatterers they meet with every where
All is romance and diftraction, the extravagance of vanity,
and the rage of conqueft   They think of nothing that is
domeftic or rational   Alas! they were never taught it.
How to appear abroad with the greateft advantage, is the
main concern   In fubferviency to that, as well as from
the general love of amufement, Parties of Pleafure, as
they are called, become the prevailing demand.   The fame
difpofitions on the fide of the men, fometimes ftimulated by
a bad defign, often feconded by good nature, and not
feldom perhaps puthed on by the fear of appearing lefs ge-

nerous

nerous or lefs gallant, prompt them to keep pace with all
this folly   They are foon fired in the chace   every thing
is gay and glittering ; prudence appears too cold a monitor ;
gravity is deemed fevere , the ladies muft be pleafed ; mirth
and diverfion are all in all   The phantoms pafs , the female adventurers muft return home , it is needlefs to fay,
with what impreffions   The young gentlemen are not always under equal reftraint , their blood boils , the tavern,
the ftreets, the ftews, eke out the evening riot and madnefs conclude the fcene ; or if this fhould be prevented, it
is not difficult to imagine the diffipation that muft naturally
grow out of thofe idle gallantries often repeated   Nor fhall
we be furprifed to find the majority of our youth fo infignificant, and fo profligate   when to thefe we join the influence of bad or giddy women grown up, the infection of
the moft peftilent books, and the pattern of veterans in fin,
who are ever zealous to difplay the fuperiority of their talents by the number of their difciples, and fecretly folicitous by the ftrength of their party to make amends for the
weaknefs of their caufe.

That men are fometimes dreadfully fuccefsful in corrupting the women, cannot be denied   But do women on the
other fide never corrupt the men ?   I fpeak not at prefent
of thofe abandoned creatures that are the vifible ruin of fo
many of our unhappy youth, but I muft take the liberty to
fay that, amongft a number of your fex who are not funk
fo low, there is a forwardnefs, a levity of look, converfation and demeanour, unfpeakably hurtful to young men.
Their reverence for female virtue it in a great meafure de-
ftroys, it even tempts them to fufpect that the whole is a
pretence, that the fex are all of a piece   The confequences
of this, with regard to their behaviour while they remain
fingle, the prejudices it muft neceffarily produce againft
marriage, and the wild work it is likely to make if they ever
enter into that ftate, I leave you to imagine.

                                            Hitherto

Hitherto I have spoken only of the interest young women
have with our sex   Let me now say something of that
which they have with their Own   It is not perhaps so ex-
tensive as the other, but for obvious reasons it cannot be in-
considerable   Do they always use it to good purposes? Do
they never corrupt one another? Do none of them assist
the common enemy, those wicked and designing men that
are combined against the sex, especially against the innocent and unwary? Do the old never initiate the young
in those low arts of dissimulation and cunning, which a wise
woman cannot want, and which a worthy woman will not
practise? Do the young—But I hasten from so painful a
topic, to consider the Importance of your sex in another light
As you have certainly great influence at present, so,

In the next place, it may be probably in your power to
communicate much happiness, or to occasion much misery
hereafter   I think now of the chances you have to be connected in wedlock.   These it is impossible to calculate, but
there are not, I suppose, many young women who, at
one time or another, unless they themselves be in fault,
may not form that connexion with the usual prospects ; and
I say, that the men you marry, the children you bring,
and the community at large, will be all deeply interested in
your conduct

As to the first, I am not ignorant that there are some
men so grossly insensible, as to be for the most part little or
nothing affected by the temper or behaviour of their wives;
provided only they do not ruin their affairs   And in truth,
if those wives be ill tempered or ill behaved, such want of
feeling is so far well for the husbands   If otherwise, how
much are they themselves objects of compassion, thus condemned to drag a wretched life with beings, on whom all
their endeavours to delight are lost! How sensibly must
such a situation pain a delicate and ingenuous mind! What

can

can reconcile her to it, but the ftrongeft principles of Religion?

Some fordid or faturnine fpirits of either fex there may
be, who can fupport a connexion of this kind with a ftupid
indifference, plodding along through a tafelefs exiftence,
without attachment or gratitude, defire or hope. Whether
the cafe be very common, I leave others to decide. Of
both fexes there are certainly many who are not made of
fuch dull materials. With refpect to them———But furely it cannot be neceffary to difplay the felicity, or the woe,
which muft unavoidably arife to them from their partners.
Here indeed, as in moft inftances where the modes of life
happen to influence, it muft be allowed the men have the
advantage. If they find themfelves unequally yoked, they
are generally furnifhed with various means of beguiling
their wretchednefs at a diftance from home: whereas, if
fuch be the fate of the poor women, they are commonly
left to pine away in folitary mifery. For them fcarce any
allowance is made; to them little or no pity is fhown.
while the former make themfelves judges in their own
caufe, and the partial world is ready to fide with them. But
yet, if the ufages of that leave them often more room to
elude the ideas of domeftic diftrefs, the feelings of nature
will never fuffer them fairly to efcape it. A woman, it is
certain, if fhe be fo minded, has ftill the power of plague-
ing her partner out of every real enjoyment,—a power
however, of which nothing can juftify the exercife, and
which when exercifed is, like every other act of tyranny,
fure to recoil upon the tyrant.

It is natural for me to wifh well to my own fex; and
therefore you will not wonder, if I be folicitous for your
poffeffing every quality that can render you agreeable companions in a relation which of all others is the moft intimate,
fhould be the moft endearing, and muft be the happieft

or

or the worst But to this solicitude my friendship for you
is at least an equal motive Were the lower springs of self-
love to have no effect on your conduct, I must yet think,
that the more refined principles of generosity and goodness
ought to prompt it Ah! my young friends, what pleasure can be compared to that of conferring felicity? What
honour can be enjoyed by your sex, equal to that of show-
ing yourselves every way worthy of a virtuous tenderness
from ours? What can be conceived so properly female as
inspiring, improving, and continuing such a tenderness,
in all its charming extent? Contrasted with this, how unamiable, and how miserable, must we pronounce the
passion for ungentle command, for petulent dominion, so
shamefully indulged by some women as soon as they find
a man in their power!

But lastly, let us suppose you Mothers, a character
which, in due time, many of you will sustain How does
your importance rise! A few years elapsed, and I please
myself with the prospect of seeing you, my honoured au-
ditress, surrounded with a family of your own, dividing
with the partner of your heart the anxious, yet delightful
labour of training your common offspring to virtue and
society, to religion and immortality, while, by thus dividing it, you leave him more at leisure to plan and provide for you all, a task which he prosecutes with ten-fold
alacrity, when he reflects on the beloved objects of it,
and finds all his toils both soothed and rewarded by the
wisdom and address of your deportment to him and to
his children

I t imagine I behold you, while he is otherwise necessarily
engaged, casting your fond maternal regards round and
round into the pretty smiling circle, not barely to supply their happy wants, but chiefly to watch the gradual
openings of their minds, and to study the turns of their

                                                    various

various tempers, that you may " teach the young idea
" how to fhoot," and lead their paffions by taking hold of
their hearts　I admire the happy mixture of affection and
fkill which you difplay in affifting Nature, not forcing
her, in directing the underftanding, not hurrying it; in
exercifing without wearying the memory, and in mould-
ing the behaviour without conftraint.　I obferve you prudently overlooking a thoufand childifh follies　You forgive any thing but falfhood or obftinacy· you commend
as often as you can · you reprove only when you muft;
and then you do it to purpofe, with moderation and temper, but with folemnity and firmnefs, till you have carried your point　You are at pains to excite honeft emulation. you take care to avoid every appearance of partiality, to convince your dear charge, that they are all
dear to you, that fuperior merit alone can entitle to fuperior favour, that you will deny to none of them what is
proper, but that the kindeft and moft fubmiffive will be
always preferred.　At times you even partake in their innocent amufements, as if one of them; that they may love
you as their friend, while they revere you as their parent.
In graver hours, you infinuate knowledge and piety by
your converfation and example, rather than by formal lec-
tures and awful admonitions.　And finally, to fecure as far
as poffible the fuccefs of all, you dedicate them daily to God,
with the moft fervent fupplications for his bleffing ———
Thus you fhow yourfelf a confcientious and a judicious
mother at the fame moment, and in that light I view you
with veneration　I honour you as fuftaining a truly glorious character on the great theatre of humanity　Of the
part you have acted I look forward to the confequences,
direct and collateral, future and remote.　Thofe lovely
plants which you have reared I fee fpreading, and ftill fpreading from houfe to houfe, from family to family, with a
rich increafe of fruit.　I fee you diffufing virtue and happinefs through the human race; I fee generations yet un-
born rifing up to call you bleffed! I worfhip that Providence

which,

which has deſtined you for ſuch uſefulneſs, for ſuch felicity
I pity the man that is not charmed with the image of ſo
much excellence, an image which, in one degree or another, has been realized by many women of worth and underſtanding in every age I will add, an image which, when
realized, cannot fail of being contemplated with peculiar
delight by all the benevolent ſpirits of heaven, with the
Father and Saviour of the world at their head! And are
there, amongſt the ſons of men, any that will preſume to
deprec ate ſuch women, to ſpeak of them with an air of
ſuperiority, or to ſuggeſt that your ſex are not capable of
filling the more important ſpheres of life?

To quote the words of an old writer· " All mankind is
" the pupil and diſciple of female inſtitution the daugh-
" ters till they write women, and the ſons till the firſt ſeven
" years be paſt, the time when the mind is moſt ductile,
" and prepared to receive impreſſion, being wholly in the
" care and conduct of the mother" Alas! my fair country - women, why are not more of you ſtruck with ſuch conſiderations? Why, ye daughters of Britain, are ſo many
of you inferible to theſe brighteſt glories of your ſex?
Where is your love for your native country, which, by thus
exceeding, you might ſo nobly ſerve? where your emulation
of hoſt Hero e Women, that have in ancient days graced
this happy land How long will you be ambitious of flaunt-
ing in French attire, of fluttering about with the levity
of that fantaſtic people? When will you be ſatisfied with
the ſimplicity of elegance, and the gracefulneſs of modeſty
ſo becoming a nation like this, ſupported by trade, poliſhed by taſte and enlightened by true religion? Say,
when will you relinquiſh deluſive purſuits, and dangerous
pleaſures, the gaze of fools, and the flattery of libertines,
for the peaceful and ſolid ſtudy of whatever can adorn your
nature, do honour to your country, reflect credit on your
profeſſion of chriſtianity, give joy to all your connections,
and confer dignity on Woman-kind?

SERMON

S E R M O N II.

ON MODESTY OF APPAREL.

1 TIM 11. 8, 9

will—that women adorn themselves in Modeſt Apparel.

LET me recall the attention of my female friends to a
ſubject that concerns them highly. I hope that hitherto I
have ſaid nothing unkind   I would not rob your ſex of a
ſingle advantage they poſſeſs from nature, providence, or
legitimate cuſtom   I would not rob you of the ſmalleſt ornament that Judgment has put on, that Prudence allows,
or that Decency warrants   On the contrary, I would
willingly add to your allurements , I want to ſee you yet
more engaging, to ſee you ſtill more completely adorned.
Superfluous, unbecoming, and unavailing decorations, it is
true, I would perſuade you to renounce , but it ſhould be
only in order to make room for ſuch as will improve beauty where found, or ſupply its place where wanting.

Your conſequence in the creation I fear not to acknowledge I feel it all. You have already heard me aſſert it. I will aſſert it ever, by pleading your cauſe againſt ignorance, prejudice
and malice   Only take care, my dear clients, not to hurt
it yourſelves. Remember how tender a thing a woman's
reputation is, how hard to preſerve, and when loſt how
impoſſible to recover ; how frail many, and how dangerous
moſt, of the gifts' you have received , what miſery and
what ſhame have been often occaſioned by abuſing them:
I tremble for your ſituation. Suffer me again to put you
on your guard   My text, you have ſeen, has nothing in
it really ſevere: St Paul is, in fact, a better friend to women than has been commonly ſuppoſed: he ſeems to have
underſtood perfectly what became them, and to have con-
ſulted their intereſts more than the moſt paſſionate of their
admirers   While theſe, by corrupting or miſleading you,

C 2   whether

whether with or without defign would leffen your influence
and obftruct your felicity; he would effectually contribute
to both, by inculcating every thing that can make you at
once more amiable and more happy

What I am now to offer will turn on the ornament he
firft mentions " I will—that women adorn themfelves
in Modeft Apparel'—in Modeft Apparel, as oppofed to
that which is Indecent, and to that which is Vain: diftinctions, whereof the theory, I muft confefs, it is in many cafes
not eafy, and in fome perhaps not practicable, to fettle with
precifion, fuch a powerful influence in thofe matters have
cuftom and the opinion of the world   But in this inftance,
as in others where the paffions are concerned, the ftricteft
cafuift will, I prefume, be generally the fafeft   The zeal of
the ancient Fathers on fuch fubjects carried fome of them
far, farther, I doubt, than the relaxation of modern manners
would well bear   Were a young woman now-a-days, from
a peculiar fenfe of the facrednefs and refinement of female
virtue, to appear with any very fingular feverity in her
drefs, fhe would hardly, I fear, efcape the charge of affectation a charge, which every prudent woman will avoid
as much as poffible   But let the licenfe of the age be what
it will, I muft needs think that, according to every rule
of duty and decorum, there ought ever to be a manifeft
difference between the attire of a Virtuous Woman, and
that of one who has renounced every title to the honourable
name It were indelicate, it is unneceffary, to explain
this difference In fome refpects, it is fufficiently difcer-
ned by the eye of the public, though, I am forry to fay,
not fufficiently attended to by the generality of women
themfelves If, in other refpects, it be not feen, or do
not ftrike, the caufe, I apprehend, muft be that declenfion
from the ftrictnefs of morals, which was hinted at a moment before, a declenfion that would have fhocked pagans
themfelves, in the pureft ftate of ancient manners, when
                                        proftitutes

proftitutes were compelled to wear a particular garb, by which they were diftinguifhed from women of virtue.

But to enter more particularly into this firft point of Modeft Apparel, as oppofed to that which a chriftian woman fhould hold Indecent.

Image to yourfelf a circle compofed only of people who are not afhamed of the gofpel of Chrift, nor in any circumftance afraid to act on that great maxim of our apoftle, "Be "not conformed to this world, but be ye transformed by "the renewing of your minds." At the fame time, let them have all the candour and charity, which the moft charitable religion that was ever known can infpire   And now fuppofe, that a young lady dreffed up to the height of the prefent fafhion, but a ftranger to moft of them, drops into their company   In what light, do ye conceive, the manner of her drefs would probably appear? The laws of chriftian candour would naturally prevent them from feeing her character in a bad light on that account, and would unqueftionably incline them to hope the beft   But can ye believe that they would approve, or juftify, the extreme gaiety and loofenefs of her attire? Suppofe, however, that her converfation difcovered a good underftanding, and that her behaviour had not the leaft tincture of that levity with which fhe feemed decked out; that, on the contrary, every part of both was wholly unlike it (a conjunction by no means impoffible,) could they forbear, in that cafe, to lament the tyranny of the mode, or to regret that a daughter of Wifdom fhould, notwithftanding her fuperior defcent and noble pretenfions, he decorated like the daughters of Folly? But whofe judgment, I befeech you, would a young woman, ambitious of regulating her appearance, as well as her difpofitions and deportment, on the pureft ftandard, prefer, that of fuch perfons as I have juft defcribed; or that of thofe who either never regarded the precepts

and

and spirit of christianity at all, or who, professing some
faint respect for them, yet scruple not to sink them in the
spirit and maxims of the world?

Let us put another case, and suppose a young lady educated by a mother, who to the best sense and truest breeding
joined the utmost reverence for religion, and the tenderest
concern for the soul of her child, qualities which, for the
honour of your sex, I hope you will not pronounce incompatible Let this accomplished parent bestow upon her
daughter a culture worthy of herself, instructing her in every thing that can become the Female and the Christian
character, among the rest, recommending a lovely Modesty
and graceful Simplicity of Apparel, and enforcing all by an
example equally unexceptionable and pleasing. Suppose
the daughter to improve these uncommon advantages (for
uncommon, I fear, they are) with the strictest care and attention. In what light do ye conceive the very free mode of
dress, so generally affected by the sex at present, would
appear to her? I am far from thinking she would assume
the airs of sanctimonious prudery, or indulge the stile of
supercilious censure, things totally different from the form
of education we have figured her to receive. But would
she admire that mode in others? Would she copy it herself?
or would she wish her companions to copy it? Would she
choose to be intimate with those young ladies that seize
every opportunity of exhibiting their charms to the public,
and vie with one another who shall most liberally display
what her honoured mother taught her more decently to
veil?

Is the mode then in question to be considered as inconsistent with the character of a Virtuous Woman? By no
means May not dispositions the most unchaste often hide
under the mask of an attire the most modest? Who can
doubt it? But what follows? That such attire is not the
properest

properest covering of Virtue, or what, if left to pursue undisturbed the dictates of delicacy and prudence, she would not readily fly to in a state of civilized society? Will any one say, that they who decline it, best consult either their safety, or their reputation amongst the wise; that they, who run into all the latitudes allowed by the wantonness of fashion, are sufficiently watchful against temptation themselves, or sufficiently careful not to throw it in the way of others, that beauty may be as secure when most exposed, as when least so, or finally, that instead of " abstaining from all appearance of evil," according to the doctrine of a religion which requires the severest vigilance, every appearance of evil may be admitted, in compliance with the practice of a world, where vice steals upon unwary mortals by persuading them to part with their outgards?

Thus far have we argued for Modesty of Apparel, in opposition to its contrary, upon the general principles of propriety and reputation, of morality and religion. She to whom these principles are familiar, and in whom the feelings that arise out of them are not blunted by too frequent intercourse with the fashionable and the gay, will on this article carry about with her a kind of living standard, which she will be enabled to apply to particular occasions, with a degree of discretion that no rules of ours can teach, and such a one will perceive in our apostle's precept a justness and solidity, of which we do not expect that any speculation of ours should thoroughly convince you, without the concurrence of a virtuous sensibility on your part.

To what has been said in favour of Modest Apparel under this head, I must not forget to add, that it is a powerful attractive to Honourable love. The male heart is a study, in which your sex are supposed to be a good deal conversant. Yet in this study, you must give me leave

to

to fay, many of them feem to me but indifferent profi-
cients To gain men's affections, women in general are
naturally defirous They need not deny, they cannot
conceal it The fexes were made for each other We
wifh for a place in your hearts why fhould not you wifh
for one in ours? But how much are you deceived, my fair
friends, if you dream of taking that fort by ftorm! When
you fhow a fweet folicitude to pleafe by every decent,
gentle, unaffected attraction; we are foothed, we are fub-
dued, we yield ourfelves your willing captives. But if at
any time by a forward appearance you betray a confidence
in your charms, and by throwing them out upon us all at
once you feem refolved, as it were, to force our admiration,
that moment we are on our guard, and your affaults are
vain, provided at leaft we have any fpirit or fentiment.
In reality, they who have very little of either, I might
have faid they who have none, even the filliest, even the
loofeft men fhall in a fober mood be taken with the bafhful
air, and referved drefs, of an amiable young woman, infinitely more than they ever were with all the open blaze
of laboured beauty, and arrogant claims of undifguifed allurement, the human heart, in its better fenfations, being
ftill formed to the love of virtue.

Let me add, that the human imagination hates to be confined We are never highly delighted, where fomething
is not left us to fancy This laft obfervation holds true
throughout all nature, and all art But when I fpeak of
thefe, I muft fubjoin, that Art being agreeable no farther
than as it is conformed to Nature, the one will not be
wanted in the cafe before us, if the other be allowed its full
influence What I mean is this, that fuppofing a young
lady to be deeply poffeffed with regard for " whatfoever
" things are pure, venerable, and of a good report," it
will lead to decorum fpontaneoufly, and flow with unftudied
propriety though every part of her attire and demeanour
                                                        Let

Let it be likewise added, that simplicity, the inseparable companion both of genuine grace, and of real modesty, if it do not always strike at first (of which it seldom fails) is sure however, when it does strike, to produce the deepest and most permanent impressions · which brings me by an easy transition to,

The second part of the present consideration, that of Modest Apparel, as opposed to what may be styled Vain I can never think of this, without recollecting in general (for who can remember the particulars of) the catalogue given by the prophet Isaiah of the various implements and instruments of dress, used by the daughters of Zion in his time Isaiah is by all acknowledged the Prince of the Prophets, in an evangelical view yet he did not deem it beneath the dignity of his commission, to descend into the most minute detail on such a subject, a circumstance which, it is hoped, may soften the severity of censure against the preacher of this hour, if the spirit of criticism or the spirit of scrupulosity, should be disposed to condemn his well-meant endeavour. The passage I now refer to is in the third chapter of Isaiah, towards the end, where the prophet having, in the name of God, complained of the pride and wantonness of those eastern females, and threatened them with disease and infamy · on that account, goes on to mention " the bravery of their tinkling ornaments about " their feet, and their cauls, and their round tires like " the moon, the chains, and the bracelets, and the muf- " flers; the bonnets, and the ornaments of the legs, and the " and the head-bands, and the tablets, and the ear-rings, " the rings and nose-jewels, the changeable suits of appa- " rel, and the mantles, and the wimples, and the crisping " pins, the glasses, and the fine linen, and the hoods, and " the veils " On the first reading of this catalogue, it must be owned, one can scarce forbear to smile But to those unhappy women who gave occasion for it, nothing, alas!

alas! could be more ferious, if you attend to the denunciations which both precede and follow it I leave you to perufe them at your leifure They are in the ftyle of the country and age in which they were uttered I am fure they convey a loud leffon to this Whether the daughters of our Zion, in the prefent very polite generation, and efpecially in this moft polite city, do or do not outftrip thofe Jew Ah ladies of old, we cannot take upon us to determine But were we inclined to indulge a vein of ridicule on female folly, here methinks we might have ample fcope We are not inclined to indulge it We reflect on thefe things with real concern, and with the utmoft ferioufnefs conjure our country women to reform whatever is indecent, and to retrench whatever is exorbitant, in their attire

That there are ftations and circumftances, in which fplendour of drefs is perfectly allowable, nay extremely proper, none, I think, but the narroweft minds, will deny For my own part, I freely acknowledge that I love to fee a woman genteely habited, if her fituation admit of it. In truth, fplendor without gentility, as well in this as in every other article where ornament is concerned, will ever feem poor and infipid to all but untaught and vulgar fpirits: whereas, on the other fide, it is certain, that the latter may very well fubfift without the former, nor is its effect ever felt more ftrongly, or more happily, than when it receives no affiftance from the other, but refults folely from our perceptions of elegant fimplicity I fay Elegant fimplicity; an object, which appears to me deferving of more attention than is commonly paid it by your fex

In affairs of this kind, it is but juft to allow to women a degree of curiofity and care, which the laws of good fenfe, found philofophy, and mafculine virtue, refufe to men a diftinction fo true, fo univerfal, and fo palpable, that moft of the laft, who betray a particular folicitude in adorning their perfons beyond cleanlinefs and a certain graceful
ease

eafe, feldom fail to make themfelves little, in the eyes of
every man who is not himfelf effeminate, and of every wo-
wan too who is not a flave to fafhion   How contemptible
many of our young men muft neceffarily appear to fuch,
it is not eafy to exprefs   But of feeing them become truly
Men in this inftance, any more than in others that might
be named, I defpair, while fo many of our young women
give fo vifible a preference to embroidery, finery, and
foppifh manners, above a plain coat, a cultivated underftanding, and a manly deportment.   It will be always fo
till they acquire a tafte for plainnefs, fobriety, and wifdom
in what relates to themfelves   But that muft begin by re-
ftraining, in every poffible way, the foolifh and pernicious
paffion I am fpeaking of, for a foolifh and pernicious
paffion I fcruple not to pronounce it.

Is there any probability, that thofe who are entirely un--
der its power will take delight in domeftic, intellectual,
or fpiritual improvements? Is not a conftant purfuit of
trivial ornaments an Indubitable proof of a trivial mind?
Will fhe that is always looking into her glafs, be much
difpofed to look into her character? Is the fpending of
whole hours every morning at the toilet, a likely method
of marking the reft of the day down for wifdom? Is vanity
favourable to devotion, or felf-conceit the parent of felf-
correction? Will that young woman who hopes to captivate by drefs, or by appearance alone, be very anxious
about any better recommendation? If to fparkle here for
a few years be the fupreme ambition, Hereafter will be
hardly thought of   The flattery of every fool will be preferred to the approbation of angels, and a connection with
fome wretched creature (wretched indeed muft he be who
is caught by mere fhow!) will be ardently fought, while
the friendfhip of God is neglected What fhall I fay more?
For a mortal and immortal being, who has many an error
to correct, many a paffion to mortify, many a virtue to
practife,

practife, and who, if she live, may probably have important fervice to render fociety—for fuch a being to lavish the principal portion of her time and ftudy on the decoration of a body that will foon, that may fuddenly, become the prey of creeping things—Gracious God, what folly, what madnefs!

Are there no allowances then to be made? Allowances for what? For the vanity of a young mind Moft certainly, if by this plea you mean to extenuate the guilt of fuch a conduct But would you offer to excufe it? Would you pretend to juftify a reafonable creature in acting habitually, and wilfully, a moft unreafonable part, in facrificing her improvement, her falvation, her profpects of ufefulnefs and dignity in life, the beft interefts of this world as well as the everlafting concernments of the next, to the idol Drefs For fo I ftate it I fuppofe, and would to God it were not too common a cafe! that this miferable idol is fuffered to fwallow up the confideration of all that is folid, rational, and praife-worthy, to confume thofe precious hours that were allotted for the moft valuable purpofes, and, in place of fecuring the great ends of exiftence both prefent and future, to pervert the capacities of nature, the acquirements of education, and the bounties of providence—to pervert them to the low defign of being admired for embellifhments that imply no merit in the wearer, and can confer no honour in the eye of any but the worthlefs and the vain Can fuch a conduct, I afk, be thought innocent, or in any refpect confiftent with the rules of chriftianity, or of confcience?

That the idol I fpeak of renders its votaries unhappy even in this world, is a fact daily experienced. But who can defcribe the profufion of expenfe, with the painful and artful fhifts that are often neceffary to fupport it, the encroachments on health, the hurry of fpirits, the travail

of

of fancy , the degredation of being frequently, for whole
hours, under the confident hands of the meaneft of mankind , together with all the anxieties of heart, the agonies
of rivalfhip, the deep-felt difgrace on being difappointed
of conqueft, or of fame , the diftraction and defpair on
being outfhone by—a Finer Gown, in a word, all the
ridiculous and all the deferved diftrefs, to which they are
perpetually expofed?

I have juft mentioned encroachments on health   Thefe
indeed, as well as the reft, are, little confidered by a
young lady, keen in the purfuit of fhow and admiration
But if fhe be not apprehenfive of their confequences, in
relation to life, and comfort, and eafe, I wonder fhe is not
immediately alarmed at their effects, with regard to that
very appearance which is her favourite object   I wonder
fhe does not perceive at once, how much her bloom and
fprightlinefs, the luftre of her eyes, and the frefhnefs of
her form, are impaired by fuch endlefs, fuch enormous
fatigue, agitation, and irregularity   I am aftonifhed fhe
does not reflect, that fhe is taking the moft effectual methods to fhorten that period of youth, on which her triumphs
depend   Miftaken creature!   thou art cruelly haftening
on the time, when thou fhalt be frightened to look at thyfelf, when not only thy mind, but thy face, fhall be
" ficklied o'er with the pale caft of thought," when languor
difeafe and depreffion, fhall undermine and deftroy every remaining allurement, and leave thee to lament too late the
jading courfe thou haft run.   You forget alfo that dreffing
up beauty continually, wears it out, that like ftrength,
or ftudy, or bufinefs, it requires the frequent intermiffion
of its toils, but that, more than any of them, it is enfeebled
by conftant exertion, and that the arts commonly made
ufe of to heighten and repair it, only accelerate and increafe its decay, while the complexion, the fkin, and the
hair, are all unnaturally difguifed and tortured

Did

Did not this shameful passion destroy, or deaden in a great measure, the worthier sensibilities of good nature, I should also mention here the more serious and important distresses, in which they involve others.—But the stretches of credit to parents, the inconveniencies to many families, the ruin to not a few, the losses to tradesmen, who are often not paid, the hardships to a vast variety of people, whose sufferings are little thought of amidst the glare of ostentation and the triumph of fancy, it were impossible fully to paint. Who does not know, that the parade of one gaudy evening shall sometimes subject a score of honest citizens to difficulties for a whole month? Is this christian? Is this humane? But where the Fury of dress tyrannizes how can the gentle pleadings of Charity hope to be heard? And as to Charity's eldest daughter, Benefi-cence, what chance has she, in general to contend with that mighty forceress, the Mode? Those streams which heaven has committed to the direction of the former, for the refreshment of industry, and the comfort of affliction; how often are they diverted with sacrilegious violence to the feeding of price!

But the present age, it will be said, is distinguished by the most diffusive, the most illustrious works of humanity both private and public. We own it, and rejoice in the effect. Far from denying the people of this country any of their just honours, we are almost tempted to speak of them with exultation. But—I wish the works in question may not be frequently performed by way of atonement for certain fashionable vices, which it too easy to reconcile with them ——" Charity hopeth all things."——I know it can do very, believe that even now, addicted, as the world is to ostentation, there are many, very many cha-racters who nobly deny themselves for the sake of others; others, who find the highest indulgence in consecrating to objects of benevolence and piety a large share of their

fortunes,

fortunes, without seeking by such means to purchase a dispensation for criminal pursuits But forgive me, if I say, with regard to numbers, that the flagrant affectation of shining in public, and the dreadful passions thence arising in private life, are not easily reconciled with real principles of religious munificence   These, I know, are unpopular ideas   I am sorry for it but their being so, is no reason why we should suppress them, it is the very reverse

To the arguments already urged several may be added It may deserve your consideration,

In the first place, that to cultivate cleanliness and finery at the same time, is rather perhaps a difficult attainment Your sex is much belied, if it be a very common one This, I think, is certain, that to attend with exactness to one object at once, is ordinarily sufficient employment for the mind.   But can any degree of finery compensate the want of cleanliness?   A dirty woman—I turn from the shocking idea, to mention,

In the next place, that engaging thing hinted at before, Simplicity of Dress In all the sciences, in every valuable profession, in the common intercourses of life, and let me add, even in the sublimest subjects, Simplicity is that which above every thing else touches and delights   Without it, indeed, all else is feeble and unaffecting   Where Simplicity is wanting, men may be dazzled for a moment Mere splendor will strike them at first: but on reflexion they will soon discover, that splendor of itself, like every other idol, is nothing   On the other hand, where Simplicity, the sister of Truth, appears, the attraction is eternal   Hence the never-failing entertainment and instruction derived from the works of antiquity in all the fine arts, of which I suppose for that reason chiefly, they remain to this day, and will ever remain, the sovereign standards Those amongst the moderns, who have in this respect

spect

spect copied them most happily, have been always most admired To instance in the art of painting, with a more
immediate reference to our subject, what honour has been
acquired by such of its professors as have approached nearest
to the noble simplicity of ancient workmanship! Its business, we know, is most particularly with Beauty, in all her
finest forms That, I presume, was never studied more suc-
cessfully by any, than by the great Raphael But who,
that has an eye for such objects, can avoid being struck with
the chaste, sober, and unaffected graces of his females? And
as to his manner of clothing them, what remarkable plainness, what delightful modesty, even where the colours and
stuff are intended to be richest! How different from those
painters of the Gothic style, who, not understanding the
distinction between ornament, and finery, which is its ex-
cess; between beauty, and show, which is the affectation
of it load their women with jewels, trappings, and other
embellishments, magnificent indeed, but tawdry!

Nor is the grand principle of Simplicity confined to the
imitative arts, it runs through all. Hence, in a great
measure, the peculiar satisfaction derived from the company of a man well bred and worthy at the same time He
looks, he speaks, he moves, with a modest ease, there is
nothing artificial or studied in his conversation and deportment. Hence too the superior pleasure from the prospect
of a garden laid out with taste, in which the views are natural, ample, and unforced, above that of seeing one cut
into a thousand little parterres, and encumbered with a
crowd of laboured conceits Let me subjoin, hence the in-
expressible power and majesty of Holy Writ itself, even ab-
stracted from its divine original And, to come to the case
directly before us, hence the resistless charm which attends
a Virtuous Woman attired with plainness and judgment;
to which, when making allowance for the mutability
                                                                and

and caprice of fashion in circumstances of less moment, will always give the most genuine and lasting content.

The neat appearance of many females belonging to a sect well known, has been frequently remarked, and greatly admired   It would be much more agreeable, could it be disjoined from the stiffness that accompanies it, a defect utterly inconsistent with the rules of taste   But those people are taught to despise every thing of this kind, and to understand literally such passages of scripture as seem to prohibit sumptuous apparel   In short, they plead religious principle for the form of their attire   We should believe them, but for the richness of the materials, and the fineness of the texture.   Many of that sect are very intelligent: can they persuade themselves, that through all their affectation of plainness the world does not perceive the utmost pride of expence?

On this article your judgment will be seen in joining frugality and simplicity together   in being never fond of finery; in carefully distinguishing between what is glaring, and what is genteel, in preserving elegance with the plainest habit; in wearing costly array but seldom, and always with ease: a point that may be attained by her who has learnt not to think more highly of herself for the richest raiment she can put on.

Were a system of this kind to prevail, I cannot help thinking, that the effects would be beneficial and happy. What sums would be saved, where they ought to be saved, for more valuable ends ! What sums would be kept at home, that now go abroad to enrich our most dangerous rivals ! French gewgaws would give place to British manufactures.   The ladies of this island, inferior to none in beauty, would be the apes of none in dress.   They would practise that species of patriotism, which is the most proper

for

for their fex , they would ferve their country in their own
way How many evils to the community, to private families, and to individuals, would be prevented' If in fome
of the moft expenfive parts of female decoration fewer
hands were employed, a much greater number on the other
fide would find exercife in cultivating an elegant propriety,
and a beautiful diverfity, through all the reft The public
tafte would be improved in a thoufand articles And is there
not reafon to hope, that the appearance, the manners, and
the minds of the Fair, would gain by the change ?

They would be lefs fhowy indeed , but they would be
more engaging Our gay affemblies, for gay affemblies
there will always be, would glitter lefs in the gaze of foolifh wonder , but they would fhine more in the eye of juft
difcernment And what honour would it reflect on your
underftandings, when in company, to fee you fuperior to
your drefs, entirely forgetting that, and every other advantage you may poffefs, in an obliging attention to all prefent, and lending luftre to each ornament, inftead of borrowing it merely from thence' Or will any of you fay,
that a woman on the contrary is likely to be more efteemed, for appearing attentive to herfelf alone, or trying to
catch by fo poor a bait, as a little gay clothing ? She who
does either, piques our pride, and offends our judgment,
at the fame inftant We are hurt by her bad breeding in
the one cafe and in the other, we are provoked to think
fhe fhould pay us fuch a forry compliment; as to fancy we
can be entangled in a cobweb

When fhall women, in general, underftand thoroughly
the effect of a comely habit, that, independent of pomp
and defpifing extravagance, is worn as the fober, yet tranf-
parent veil of a more comely mind? Be affured, my
young friends, it is thus that you will captivate moft, and
pleafe longeft By purfuing this plan, you will preferve

an

an equality in that great indispensible article of neatness. You will be clean, and you will be easy, nor will you be in danger of appearing butterflies one day, and slatterns the next. You will be always ready to receive your friends, without seeming to be caught, or being at all disconcerted on account of your dress. How seldom is that the case amongst the flutterers of the age! I wish we could say, amongst them only For young ladies of more sobriety to be found so often slovenly, I might have said downright squalid and nasty, when no visitors are expected, is most peculiarly shameful I cannot express the contempt and the disgust I feel, when I think of it. I will not think of it

I proceed to observe, that what you take from tinsel trappings you will gain in time, in saving, and in real loveliness. The less vanity you betray, the more merit we shall be always disposed to allow you We shall be doubly charmed, first with finding young women that are not slaves to show, and next with your putting so much respect on our heads and hearts, as to suppose we are only to be gained by better qualities

Add to this, that men of ordinary fortunes, and proper sentiments, will not be afraid of connecting themselves with persons too prudent to be profuse, and too wise, as well as too worthy, when married to court the admiration of all—but their husbands.

The unbounded and undistinguishing love of admiration, has been thought the most common, the rankest, and the most noxious weed, that grows in the heart of a female. It is nourished by nothing more than by the love of finery. In effect, they depend on each other. But if you will begin by crushing the latter, the former, I am persuaded, will quickly decay, and at last fall to the ground. The

D 2 love

love of finery naturally prompts the passion to be seen, that
is, to be admired; for between these a conceited young
creature makes no distinction   Alas! what woman is
there at any age, who, if devoted to dress; burns not with
impatience to display in public a new fashion, or a new
any thing, which she has been told by those about her, or
by her own imagination, *looks exceeding fine?*   And of
this impatience what is the source, but that very passion
which I just now called The unbounded and undistinguishing love of admiration?   The mischiefs flowing from
thence have been touched upon in part   They will be farther traced hereafter.   At present I shall only add, what
ought to alarm women of decency, that an immoderate
fondness for external embellishment is a strong temptation
to a light and lascivious mind.

From the passage of Isaiah before quoted, compared with
the verse immediately preceding, it appears that, in the
case there pointed to, an indecent deportment was closely
connected with an excessive vanity in apparel   And from
the whole of that discourse it is manifest, the behaviour of
the daughters of Zion at that time was highly displeasing
to the Almighty ; which could only proceed from the influence their behaviour had upon their dispositions, or reci-
procally from the latter as giving birth to the former. How
applicable the observation to the case of many females at
this day !

But has it not been too much the manner amongst preachers of every age, to decry that in which they lived, as having remarkably degenerated from those that went before, and
to denounce peculiar judgments accordingly? It often has,
no doubt And so far certainly they have forgotten the caution of Solomon , " Say not thou, What is the cause that
" the former days were better than these?   For thou dost
" not enquire wisely concerning this." A mistake we would
                                                        willingly

willingly avoid. Such complaints, when indulged indiscriminately, are either the dictates of a gloomy and querulous temper, or the trite and unmeaning declamation of mere popular preaching. I trust, we shall be charged with neither in saying, that to this nation there can accrue no good from the spirit of luxury, of levity, and of vice, so prevalent, and so spreading, in a sex that leads the world.

SERMON

S E R M O N III.

ON FEMALE RESERVE.

1 TIM 11 8, 9

I will———that women adorn themselves with Shamefacedness.

MANY of you, my honoured hearers, have been addressed in the style of love and admiration   I have taken the
liberty to address you in that of zeal and friendship, a style
not the less sincere, or the less worthy of your attention,
for being sober and impartial   Will you permit me to proceed in the same manner ? Suppose me speaking to you as
a brother   It will be more than a supposition. Have we
not all one father by creation, even the great GOD ? and
by religion, is not the new Jerusalem the mother of us all ?
With a brother's affection then I will go on to lay before
you some better ornaments than wealth can purchase, in
which I wish my beloved sisters to shine, that they may appear as becomes their high birth, and the noble expectations they are encouraged to entertain

After modest apparel our apostle mentions Shamefacedness   " I will—that women adorn themselves in modest
" apparel, with Shamefacedness " This lovely quality,
in its largest extent, and in its most pleasing effects on female manners, shall be the subject of our present meditation   It is an ornament equally necessary and wise.

I   It is a necessary ornament, considered, I mean, in a
moral and religious light   I would only premise, that the
amiable reserve, termed by St Paul, Shamefacedness, is
something widely distant from those airs of disdain, those
pretences of aversion to men, which we now and then meet
with in your sex   I said Pretences , For no degree of candour can persuade us to believe that such women, generally

ly fpeaking, do not play a part, and under the maſk of this feeming feverity, this violent affectation of virtue, harbour paſſions of a very different kind Who does not know, that the greateſt prudes have often dropt their diſguiſe at laſt, and betrayed ſuch diſpoſitions as many a young woman of good nature, and courteous behaviour, is incapable of indulging? Every thing overdone is liable to fuſpicion Innocence in women wants not the aid of oſtentation, like integrity in men, it reſts in its own conſciouſneſs Not ſo, however, as to neglect the rules of prudence and circumſpection. To ſay the truth, prudery is not the prevailing evil of the times. Female modeſty, even where it is moſt real, is in little danger, as the world goes, of being carried to an extreme In the gayer part of the world, how ſeldom, alas! does it riſe to the Shamefacedneſs enjoined in our text, and which on the very firſt hearing ſuggeſts the idea of a virtuous baſhfulneſs This beautiful grace,

> " Clear Chaſtity
> " With bluſhes redd'ning as ſhe moves along,
> " Diſorder'd at the deep regard ſhe draws,"

whither is ſhe retired? Where is the charming original, from which the poet drew ſo ſweet a picture?——Has virtue then forſaken the ſex? GOD forbid But I am bold to ſay, her favourite walks are not in thoſe places of public entertaiment, now ſo fondly frequented by ſo many women She loves the ſhade There ſhe finds herſelf moſt ſecure from the blights of calumny, and the heats of temptation Ah! ye mothers of this land, how can you expoſe ſo raſhly thoſe tender bloſſoms committed to your care? Have ye forgotten that every unkindly breath is ready to blaſt them? Are ye ignorant, how ſoon the whiteſt innocence may be ſullied, that it is poſſible even for the ſtricteſt principles to be corrupted? Is there nothing in your own minds that whiſpers the frailty of your ſex?

But

But you plead the neceffity of allowing to youth a little amufement, of fhowing your daughters a little of the world, of preventing, or rubbing off the awkwardnefs, that is apt to adhere to young perfons who are confined at home. You urge the propriety of convincing them by comparifon, how much the calm and rational pleafures of that home are preferable to the noify and giddy diverfions ufually found abroad, that in the latter there is nothing fo wonderfully fine, fo irrefiftably alluring, as their youthful fancies, or the information of others, might lead them to fuppofe.

We admit your arguments, fo far as they go Keep within thefe bounds, and be blamelefs But do the parents of the prefent generation commonly keep within them? Are not many of thofe parents as fond of gaiety and fhow, as the mereft girl can poffibly be? Is it furprifing to fee the daughters of fuch become very early the votaries of Folly, when every other day or night they are conducted in triumph to her temples, without any precaution, any previous pains taken to inftruct them in the emptinefs and worthleffnefs of the object worfhipped there, worfhipped with every circumftance that can ferve to propagate the idolatry, while the poor innocents are inflamed by the concurrence of company, drefs, flattery, example, the example of thofe whom, by nature and education, they are difpofed to refpect moft highly, and to imitate moft implicitly? It were ftrange indeed, if in this fituation their too fufceptible hearts fhould efcape the fafhionable contagion. But what can be faid for thofe who thus directly, and with their eyes open, lead their children into a fnare?—Ceafe, thou reftlefs and raging fpirit of hell, who art "going "about feeking whom thou mayeft devour," ceafe thy cruel toil The parents of Britain render it needlefs The mothers of the church haften to bring thee their little lambs, as if impatient for the pleafure of prefenting them —Excufe, ye better characters, this tranfport of indignation, kindled

by

by an impiety which you are not capable of committing.
I think with honour of all who truly merit the parental name.
May the Father of the world encreafe their number, and
multiply their joys! But for thofe wicked——I turn from
them to you, ye pretty helplefs creatures, who have loft—
it may be, happily——merciful heaven! muft I fay, Happily loft your parents? or whofe parents yet alive, but loft
to themfelves and to their offspring, have in the blindnefs
of indulgence, or the barbarity of neglect, abandoned you
to your own untutored conduct. Let me warn you of your
danger If there be no other friend to fhow a folicitude for
your welfare, allow me at leaft to have that fatisfaction.

Reflect, my fifters, on all I have faid concerning your
importance in life. and look beyond life's narrow bounda-
ry Confider everlafting confequences Contemplate ap-
proaching judgment You have received from the almighty your bodies and your fouls, unftained by difhonour.
You will be foon required to reftore them immaculate.
You belong to a fociety, for which your Saviour " gave
" himfelf, that he might fanctify and cleanfe it with the
" wafhing of water by the word, that he might prefent it
" to himfelf a glorious church, not having fpot, or wrinkle,
" or any fuch thing" Think of this. " Watch and pray,
" that ye enter not into temptation

The love of promifcuous amufement, how innocent foever it may often feem, and fometimes be, enfnares multitudes of your fex Their earlieft days are marked by a
mixture of fprightlinefs and fimplicity They run, they
laugh, they prattle, and then they often blufh for fear of
having offended. As they grow up, their fenfibilities become more enlightened, and more awake They blufh oftener It is the precious colouring of virtue, as one has
happily phrafed it. They contract a quicker perception of
what is decent, and of what is wife. A fweet timidity

was

was given them to guard their innocence, by inclining
them to shrink from whatever might threaten to injure it.
Their passions, as they rise, are restrained from exorbitance,
by a secret sentiment of shame and honour   In this state of
mind they come to hear much concerning public diversions.
The description is frequently repeated, and always exagge-
rated   Their curiosity takes fire, they are eager to parti-
cipate   The are indulged once, a second, a third time,
often, without controul   By little and little their natural
fearfulness begins to abate   For a while they are shocked
at signs of rudeness   Their ears are wounded by the language of vice   Oaths, imprecations, double meanings,
every thing obscene fills them with disgust and horror   But
custom soon begets familiarity, and familiarity produces indifference   The emotions of delicacy are less frequent, less
strong   And now they seldom blush, altho' perhaps they
often affect it   At the image of sin they tremble no longer   their minds are already debauched   All the internal
fences of modesty are broken down   Can you wonder, if
it be then easily assailed from without?   But what if it be
not?   What if appearances be still preserved, if open
scandals be not incurred, or if secret enormity should be always avoided?   Is it enough for a young woman to be free
from infamy, from crimes?   Between the state of virgin
purity and actual prostitution are there no intermediate degrees?   Is it nothing to have the soul deflowered, the fancy polluted, the passions flung into a ferment?   Say, is it
nothing to forfeit inward freedom and self-possession?   The
beauty, the dignity, the tranquillity of conscious virtue—
are all these of no account?   Such indeed one would think
were the opinion of those, who imagine there can be no
harm in a passion for places of entertainment.   Because,
say they, all attacks on the honour of persons who resort
thither are precluded   Be that as it may, I must ever maintain   that young women of principle will be cautious of
frequenting scenes where shamefacedness, at once the companion

panion and the guardian of female innocence, is in danger
of being lost But I add, that every prudent young woman
also will be extremely wary in this particular, because,

II The ornament we now recommend is as Wife, as
it is Necessary There is nothing so engaging as bashful
beauty The beauty that obtrudes itself, how considerable
soever, will either disgust, or at most excite but inferior de-
sires Men are so made They refuse their admiration,
where it is courted where it seems rather shunned, they
love to bestow it The retiring graces have been always the
most attractive

You remember the representation which Milton puts into Adam's mouth of his first meeting with our general mother. How beautiful, and how delicate!

" She heard me thus, and though divinely brought,
" Yet innocence and virgin modesty,
" Her virtue and the conscience of her worth,
" That would be woo'd, and not unsought be won,
" Not obvious, not obtrusive, but retir'd,
" The more desirable, or, to say all,
" Nature herself, tho' pure of sinful thought,
" Wrought in her so, that seeing me she turn'd.
" I follow'd her She what was honour knew,
" And with obsequious majesty approv'd
" My pleaded reason To the nuptial bower
" I led her blushing like the morn "

But this was only the poets fancy True Yet the poet knew the sexes well, and seems to have studied yours
particularly He painted from the completest standards he
could find His picture of Eve, in her state of innocence,
may be considered as the model of a woman most amiably
feminine, in whom his imagination, alike exalted and
correct, could figure nothing so alluring,

" As

" — thofe graceful acts,
" Thofe thoufand decencies that daily flow
" From all her words and actions "

What mind of any worth can forbear to be charmed with the defcription you have juft heard?

To fay the truth, there is not, I verily believe, a man living, who in his fober fenfes, would not prefer a modeft to an impudent woman. An impudent woman——Who can tell which is greater, the difgrace thrown upon humanity, by fuch a character, or the honour reflected on our natures by that abhorrence, which is raifed by the bare idea in every breaft not totally degenerate?

Surely it deferves your notice, what pains the all prefiding power has gracioufly taken to fhow his care of female virtue, not only by impreffing the minds of your fex with that deep and lively fenfe of reputation, which is one of its moft powerful prefervatives, but alfo by forming the minds of ours with fo high an efteem for every indication of chaftity in women, and with fo ftrong a difapprobation of the contrary. That efteem, and this difapprobation, it is certain. are felt by the men, whenfoever reafon is permitted to take place of appetite; and thefe indications are perfectly and univerfally intelligible. I fay not, that thofe of the laft kind are always apparent, where women have given themfelves up to vice; but I apprehend, they are fo for the greater part. This breach of her moft facred law, the juftice of Nature has generally branded with a look and manner peculiarly characteriftic and fignificant; as on the other fide, fhe has always (I think, always) marked the genuine feelings of modefty with a look and manner no lefs correfpondent and expreffive.

In the latter cafe, fhe feems to fay to us men, pointing

to

to her yet uncorrupted daughters; ' Behold thefe fmiling
' innocents, whom I have graced with my faireft gifts, and
' committed to your protection, behold them with love and
' refpect, treat them with tendernefs and honour They
' are timid, and want to be defended They are frail, O
' do not take advantage of their weaknefs. Let their fears
' and blufhes endear them. Let their confidence in you
' never be abufed—But is it poffible, that any of you can
' be fuch barbarians, fo fupremely wicked, as to abufe it?
' Can ye find in your hearts to defpoil the gentle trufting
' creatures of their treafure, or do any thing to ftrip them of
' their native robe of virtue? Curft be the impious hand
' that would dare to violate the unblemifhed form of Chafti-
' ty! Thou wretch! thou ruffian! forbear! nor venture
' to provoke heaven's fierceft vengeance '

In the other cafe, the fame parental power, equally
watchful for all her children, feems to caft an eye of awful
reproach on fuch of her daughters as are unhappily abandoned, and, raifing her voice, to addrefs our fex to this purpofe ' Flee, my fons, Flee thefe deftructive Syrens
' They fmile, only to tempt, and they tempt, in order to
' devour. Once indeed they fhone in many of my fweeteft
' charms. Thefe are no more They have forgotten to
' blufh, their foreheads are hardened into fhamelffnefs.
' Their eyes formerly foft, virtuous, and downcaft, thofe
' very eyes that effufed the foul of innocence, have learnt
' to ftare, and roll with unbounded wantonnefs, to dart no-
' thing but unholy fire. Their hands are the hands of Har-
' pies. Their feet go down to death, and their fteps take
' hold on hell '

This account of thofe wretched beings will be always
true in part The profligate and the foolifh, that are taken in their toils, fhall fome time or other be fure to repent
it Neverthelefs it muft be owned, there are of them
who

who, with hearts of adamant to the best impreffions, and without any remains of natural modefty, yet practife the art of feigning its decent demeanour; one of the ftrongeft arguments that can be conceived in its favour!

Yet, thofe more accomplifhed enfnarers are fufficiently aware, that there is no allurement equal to that of maiden virtue, and therefore. having, loft the reality, they ftudy to retain the appearance In this inftance, no doubt, as in numberlefs others, the operations of Nature may be counteracted by violence, and her moft fpeaking features filenced by diffimulation But, ah, how much more eafy, pleafant, noble, and happy, to be virtuous, than only to feem fo! That vicegerent of God within us, Confcience, will not bear the abufe calmly All effential tranfgreffions of order how fuccefsful foever they may outwardly appear, fhall certainly be punifhed by inward difquietude, and home-felt meannefs But the truth is, that the art of diffembling in the cafe before us, feldom fucceeds fo far, as not to be feen through on many occafions and when it is, the con-tempt and averfion produced by it, are only heightened by thofe attempts to impofe Of this be affured, that to the fo fe of decency there is no hing more difgufting, than the notion of a young woman who cannot be put out of coun-tenance In our fex, the character of being loft to fhame s fcandalous, but in yours—who can defcribe the detefta-tion it excites?

Next to this is the d flike we feel to her who has contrac-ted a certain brifknefs of air, and levity of deportment, which, though by good nature, or the courtefy of cuftom, diftinguifhed from the brazen front and bold attack of the proftitute, does yet, I cannot help faying, approach too near them, and can never, I am fure, be pleafing to men of fentiment. Such an air and deportment, I well know are by many efteemed marks of fpirit It may be fo, I am willing at leaft to believe, that no real harm is meant

by

by numbers who affect them   But furely they are the worft
kind of affectation   I had rather a thoufand times fee a
young lady carry her bafhfulnefs too far, than pique herfelf on the freedom of her manners.

A Mafculine woman muft be naturally an unamiable
creature   I confefs myfelf fhocked, whenever I fee the
fexes confounded   An effeminate fellow, that, deftitute
of every manly fentiment, copies with inverted ambition
from your fex, is an object of contempt and averfion at
once. On the other hand, any young woman of better
rank, that throws off all the lovely foftnefs of her nature
and emulates the daring intrepid temper of a man—how
terrible!   The transformation on either fide muft ever be
monftrous   Is not this fhadowed out to us in that particular
prohibition of the Jewifh law, which fays, "The woman
"fhall not wear that which pertaineth unto a man neither
"fhall a man put on a woman's garment   For all that do
"fo are abomination to the Lord?" Such confufion of apparel was to be confidered as renouncing, in effect, the
diftinction of form, which the Almighty had eftablifhed in
the creation   To this unnatural mode do we not fometimes
obferve a vifible tendency in our days? But what though
the drefs be kept ever fo diftinct, if the behaviour be not,
in thofe points, I mean, where the character peculiar to
each fex feems to require a difference? There, a meta-
morphofis in either will always offend an eye that is not
greatly vitiated   It will do fo particularly in your fex.
By dint of affiduity and flattery, fortune and fhow, a
Female Man fhall fometimes fucceed ftrangely with the
women but to the men an Amazon never fails to be
forbidding. Are none of you, my fair hearers, in danger
of roughening into this ungracious figure? How readily it
is affumed, in thofe fcenes where the ignorance of youth
co-operates with the magic of fafhion, many of you perhaps will not fufpect

Men

Men, I prefume, are in general better judges than women, of the deportment of women Whatever affects them from your quarter they feel more immediately. You fl de infenfibly into a certain caft of manners; you perceive not the gradations, you do not fee yourfelves at a proper diftance If the effect produced be on the whole difagreeable, felf-love will not be the firft to difcover it Men, it is true, are often dazzled by youth, vivacity, and beauty but yet at times they will look at you with a cooler eye, and a clofer infpection, than you apprehend; at leaft, when they have opportunities of feeing you in private company.

In fplendid crowds all is diffipated, becaufe all is garnifh. The multiplicity of the object fcatters and diftracts: nothing is felt or thought of, in the way of either ferious reflection, or ferious paffion How much misjudged is an exceffive fondnefs for fuch fcenes! Believe me, they are not the places, where the heart is moft apt to be touched

At any rate, the majefty of the fex is fure to fuffer by being feen too frequently, and too familiarly. Difcreet referve in a woman, like the diftance kept by royal perfonages, contributes to maintain the proper reverence Moft of our pleafures are prized in proportion to the difficulty with which they are obtained. The fight of beauty may be juftly reckoned in that number Nothing can be more impolitic in young ladies, than to make it cheap. " So long," fays a lively author, " as they govern them- " felves by the exact rules of prudence and modefty, their " luftre is like the meridian fun in its clearnefs, which, " though lefs approachable, is counted more glorious, " but when they decline from thofe, they are like that fun " in a cloud, which, though fafelier gazed on, is not half " fo bright "

Even the worft men are ftruck by the fovereignty of
female

female worth unambitious of appearing. But if a young perſon (ſuppoſing her diſpoſitions in other reſpects ever ſo good) will be always breaking looſe through each domeſtic incloſure, and ranging at large the wide common of the world, thoſe deſtroyers will ſee her in a very different point of light They will conſider her as lawful game, to be hunted down without heſitation. And if her virtue, or (which to a woman is in effect nearly the ſame) her reputation, ſhould be loſt, what will it avail the poor wanderer to plead that ſhe meant only a little harmleſs amuſement, and never thought of ſtraying into the abhorred paths of vice?

With regard to the opinion of the better ſort of men, I will tell you a ſecret. If in the flutter of too public a life you ſhould at any time ſo far forget yourſelves, as to drop that nice decorum of appearance and manner, which is expected from your ſex, particularly from the younger part of it, they will be tempted to harbour ſuſpicions which I dare not name, that is, many of them will The reſt, who know you better, or have more charity, will be hurt to think you ſhould expoſe yourſelves to a degree of cenſure which in reality you do not deſerve. Yet none of them hardly will be kind enough to offer you a friendly hint of what ſo much concerns you, not even where it might be done with the moſt perfect propriety. Their general inclination to good nature, their love of amuſement in their turn, and their finding it moſt readily in the ſociety of your ſex, will diſpoſe them to laugh with you very freely. Intimacy will lead on to a kind of attachment. They will often entertain you with no little gallantry; ſometimes perhaps at an expence which they can ill afford. In a word, they will be mightily pleaſed with you—as the companions of an hour Companions for life, if they ever think of ſuch, they will look out for elſewhere They will then make the neceſſary diſcrimination, I mean, if

E

they

they be wife and honeft enough to marry from choice
They will then try if they can find women well-bred and
fober-minded at the fame time, of a chearful temper with
fedate manners, women, of whom they may hope that
they will love home, be attached to their hufbands, attentive to their families, reafonable in their wifhes, moderate
in their expences, and not addicted to eternal fhow   Having found them, whether with or without fortune (that
will never be their prime confideration) they will endeavour
to gain them by another fort of ftyle and behaviour, than
they ufed towards you   Far other fentiments, far other
emotions, will then poffefs them   In fhort, their hearts
will be then engaged; and if they fhould be happy enough
to obtain the much wifhed for objects, then, with a joy
unfelt before, they will form the tendereft of all connexions, leaving you where they found you, as widely removed as ever from the trueft pleafures, and the faireft
profpects, that humanity knows, the pleafures which
are enjoyed at home, and the profpects which include a family

But many of you, I fear, will fmile at all this, trufting to the
flatterer Beauty, that, whenever you fhall pleafe, you cannot fail to fix your men, and fo, in the gaiety of your fpirits, you continue to exhibit that beauty as ufual, and to
dance along through the giddy maze. Not to infift, at
prefent, how precarious and tranfient an attendant this
arch-flatterer has always proved ; I muft remind you, that
a face hackneyed in the public eye, how ftriking foever when
firft feen, or how handfome foever it may yet remain, lofes
much of its power to pleafe   Every new appearance
takes fomething from its charms; and for one inftance
wherein this kind of exhibition fucceeds, how many might
be named in which young women once extolled, and run
after every where, have lived to tread the beaten round,
unpraifed, neglected, forlorn !

No,

No, those large promiscuous circles are not the scenes where the heart is commonly interested Virtuous love, like true devotion, flies from noise, seeks retreat, and delights to indulge itself, unobserved by all but the object of its veneration That respectful modesty, which attends it on the part of a man, is maintained and exalted by nothing so much as an unaffected bashfulness on the woman's side. But this last, which properly speaking is the flower of female chastity, is of a nature so delicate and tender, as always to thrive best in places the least frequented. What pity, when, instead of being sheltered and cherished with care, it is heedlessly exposed to the wanton gaze of every wandering eye, to the cruel hand of every rude, or of every sly invader! Can any entertainment, or any admiration, the public has power to offer, compensate the loss of this enchanting quality?

Say not that it is incompatible with politeness, or with affability. We have seen it accompanied with the sweetest affability, and with the most perfect politeness Depend upon it, that the best breeding is not learnt by rambling from one assembly, and one diversion, to another, but by living among the best bred people, by cultivating a fund of goodness in the heart, and possessing the advantage of a well educated mind.

After what you have heard, I hope you will not imagine, that the Bashfulness I plead for tends to obstruct any one view, which it becomes a wife and worthy woman to entertain. Some men, I confess, may be flattered by forward advances from those of your sex, whom the ingenious Mr Richardson used to term Seekers But is there not reason to apprehend, that when they come to reflect coolly, their esteem will not be lasting, where the foundation of it is not natural ? There are other men, it is but fair to tell you, who will appear delighted with this kind of

E 2   courtship,

courtship, pretend the higheſt regard, pay you a world of
compliments by which they mean nothing, and ſwear to
the firſt worthleſs companion they meet, that you have a
deſign upon them   Can you bear the thought of expoſing
yourſelves to ſuch an imputation? How mortifying, on
thoſe occaſions, to hear a girl ſeriouſly boaſt of her imaginary conqueſts? How weak in her, to fancy that every man
who flatters her, not to ſay every man who treats her with
the attention to which your ſex are entitled, is a lover!

I ſpeak not of thoſe more deſerving females, whoſe
peace of mind has been cruelly ſported with by a ſpecies of
men ——, the diſgrace of their ſex, the reverſe of all that
is brave or humane, whoſe buſineſs and boaſt it is, to in-
veigle the affections of virtuous women by endleſs obſequi-
ouſneſs and ſolemn profeſſions, that ſeem to imply every
thing juſt and kind, till they have undone the credulous
believers, whom they then barbarouſly conſign to infamy
and woe or elſe, finding that they have gone too far in
the purſuit of thoſe who will not yield but on honourable
terms to which they have not the ſpirit or probity to agree,
they meanly and baſely relinquiſh them, after having ſtolen
their hearts   Happy creatures, to be ſo relinquiſhed,
though not happy to be ſo inveigled! What an eſcape have
ye made from wretches that never deſerved you! If your
reſentment there riſe at firſt, as it cannot fail of being, that
——— ————— ſhould inſpire you with a generous contempt,
——— ————— fit to be retained on ſuch a ſubject

To ſuch of our ſex, whom a rage for amuſe-
——— ———— has robbed of one of the fineſt orna-
——— ———— on them, the Shamefacedneſs I have
——— ———— during to inculcate   After having ſaid ſo much
to her to ſhew how they are to blame, what ſhall I ſay to
——— ——— that it is to adviſe them better, but who have
——— ———— ————— Surely it might be thought, that
                                                      ſuch

fuch of their female acquaintance, and fuch efpecially of
their female relations as are advanced in life, would, from
their fuperior ftore of judgment and obfervation, be friendly enough to communicate to thofe ignorant or unexperienced young creatures, fome falutary counfel on this and
other important articles. I know they will excufe themfelves
by pleading the difficulty of the taſk   I own it difficult. To
advife well was always fo, and who can be fure of advi-
fing fuccefsfully ? Is it therefore never to be attempted ?
In the prefent cafe, I cannot doubt but good counfel, offered
with prudence and affection, would often fuccced.

St Paul, who held it not unworthy of an Apoftle to enter
with the greateft particularity into the concerns of common life, directs Titus to remind the aged women of their
duty on this very head   His words are remarkable : " Speak
" thou the things that become found doctrine ;"—among
the reft—" that the aged women may teach the young
" women to be fober, to love their hufbands, to love
" their children"———What follows ?—" to be difcreet,
" chafte, keepers at home " The precept indeed points
to young women in the ftate of wedlock   But will any fuppofe the apoftle meant to exclude women yet unmarried
from that part of it, which on his principles, muft neceffarily be applicable to them ? That women who, having
families of their own, go much abroad, and affect to fhine
any where but in their proper fphere, are peculiarly to blame,
muft, I think, be acknowledged   But will you thence infer, that they who have none are at liberty to ftroll about
perpetually, to prefer every place to home, and neglect
the moft refpectable virtues, the moft valuable accomplifhments, for the parade of drefs, the difplay of beauty, and
the tricks of affectation ?

It is truly fad to fee fo many young ladies, fhowing
themfelves every day in the markets of Vanity, who by

a proper deportment elfewhere might render themfelves a-
greeable and happy ; to fee them trifling away the opportunities of doing both, and facrificing to a falfe ambition
the real importance of their fex   But it is no lefs furprifing
than fad, to find amongft women of age and experience fo
few, comparatively fpeaking, who have the confcience
or the humanity to contribute to their reformation and welfare

Imagine a fet of chafte matrons, anciently mothers in
this metropolis, who lived and died in facred obfcurity,
were feldom found from their own houfes, but placed
their humble glory in fhining there, particularly in breeding
their children to every thing prudent and praife-worthy ;
imagine them for a little to return to life, and to obferve
unknown the manners of the prefent age   When, amongft
other things, they faw the daughters of many a citizen,
glittering in gorgeous apparel not paid for, rolling their
eyes on every fide through a large affembly, ftudying by
every childifh art to draw the notice of the men, contending with one another who fhould be moft the objects of
attention, catching with a kind of triumph each tranfient
glance, nor fhewing the fmalleft uncafinefs even to be fta-
red at by the moft licentious eye, or to be blown upon by
the moft corrupted breath of every vile betrayer—I purfue
the defcription no farther—what would our venerable fpec-
tators think of their pofterity ! What grief would fill their
hearts on the occafion! But how great would be their
aftonifhment and horror, when informed, that numbers
of thofe young perfons, whofe behaviour was fo unbecoming, had not been taught by their mothers, their grand
mothers, or any other friend in the world, one folid leffon
of wifdom or frugality, of female decorum or Amiable
Referve!

SERMON

SERMON IV.

ON FEMALE VIRTUE.

1 TIM ii 8, 9

I will—that women adorn themfelves with Sobriety.

A PLAIN drefs you have often found extremely pleafing
What fuch a drefs is to the perfon; that, and much more,
is Sobriety to the mind   Sobriety is a fort of fpiritual vef-
ture entirely void of fhow, fubftantial, home-fpun, and
hardy; calculated to defend againft the injuries of the
world, as well as to cover the nakednefs of the foul, proper to be worn every day, and not unfit for any place where
a reafonable being ought to appear; perfectly decent, and
to a judicious eye extremely beautiful; in a word, fo in-
difpenfible and becoming, that fhe who is without it has
been ever deemed, by the virtuous and wife, an object of
deformity, loathing and wretchednefs Like every thing elfe
of greateft value, its worth is beft known by its lofs That
this quality, which like your daily clothing anfwers fo many ufeful and neceffary ends, fhould like that too not ftrike
the generality of beholders, reflects in my opinion honour
on your fex It would be more efteemed, were it lefs common   And here I muft complain of thofe men who will allow little or no merit to a young woman for being fober,
when, if fhe were not, they would condemn her loudly
If the vice be fcandalous, can the virtue fail of being honourable ?

To argue from an inftance fomewhat fimilar. Becaufe difobedience to parents is unnatural and vile, does it
follow that filial piety deferves little or no praife ? But the
temptations to this crime are ufually inconfiderable, frequently none at all, whereas to indecorum, intemperance,
and incontinence, it is certain many women are under
ftrong

ftrong temptations, it is alfo certain, that many have given way to them, it is probable there are but few, whofe
virtue in thofe particulars has not been expofed to very dangerous fnares, yet the far greater part preferve it entire,
and fhall we deny them our tribute of approbation? Forbid
it Generofity and Juftice!

The fpeaking with contempt of what is commonly called Negative Virtue, is often the mere rant of an affected
philofophy   To make fome allowance for the condition of
humanity, were furely more modeft and candid   Where
does he live, and what is his name, who dares be confident, that in any given circumftance of critical trial, his
own refolutions would remain unfhaken?   For vice and
immorality, though there may be alleviations, there can
be no excufe   But yet, on the other hand, fituated as mortals are, a moral, or inoffenfive conduct is fairly entitled to
commendation from mortals   Your fituation, my young
friends, demands much candour from us, and mighty caution in you

The ornament of Sobriety, which comes next to be confidered, is by no means a cheap one. But though it be pur-
chafed with difficulty, it is loft with eafe   To pieferve it,
will require the unremitted exercife of prudence, vigilance,
and fevere circumfpection, or to fpeak more properly,
thefe are parts of this quality, which in effect is of a mixed
and comprehenfive nature.   To defcribe it at large, is not
my defign   The attempt would lead into a difcuffion much
too dry and uninterefting   If poffible, I would engage your
attention to truth, and your hearts to goodnefs, in a different way, by fentiment, perfuafion, and the native influence
of fraternal counfel   Come then, my fifters, and hearken
to a brother, while he endeavours to fhow you on one
fide thofe things which you ought principally to fhun, in
order to the maintaining of your Sobriety, and to point out

on

on the other that positive discipline, which must co-operate
for this purpose   At present we can only undertake the
former of these points But before we proceed to that, let me desire you to take notice with what propriety the apostle's ideas
seem to rise one above another   He begins with that
which is most directly obvious, and the very first precaution to be observed, Modesty of Apparel Then he mentions
Shamefacedness which, though sometimes less apparent,
yet when observed cannot fail of recommending itself to
every eye, and without which decency of garb is mere affectation   Shamefacedness, as he has ranked it, appears
like a kind of finer covering, the virgin veil of chastity to
to be thrown over all the rest   But that it may be a
veil in the best sense, a holy veil and no mask, he subjoins
Sobriety as the more inward habit (so to speak) which
must support and give value to the whole , or, to drop the
metaphor, as that internal and prevailing character, by
which every part of a woman's dress and demeanour must
ever be regulated   Now to cultivate this character, it is
of infinite consequence.

In the first place, to avoid Dangerous Connexions If
that be not done, what is there on earth, or in heaven
that can save you? Of miraculous interposition I think
not at present   She can have no right to expect it, who
throws herself into the broad way of temptation.   What
those dangerous connexions are, it may not be always easy
to explain, when it becomes a question in real life   Unhappily for young women, it is a question sometimes of very nice decision   Cases there are, in which nothing can be
clearer   The man that behaves with open rudeness, the
man that avowedly laughs at virtue, the man that impu-
dently pleads for vice ; such a man is to be shunned like a
rattle-snake   In this case, " The woman that deliberates
" is lost "   What ! would you parley with the destroyer,
when he gives you warning ? Then you are not ensnared,

you knowingly and wilfully expose yourselves If you be poisoned, if you be lost, your folly is without excuse, and your destruction without alleviation.

But in this manner none will proceed, except wretches alike licentious and imprudent Of artful men, the approaches will be silent and slow all will be soft insinuation; or else they will put on a blunt face of seeming good humour, the appearance of honest franknefs, drawing you to every scene of diffipation, with a kind of obliging violence, should violence of any kind be neceffary. If they be also agreeable in their persons, or lively in their conversation; above all, if they wear the air of gentlemen, which, unfortunately for your sex, is too often the case. then indeed your danger is extreme Thus far the trap is concealed. You apprehend nothing, your unsuspecting hearts begin to slide. they are gone before you are aware. The men I am speaking of perceive their advantage the moment it appears I have supposed them destitute of worth. If they be also unchecked by fear, what can preserve you? A sense of reputation the dread of ruin? Perhaps they may, but perhaps not They have often, no doubt, come in to prevent the last excefs And, but for such restraints, what would become of man, a woman who is not under that best one, religious principle? The experiment, however, you will own is hazardous Multitudes have trufted to it, and been undone.

But to those, who in the world's sense are not undone, escape, that is, unhurt: unhurt in their health and spirits, in their serenity and self-enjoyment, in their sobriety of mind and habits of self controul? You cannot think it very feldom at least can you suppofe, that, where there is much fensibility of temper, an ill placed paffion shall not leave behind it, in a youthful breast, great diforder and decay of quiet.

But

But how, you will afk, is the fnare to be eluded, hidden as it frequently is? Not fo hidden throughout, as to be invifible, unlefs you will fhut your eyes Is it not your bufinefs to enquire into the character of the man that profeffes an attachment? Or is the character nothing? Is there no effential difference between a man of decency and honour, or who has all along paffed for fuch, and a man who is known to lead an irregular life, or who is fufpected, however, to be the fmiling foe of female virtue? May you not learn, if you pleafe, with whom the perfon in queftion affociates? Or is a man's choice of company nothing? If not refolved to be blind, you may furely difcover whether fuch a perfon proceeds by little and little to take off the vifor, and appear what he is, by loofe fentiments, indecent advances, an ambiguous ftyle, an alarming affurance, " foolifh talking, and jefting which is not convenient "— I blufh for numbers of your fex, who not only exprefs no difpleafure at thefe things, but by a loud laugh, or childifh titter, or foolifh fimper, or fome other indication of a light mind, fhow real fatisfaction, perhaps high complacence.

Another thing, no lefs abominable, I cannot forbear to mention How common is it to fee young ladies, who pafs for women of reputation, admitting into their company in public places, and with vifible tokens of civility and pleafure, men, whom the moment before they faw herding with creatures of infamous name! Gracious Go D, what a defiance to the laws of piety, prudence, character, decorum! What an infult, in effect, to every man and woman of virtue in the world! What a palpable encouragement to vice and difhonour! What a defperate attempt to pull down, in appearance, and with their own hands, the only partition that divides them from the moft profligate of their fex! Between the bold and the abandoned woman there may ftill remain, notwithftanding fuch behaviour, a diftinction

truction in the world's eye, but we fcruple not to declare, that religion, purity, delicacy, make none

To return from this digreffion, if it be one, we will allow it poffible to put cafes wherein no particular rules of difcovery, no determinate modes of judgment, will enable a young woman, by her own unaffifted fkill, to difcern the dangers that lie in her way. But can a young woman be juftly excufed, or can fhe fairly excufe herfelf, if, where all is at ftake, fhe call not in the joint aid of wife fufpicion, friendly counfel, and grave experience, together with prayers for God's protection more than ordinarily fervent.

But methinks, I hear fome of you afk, with an air of earneft curiofity, Do not reformed libertines then make the beft hufbands? I am forry for the queftion. I am doubly forry, whenever it is ftarted by a Virtuous Woman. I will not wound the ear of modefty by drawing minutely the character of a libertine; but give me leave to anfwer your enquiry, by afking a queftion or two in my turn. In the firft place, we will fuppofe fuch a one really reformed, fo far as to treat the woman he marries with efteem and feeling, and that he gives up for ever his old companions, as far as to an chofen intimacy, or preference of their company to hers. We grant it poffible; we rejoice when it happens. It is certainly the beft atonement that can be made for his former conduct. But now let me afk you, or rather let me defire you to afk your own heart, without any regard to the opinions of the world, which is moft defirable on the fcore of fentiment, on the fcore of that refpect which you owe to yourfelves, to your friends, to your fex, to order, rectitude, and honour; the pure unabufed affection of a man who has not by intemperance and debauchery, corrupted his principles, impaired his conftitution, enflaved himfelf to appetite, fubmitted to fhare with the vileft and loweft of mankind, the

mercenary

mercenary embraces of harlots, contributed to embolden
guilt, to harden vice, to render the retreat from a life of
scandal and misery more hopeless; who never laid snares
for beauty, never betrayed the innocence that trusted him,
never abandoned any fond creature to want and despair,
never hurt the reputation of a woman, never disturbed
the peace of families, or defied the laws of his country,
or set at nought the prohibition of his God,————which,
I say, is most desirable, the affection of such a man, or
that of him who has probably done all this, who has
certainly done a great part of it, who has nothing now to
offer you, but the shattered remains of his health, and of
his heart ? How any of you may feel on this subject, I
cannot say But if, judging as a man, I believed, what
I have often heard, that the generality of women would
prefer the latter, I know not any thing that could sink
them so low in my esteem.

That he who has been formerly a rake may after all prove
a very tolerable husband, as the world goes, I have said already
that I do not dispute But I would ask, in the next place,
is this commonly to be expected ? Is there no danger
that such a man will be tempted by the power of long
habit to return to his old ways , or that insatiable love of
variety, which he has indulged so freely, will some time
or other lead him astray from the finest woman in the
world? Will not the very idea of a restraint, which he
could never brook while single, make him only the more
impatient of it when married ? Will he have the better
opinion of his wife's virtue that he has conversed chiefly
with women who had none, and with men with whom it
was a favourite system, that the sex are all alike? But it is
a painful topic Let the women who are so connected
make the best of their condition, and let us go on to something else If you, my honoured hearers, would preserve
your sobriety, I would warn you,

In

In the fecond place, againft a Diffipated Life , into which many, who I verily believe have no ill intentions, are unhappily drawn by one engagement or another. Youth, fprightl nefs, the love of fociety, the love of fhining, (the laft parparticu ary ftrong in minds were imagination predominates) joined with a tafte for amufement, which the circumfcribed fituation of the fex ferves perhaps only to increafe——— all thofe put together lead them very readily into fuch a tract moft efpecially if their education has lain in that line, or if their connexions, whether natural or accidental, have concured to ftreng ! en the bias But how innocent foever it may be in the firft inftance, who does not know, that in its after confequences it is often to the laft degree hurtful ?

Does it not manifeftly breed an impatience of home and fuch a propenfity to fhow, as, rather than not be gratified, fhall balk the moft important duties, and court the moft improper company ? Does it not tend directly to expence and profufion ? Does it not unavoidably cherifh the paffion for dlenefs and fauntering, fo inconfiftent with every thing folid, ufeful and improving ? Not to fpeak now of the prejudice done by it to the health and conftitution is fuch a temper, and fuch a conduct, agreeable to the great rules of moderation ? Will that mind be acquainted with wifdom, which is averfe to thought ? Will felf-government be her ftudy, who, flies from felf-infpection ? Can Religion or Virtue hope to make any lafting impreffion on a fpirit, that by perpetual agitation is wrought up into mere froth ? What imaginable folly is there that may not find its way into a heart, like the garden of the fluggard, thrown open to every incurfion ? If your mornings be fpent in rambling and dreffing, your evenings in vifits and cards, or public entertainments , if this be the general tenour of your tranfactions, on which fide, I befeech you, can the balance be expected to lie at the bottom of the account ?

Buf

But that perhaps is not your care. ' What have the
' young and the gay to do, but to divert themselves?' Indeed? Were you fent then into this world for no
other purpofe? Do you defign to apply to nothing
ferious? ' Yes, certainly, when we are fettled, and have
' families' But pray, tell me . To act your parts properly then, is there no preparation neceffary now? Is ro-
ving about continually, the way to grow either fond of
domeftic employments, or fit for them? Will neglecting
the leffer affairs committed to you at prefent, difpofe or
qualify you for a larger fphere of activity hereafter?

But have we not often feen young women, that were
thoughtlefs and profufe, turn out very prudent and œconomical wives? We have, and what then? Would you
build a fyftem of action on events fo precarious and unlike-
ly? Becaufe by the force of genius, or a felicity of circumftances, boys who were good for little or nothing at
fchool, have not unfrequently, in procefs of time, fhot up
into men of ability or fpirit, would you thence infer that
youth may fafely trifle away their early years?

But is it certain, after all, that you are to change your
ftate, as well as your character? Will the train of life we
are confidering recommend you much to young men? I
have converfed with many of them on this fubject Shall
I tell you their opinions? Some, I find, would like a
fprightly companion in marriage, but none a diffipated one,
and all of them, to a man, dread a woman of expence. I
fay not, that it is right in this cafe to count the coft too
nicely ; but men that are not very violent lovers, or very
great fools, will not overlook it Our fex of late years
have been by many thought more backward than formerly
to enter into the holy bands of wedlock; and what I hint
at has been affigned as a principal caufe.

It is too common, I confefs, to hear thofe who have
been

been addicted to vagrant pleafures, and vain profufion,
plead the fmallnefs of their fortunes as an excufe for not marrying, when, if they connected themfelves with women of
fobriety and difcretion, it is perhaps demonftrable that they
would live cheaper. But what, fay they, if, hoping to
find a help mate, we fhould wed our ruin? I anfwer them,
Choofe the better Shall I give you their reply? ' The
' ladies of the prefent age are fo immoderately expenfive'
—You may guefs the reft.

But it is not only fuch men that fpeak this language.
There are of a different character not a few, who, ftrongly
attached to the worthier part of the fex, wifh for nothing
fo much as an honourable connexion with them, but are
reftrained by the very confideration in queftion We
could eafily convince them, that they carry it too far.
They appeal to facts, and perfift in the argument We
are weary of the difpute It is inconceivable what frivolous articles of parade are infifted on by fome women, of
whom better things might be expected But rivalfhip in
fhow is the ruling paffion of the times, and how much is
it nourifhed by diffipation!

I cannot leave this point without obferving, that one
of the worft confequences attending fuch a courfe is its
throwing many young ladies into the company of women
who with the general reputation of virtue, or under the
particular fhelter of matrimony, are often the very quin-
teffence of vice, a fet of fmooth pernicious tempters, like
Satan to Eve, winding themfelves by flattery into the hearts
of their heedlefs daughters, defcanting on their beauty,
perfections, profpects, and I know not what, firft exciting and then gratifying their youthful curiofity, with
fuch fuggeftions, and fuch tales, as fet their fancies all on
fire, by which any little ftructure of modefty, that Nature
and Education may have raifed, is confumed in a moment.
                                                    Which

Which contribute moſt to their fall from innocence, thoſe
the ſerpents, or the male ones mentioned before, I will
not determine ; but remember I have warned you againſt
both

Permit me farther, on this occaſion, juſt to remind
you of poor Dinah   Secure as you may think yourſelves,
none of you, I ſuppoſe, have been trained more virtuouſly
than it is probable ſhe was under the eye of a pious father.
But, alas ! the ſpirit of wandering ſeized her   " She
" went forth to ſee the daughters of the land "   She met a
betrayer, and loſt her honour.   But I proceed,

In the third place, to caution you againſt that fatal poi-
ſon to virtue   which is conveyed by Profligate and by Improper Books

When entertainment is made the vehicle of inſtruction
nothing ſurely can be more harmleſs, agreeable, or uſeful
To prohibit young minds the peruſal of any writings, where
Wiſdom addreſſes the affections in the language of the imagination, may be ſometimes well meant, but muſt be
always injudicious   Some ſuch writings undoubtedly there
are ; the offspring of real genius enlightened by knowledge
of the world, and prompted, it is to be hoped, by zeal for
the improvement of youth

Happy indeed, beyond the vulgar ſtory-telling tribe,
and highly to be praiſed, is he who, to fine ſenſibilities
and a lively fancy ſuperadding clear and comprehenſive
views of men and manners, writes to the heart with ſimplicity and chaſteneſs, through a ſeries of adventures, well
conducted, and relating chiefly to ſcenes in ordinary life;
where the ſolid joys of Virtue, and her ſacred ſorrows,
are ſtrongly contraſted with the hollowneſs and the horrors
of vice, where, by little unexpected yet natural incidents
of the tender and domeſtic kind, ſo peculiarly fitted to

                                F   touch

touch the foul, the moft important leffons are impreffed,
and the moft generous fentiments awakened, where, to
fay no more, diftrefs occafioned often by indifcretions,
confiftent with many degrees of worth, yet clouding it
for the time, is worked up into a ftorm, fuch as to call
forth the principles of fortitude and wifdom, confirming
and brightening them by that exertion, till at length the
burfting tempeft is totally, or in a great meafure difpelled,
fo that the hitherto fufpended and agitated reader is either
relieved entirely, and delighted even to tranfport, or has
left upon his mind at the conclufion a mixture of virtuous
fadnefs, which ferves to faften the moral deeper, and to
produce an unufual fobriety in all his paffions

Amongft the few works of this kind which I have feen,
I cannot but look on thofe of Mr. Richardfon as well entitled to the firft rank, an author, of whom an indifputable
judge has with equal truth and energy pronounced, " that
" he taught the paffions to move at the command of rea-
" fon " I will venture to add, an author, to whom your
fex are under fingular obligations for his uncommon attention to their beft interefts, but particularly for prefenting
in a character fuftained throughout with inexpreffible
pathos and delicacy, the moft exalted ftandard of female
excellence that was ever held up to their imitation I would
be underftood to except that part of Clariffa's conduct,
which the author meant to exhibit as exceptionable. Setting this afide, we find in her character a beauty, a fweetnefs, an artleffnefs————what fhall I fay more?——
a fanctity of fentiment and manner, which, I own for my
part, I have never feen equalled in any book of that fort;
yet fuch, at the fame time, as appears no way impracti-
cable for any woman who is ambitious of excelling.

Befide the beautiful productions of that incomparable pen,
there feem to me to be very few, in the ftyle of Novel,
that

that you can read with fafety, and yet fewer that you can read with advantage ——What fhall we fay of certain books, which we are affured (for we have not read them) are in their nature fo fhameful, in their tendency fo peftiferous, and contain fuch rank treafon againft the royalty of Virtue, fuch horrible violation of all decorum, that fhe who can bear to perufe them muft in her foul be a proftitute, let her reputation in life be what it will But can it be true—— fay, ye chafte ftars, that with innumerable eyes infpect the midnight behaviour of mortals——can it be true, that any young woman, pretending to decency, fhould endure for a moment to look on this infernal brood of futility and lewdnefs?

Nor do we condemn thofe writings only, that, with an effrontery which defies the laws of God and men, carry on their very forehead the mark of the beaft We confider the general run of Novels as utterly unfit for you. Inftruc- tion they convey none They paint fcenes of pleafure and paffion altogether improper for you to behold, even with the mind's eye. Their defcriptions are often loofe and lufcious in a high degree, their reprefentations of love between the fexes are almoft univerfally overftrained. All is dotage, or defpair, or elfe ranting fwelled into burlefque. In fhort, the majority of their lovers are either mere luna- tics, or mock-heroes. A fweet fenfibility, a charming tendernefs, a delightful anguifh, exalted generofity, heroic worth, and refinement of thought, how feldom are thefe beft ingredients of virtuous love mixed with any judgment or care in the compofition of their principal characters

In the Old Romance the paffion appeared with all its enthufiafm But then it was the enthufiafm of honour, for love and honour were there the fame The men were fincere, magnanimous, and noble; the women were pat- terns of chaftity, dignity, and affection They were

only

only to be won by real heroes, and this title was founded
in protecting, not in betraying, the sex   The proper
merit with them consisted in the display of disinterested goodnefs, undaunted fortitude, and unalterable fidelity   The
turn of those books was influenced by the genius of the
times in which they were composed, as that, on the other
hand was nourished by them   The characters they drew
were, no doub, often heightened beyond nature, and
the incidents they related, it is certain, were commonly
blended with the moft ridiculous extravagance   At prefent,
however, I believe they may be read with perfect fafety,
if indeed there be any who choofe to look into them

The times in which we live are in no danger of adopt-
ing a fyftem of romantic virtue   The parents of the prefent generation, what with felling their fons and daughters
in marriage, and what with teaching them by every poffible means the glorious principles of Avarice, have con-
trived pretty effectually to bring down from its former
height that idle, youthful, unprofitable paffion, which has
for its object perfonal attractions, in preference to all the
wealth of the world   With the fuccefsful endeavours of
thofe profoundly politic parents, the levity of diffipation,
the vanity of parade, and the fury of gaming, now fo
prevalent, have concurred to cure completely in the fafhionable of both fexes any tendency to mutual fondnefs

What has a modifh young gentleman to do with thofe
antiquated notions of gallantry, that were connected with
veneration for female excellence, invincible honour, and
unfpotted fame? Is it not enough for him, if he intended
to ftrike the matrimonial bargain, that by himfelf, or an
old cunning father, he can drive a good one, to get poffeffion of fome woman, whofe fortune joined to his own, if
any fhe have, fhall enable him to glitter in public, and in
private to gratify other favourite inclinations more freely?
Provided thefe grand points are gained, in the perfon he
                                                    thus

thus trafficks for to be the partner of his life, what signifies her appearance, her understanding, or her character? And those Fine Ladies who seek conquest only for show, too well instructed in the superior consequence of that, to put any value on so simple a thing as a Heart, merely for its own sake, what else have they to mind but securing, by what ever arts, such settlements as shall place them, when married, on a level with their companions, or if possible above them, in the all-important articles of gaiety and splendor? As to men's hazarding any thing in the defence of girls, who may take it into their heads to think of reputation, delicacy, sentiment, and other such exploded ideas, what can be so foolish?—although to hazard their lives in a drunken quarrel for a prostitute might, perhaps, be brave?

That in so polite an age the elevations of love, the sanctity of truth, and the majesty of virtue, should pass for knight-errantry, cannot be surprising, nor is it any wonder, that the very best things, in the productions last mentioned, should be no way interesting to a modern reader, whose taste and manners are formed on standards far different Some, however, may not be displeased to hear the opinion of no less a judge than Milton concerning them. It seems they were one of his early studies, and that on a moral account As his words to this purpose are remarkable, and not much known, I shall take the liberty to quote part of them   " I betook me among those lofty fables and " romances, which recount in solemn cantos the deeds of " knighthood, founded by our victorious kings, and from " hence had in renown over all Christendom   There I " read it in the oath of every knight, that he should de- " fend, to the expence of his blood, or of his life, if it so " befell him, the honour and chastity of virgin or matron. " From whence, even then, I learnt, what a noble virtue " chastity sure must be, to the defence of which, so many
                                             " worthies

" worthies by fuch a dear adventure of themfelves had
" fworn. And if I found in the ftory afterwards, any of
" of them by word or deed breaking that oath, I judged it
" the fame fault of the poet, as that which is attributed to
" Homer, to have written undecent things of the Gods
" Only this my mind gave me, that every free and gentle
" fpirit, without that oath, ought to be born a knight,
" nor needed to expect the gilt fpur, or the laying of a
" fword upon his fhoulder, to ftir him up both by his coun-
" fel and his arm to fecure and protect the weaknefs of any
" attempted chaftity.

To come back to the fpecies of writing which fo many
young women are apt to doat upon, the offspring of our
prefent Novelifts, I mean the greater part' with whom
we may join the common herd of Play-writers Befide
the remarks already made on the former, is it not manifeft
with refpect to both, that fuch books lead to a falfe tafte
of life and happinefs, that they reprefent vices as frailties,
and frailties as virtues, that they engender notions of love
unfpeakably perverting and inflammatory; that they overlook in a great meafure the fineft part of the paffion, which
one would fufpect the authors had never experienced, that
they turn it moft commonly into an affair of wicked or of
frivolous gallantry, that on many occafions they take off
from the worft crimes committed in the profecution of it,
the horror which ought ever to follow them; on fome occafions actually reward thofe very crimes, and almoft on
all leave the female readers with this perfuafion at beft, that
it is their bufinefs to get hufbands at any rate, and by
whatever means? Add to the account, that repentance
for the fouleft injuries which can be done the fex, is generally reprefented as the pang, or rather the ftart, of a moment, and holy wedlock converted into a fponge, to wipe
out at a fingle ftroke every ftain of guilt and difhonour,
which it was poffible for the hero of the piece to contract—

—Is

—Is this a kind of reading calculated to improve the principles, or preferve the Sobriety, of Female minds? How
much are thofe young women to be pitied, that have no
wife parents or faithful tutors to direct them in relation to
the books which are, or which are not, fit for them to
read! How much are thofe parents and tutors to be commended, who with particular folicitude watch over them
in fo important a concern!

I conclude with faying, that the fubject of this difcourfe
has unavoidably fuggefted fome ideas which, had we not
undertaken to addrefs young women at large, we fhould
have certainly fuppreffed for the fake of more modeft natures, whom we would not willingly pain, no not for a
moment But fuch we hope will be candid enough to excufe us, if, by throwing out to others what to them would
have been unneceffary, we may be happily inftrumental in
refcuing were it but one of their fex from the flavery of
vice, or defending a fingle innocent from its fnares.

SERMON

SERMON V.

On female Virtue, Friendship, and Conversation

I TIM ii 8, 9

I will—that women adorn themfelves with Sobriety

COL v 6

Let your Speech be always with Grace, feafoned with Salt

To preferve the Sobriety enjoined by our apoftle, there is required a pofitive difcipline, as well as the negative part already explained · Be not alarmed at the name of Difcipline, In what we are going to propofe you will find nothing forbidden or harfh We do not, you may beLeve, wifh to fee you cut off from the friendly intercourfe and innocent delights of fociety, confined to convents, as millions of your fex moft unnaturally are in popifh countries, and there condemned to the idle yet fatiguing tafk of a devotion unreafonable in many refpects, uninterefting in moft, feeble for want of temptation, vifionary and dry at the fame time The genuine intention of piety was certainly to make its difciples amiable, ufeful, and happy; to give folidity to every virtue, and grace to every relation of human life Is it poffible to reflect on the prodigious multitudes of women fhut up in thofe dens of fuperftition, without feeling horror at a fyftem which, under the guife of super or fanctity, facrifices to hopelefs folitude, frequently all the flower of youth and beauty, fuch fwarms of helplefs beings, who, had they remained in the world, might have been the ornament of their own fex, the delight of others, the mothers of a numerous race, and bleffings to every country where they dwell?

Of the colours with which this cruel practice is difguifed by the church of Rome we are not ignorant and we can even conceive, that the prepoffeffions of art, and the foft-

cerings

enings of habit, their Commerce with one another, their employments in their priſon, and often, I doubt not, the ardour of a well-meaning though much miſtaken zeal, that all theſe may have the power to reconcile many of them to a ſtate, otherwiſe gloomy beyond expreſſion. But what ſhall be ſaid for the ſituation of the reſt, and what can juſtify the flagrant oppoſition of ſuch a ſyſtem to the ſacred laws of ſocial duty, and the truly benevolent, joyful, and active ſpirit of the religion of Jeſus, as taught and exemplified by himſelf and his apoſtles ?

But to proceed in our plan. From dangerous connections, from a diſſipated life, and from books of a corrupting tendency, we attempted to put you upon your guard in our laſt diſcourſe. In the preſent we will endeavour to point out that Society or Converſation, and in ſome following ones thoſe Talents or accompliſhments, which will contribute at once to fortify you againſt ſuch ſnares, if they ſhould fall in your way, to ſubdue any propenſities that might expoſe you too raſhly to their influence, to ſtrengthen all your virtuous reſolves, and to ſupply inexhauſted ſources of ſolid, rational, and refined entertainment.

As to the Converſation which you ought with theſe views to cultivate, it may be proper,

Firſt of all, to ſay ſomewhat concerning thoſe Early Friendſhips with one another, that uſually lead you to the moſt intimate communications. I take it for granted there is no young woman who has not, or wiſhes not to have, a companion of her own ſex, to whom ſhe may unboſom herſelf on every occaſion. That there are women capable of friendſhip with women, I cannot for my part, queſtion in the leaſt. I have ſeen indubitable proofs of it, and thoſe carried as far as ſeemed compatible with

the

the imperfections of our common nature. I know it is
questioned by many men; while others believe, that it
happens exceedingly seldom Between married and unmarried women, I hope it happens very often. Whether
it does so between those that are single, I confess myself a
little doubtful The preacher will be probably charged
with partiality to his own sex, when he adds, that, so
far as he has been able to observe, young men have appeared more frequently susceptible of a generous and steady
friendship for each other, than females as yet unconnected;
especially if the latter have had, or been supposed to have
pretensions to beauty not yet adjusted by the public

Having professed himself however, what (as often as
truth will permit him) he really is, an advocate for the sex,
and this being the feature in their character which seems
to him the most unfavourable, he is willing to find out
whether in their frame and condition, compared with
those of the men, there be any circumstances which may
help towards an apology, and he argues in the following
manner

The state of matrimony is necessary to the support,
order, and comfort of society. But it is a state, that
subjects the women to a great variety of solicitude and
pain Nothing could carry them through it with any
tolerable satisfaction or spirit, but very strong and almost
unconquerable attachments To produce these, is it not
fit they should be peculiarly sensible to the attention and
regards of the men Upon the same ground, does it not
seem agreeable to the purposes of Providence that the securing of this attention, and these regards, should be a prin-
pal aim But can such an aim be pursued without frequent
competition And will not that too readily occasion jea-
lousy, envy, and all the unamiable effects of mutual rival-
ship I mean, without the restraints of superior worth
and

and sentiment   But can these be ordinarily expected from
the prevailing turn of female education, or from the little
pains that women, as well as other human beings, commonly take to controul themselves, and to act nobly ? In
this last respect, the sexes appear pretty much on the same
footing   in others, it is manifest that the nature and situation of the men are very different   Their constitution of
mind, no less than of body, is for the most part hardy and
rough   By means of both, by the demands of life, and
by the impulse of passion, they are engaged in a vast diversity of pursuits, from which your sex are precluded by decorum, by softness, and by fear   This diversity of daily
pursuits, joined with the multiplicity of female objects,
that freer modes of living present to their imagination, and
the power they have of unlimited choice whenever they
are disposed to make it (a power which Nature probably,
and Custom certainly, have denied to the others), all this
put together, must in the case of our sex, be productive
of every different effects

Do I mean by this reasoning to justify in yours the indulgence of those little, and, I must needs say, in many instances, base passions towards one another, with which
they have been so generally charged ? God forbid. I only
mean to represent such passions in the first approach, and
while not entertained, as less criminal than the men are apt
to state them, and to prove, that, in their attachment
to each other, the latter have not always that merit above
the poor women, which they are apt to claim   In the
mean time it will be your business, by emulating them
where they appear good-natured and disinterested, to dis-
prove their imputation, and to shew a temper open to
Friendship, as well as to Love

To talk much of the latter is natural for both, to talk much
of the former, is considered as one way of doing themselves
honour.

honour. Friendship, they well know, is that dignified form, which in speculation at least every heart must reverence But in friendship, as in religion, which in many respects it resembles, speculation is often substituted in the place of practice People fancy themselves possessed of the thing, and hope that others will fancy so too, because they are fond of the name, and have learnt to talk about it with plausibility Such talk indeed imposes, till experience gives it the lie

To say the truth, there seems in either sex but little of what a fond imagination, unacquainted with the falshood of the world, and warmed by affections which its selfishness has not yet chilled, would reckon Friendship In theory the standard is raised too high, yet, methinks, I would not have it set much lower I would not, on any account have the honest sensibility of ingenuous nature checked by the over-cautious documents of political prudence No advantage, obtained by such frigidity, can compensate the want of those warm effusions of the heart into the bosom of a friend, which are doubtless among the most exquisite pleasures, at the same time that it must be owned, they often, by the inevitable lot of humanity, make way for the bitterest pains which the breast can experience Happy beyond the common condition of her sex is she, who has found a Friend indeed, open-hearted, yet discreet, generously fervent, yet steady, thoroughly virtuous, but not severe, wise and chearful at the same time ! Can such a friend be loved too much, or cherished too tenderly ? If to excellence, as well as happiness, there be any one way more compendious than another, next to friendship with the great Almighty, it is this

But when a mixture of minds so beautiful and so blessed takes place, it is generally, if not always, the result of early prepossession, casual intercourse, secret sympathy, inexplicable

cable

cable attraction, or elfe a combination of fuch caufes as are
not to be brought together by management or defign This
noble plant may be cultivated ; but it muft grow fpontaneoufly. I can only therefore wifh to each of you, beloved,
the felicity of finding fuch a friend , and, having found
her, the wifdom to ufe her well

For the more general commerce of focial life, a few
advices may not be improper That, like the ordinary
duties of religion, may be directed with tolerable advantage
by human precepts The harmonies of holy friendfhip,
like the fublimer contemplations of the Divinity, muft depend more immediately on that hand, which can alone
attune the finer movements, and exalt the beft conceptions
of the foul. Let us go on then,

In the fecond place, to what he may term the common
tenor of your company, which, for the fake of our fubject,
we muft fuppofe left in fome meafure to your own choice.
That it ought to be fuch as fhall not corrupt your good
manners, is a principle already eftablifhed. It will be
likewife underftood that, in the fociety you choofe to frequent, you will feek for that ftyle of virtue which is moft
adapted to the turn of your own minds. But this laft propenfity fhould not, I apprehend, be indulged too far. I
will explain myfelf

The more intimate reciprocations of a clofe friendfhip
are now, as you know, out of the queftion That at your
time of life you fhould be particularly fond of fprightly
converfation, where all is enlivened and joyful, and where
Wifdom, when allowed to enter, puts on her gayeft garb,
is perfectly natural. To advife you againft it were as
weak, as it would be unfriendly Such fprightlinefs and
freedom, when fupported by fenfe, and chaftened by decency, have always, I frankly acknowledge, appeared to
me

me delightful. Dulnefs and infipidity, morofenefs and rigour, are dead weights on every kind of focial intercourfe, nor will I conceal it from you that I wifh, as much as any of you can do, to make my efcape from them on all occafions But tell me, my lively friends, when the heart overflows with gaiety, is there no danger of its burfting the proper bounds? Is not extreme vivacity a near borderer on folly? To prevent its breaking loofe, and throwing itfelf into very ferious inconveniencies, into a very hurtful conduct, will furely require the check of felf-command. But how is that to be attained? By affociating only with the fanciful, the vivacious, or the witty? Is hazard to be fhunned by rufhing into the field of battle? Or, to reprefent things at the beft, is familiarity with Wifdom to be contracted moft readily, where Wifdom appears moft feldom? Would ye form habits of fobriety, a fpirit of fedatenefs, no way inconfiftent with innocent mirth, you muft frequently refort to the company of the fober and the fedate But will not thefe be chiefly found among fuch as are farther advanced in years than yourfelves? Should not you be ambitious of profiting by their experience and knowledge? And will not a refpect for fuperior age, when poffeffed of fuperior difcretion, often prove a feafonable reftraint on the wildnefs of more youthful fallies? "He that walketh with wife men fhall be wife," faid the wifeft of mortals Is not the maxim equally applicable to women?

Will you give me leave on this occafion to mention what is much to the honour of our fex, that all the moft fenfible and worthy of yours, have ever profeffed a particular relifh for the converfation of men of fenfe and worth. Such men, I prefume, are attached to the fociety of fuch women beyond every thing elfe in the world And when circumftances favour, this mutual tendency cannot fail to be a rich fource of mutual improvement. Was not fuch reciprocal aid a great part of Nature's intention in that mental and mortal difference of fex, which fhe has marked by characters no lefs diftinguifhable, than thofe that diverfify their outward forms?

To adopt the language of an amiable writer, who has ftudied the human heart with fuccefs. " We believe that " it is proper for perfons of the fame age, of the fame fex, " of fimilar difpofitions and purfuits, to affociate together. " But here we feem be deceived by words If we con- " fult nature and common fenfe, we fhall find, that the " true propriety and harmony of focial life depends upon " the connection of people of different difpofitions and cha- " racters judicioufly blended together. Nature hath made " no individual, nor no clafs of people, independent of " the reft of their fpecies, or fufficient for their own hap- " pinefs. Each fex, each character, each period of life, " have their feveral advantages and difadvantages, and that " union is the happieft and moft proper, where wants are " mutually fupplied. The fair fex fhould naturally expect to " gain from our converfation, knowledge, wifdom, and fe- " datenefs and they fhould give us in exchange humanity, " politenefs, chearfulnefs, tafte, and fentiment " He adds, " The levity, the rafhnefs, and folly of early life, are tem- " pered with the gravity, the caution, and the wifdom of " age ; while the timidity, coldnefs of heart, and languor " incident to declining years, are fupported and affifted by " the courage, the warmth, and the vivacity of youth."

The converfation of people older than yourfelves will be often accompanied with lefs joy at the moment, but afterwards it will make abundant compenfation It will produce more recollection and be affured, my fifters, thofe are the trueft pleafures which are tafted by a mind compofed and ferious. In that fituation, every thing is felt more ftrongly A diffipated fpirit is too fuperficial to be capable of deep or permanent delight. Befides, as

has

has been already hinted, the experience and maturity of
more years will enlarge your underſtandings, at the ſame
time that they will repreſs your vanity and preſumption;
while the ſportiveneſs peculiar to youth will, on your
part, enliven the ſeriouſneſs of age   And if thoſe, whom
you thus reſpectfully cultivate, have any good nature,
they will certainly treat you with condeſcenſion and forbearance   I ſaid Good Nature, for whatever excludes
that, is ſure to loſe all the influence, as well as praiſe of
wiſdom.

On this principle, I would particularly recommend to
you the company of thoſe, whoſe piety is of the moſt chearful and moſt charitable ſtrain   They are ſtrangers to human nature, who would affright the young by the frown
of auſterity.   True religion ever was, and ever will be, of
the friendly kind   It is not zeal, but bigotry, that refuſes
to make allowance for juvenile ſpirits and gayer tempers.
Could the old be convinced by us, there is nothing we
ſhould be at greater pains to impreſs upon them than this,
That as chearfulneſs is the moſt natural effect of real goodneſs, it is alſo its moſt powerful recommendation   Wiſdom is never ſo attractive as when ſhe ſmiles.

But do not, my dear hearers, conceive an unfavourable
opinion of that venerable form, if in the virtue of your mothers and aunts you ſhould happen to find a defect of good
humour   Conſider the conſequences of declining health,
diſagreeable accidents, the death of their beſt friends, frequent inactivity, and depreſſion after a life of action and enjoyment   If you can look forward ſo far as a few years at
moſt, it will be right for you to think what you may probably feel at their age   And pray remember, that if you
require and expect allowances to be made for ſtarts of ill-hu-
mour in yourſelves, at a ſeaſon when all ſhould be naturally ſoft and gentle, it is but fair at leaſt that you ſhould ex-
cuſe

cuſe the ſame in thoſe who, not to inſiſtnow on their other claims, are objects of tender ſympathy, as being invaded by languor, infirmity, and affliction

I cannot, however, omit to caution them againſt giving way too eaſily to that peeviſhneſs, which is apt to grow upon them from theſe circumſtances and to remind them, that in ſuch as have ſurvived the lively taſte of delight themſelves, there is nothing ſo noble or pleaſing, as not to diſcourage others who ſtill retain it, but on the contrary to ſhow a generous ſat'sfaction in ſeeing and making young people happy   Ah! my reſpected friends, why would you ever forfeit this higheſt honour of an excellent temper? Why would you ever render your company forbidding, or aſſiſt in the ravage which Nature is unavoidably making on your attractions?   Why rob Religion of that engaging appearance, which is not only her native appearance, but ſo peculiarly neceſſary to promote her intereſt with unexperienced minds, in oppoſition to the wiles of her laughing rival?   You will hardly believe how much harm is done by this conduct to the beſt of cauſes.

The world will judge of piety by its profeſſors   The proceeding is often unfair, becauſe they are often unlike that which they profeſs.   But there is no poſſibility of preventing it.   The young have heard religion repreſented as an enemy to joy and affability   Nothing can be more unjuſt.   Inſtead therefore of confirming thoſe prejudices, it becomes you to confute them by the only argument that will thoroughly convince, the chearfulneſs of your diſcourſe, and the mildneſs of your demeanour   In this way you may hope to do great good.   When " Wiſdom is thus " juſtified of her children," they who are yet ſtrangers to her will be induced to venerate an authority that appears ſo condeſcending, and to ſtudy precepts that are productive of ſuch happineſs   But to return to my young hearers, allow me,

In

In the third place, to offer you a few hints on the ſpirit
and manner, in which I conceive your Converſation
ſhould be conducted And now perhaps you imagine we
want to preclude every degree of that which paſſes under
the name of Trifling You are miſtaken We do not
expect that women ſhould always utter grave ſentences,
nor men neither It were inconſiſtent with the ſtate of
mankind It cannot be expected from philoſophers of the
firſt rank, nor if it could, do I know that it would be de-
ſirable I am even inclined to believe, that they who underſtand the art of what has been termed Trifling agreeably,
have gained a very conſiderable point. The frailty of human nature, and the infelicity of human life, require to
be relieved and ſoothed There are many occaſions, on
which this is not to be done by ſage admonitions, or ſolemn reflexions Theſe, to well diſpoſed minds, are often
highly ſolacing, but to dwell on them always, were to
ſtrain the machine beyond its powers Beſides, in fact,
a ſeaſonable diverſion to anxiety, a temporary forgetfulneſs
of grief, is frequently a far better method to remove it,
than any direct application or laboured remedy. To
change the metaphor, when the road proves rugged, or
is in danger of growing tedious, one ſucceſsful method of
beguiling it is for the travellers to chear and amuſe one another by the play of fancy and the facetiouſneſs of mirth.
But then the end of the journey muſt not be forgotten
Becauſe we are weak there is no reaſon why we ſhould be
ſilly The brow of care may ſurely be ſmoothed without
converting it into the laugh of folly While we indulge
the recreation neceſſary for mortals, let us maintain the
temper requiſite in immortal beings To reconcile theſe
two things, and to blend them happily ſeems the proper
ſcience of creatures on their progreſs through time to eternity From you, my gentle friends, we look for every
thing that, next to the diviner influence of religion, can
ſoften the inequality, and animate the dulneſs of the way
We

We wish to see you often smile, but we would not have you smile always, if it were possible There are many scenes that demand a grave deportment, there are not few that call for a mournful one She that cannot distinguish between laughter and happiness, never knew what the latter means She that cannot " weep with them that weep," as well as " rejoice with them that rejoice," is a stranger to one of the sweetest sources of enjoyment, no less than to one of the noblest lessons of Christianity Those are the happiest dispositions, which are the best Benevolence is the supreme perfection of the ever blessed Deity He is infinitely removed from every painful impression Yet scripture, in the style of accommodation, ascribes to him all the guiltless emotions of humanity and we know that our SAVIOUR was formerly on earth, and is now in heaven, " touched with the feelings of our infirmities."

With the character of a Christian Woman nothing, methinks, can better correspond than a propensity to melt into affectionate sorrow It becomes alike her religion and her sex. Never, my fair auditory, never do your eyes shine with a more delightful effulgence, than when suffused with all the trembling softness of grief, for virtue in distress, or of solicitude, for friendship in danger Believe me, if the gaiety of conversation gave place somewhat oftener to the tender tale of woe, you would not, to such at least of your male acquaintance as have hearts, appear at all the less lovely The sigh of compassion stealing from a female breast on the mention of calamity, would be rather more musical in their ears, than the loud bursts of unmeaning laughter, with which they are often entertained Let me add here, that the charms of innocence and sympathy appearing in your discourse, will, to every discerning man, spread around you a lustre which all the jewels in the world cannot bestow

The diamond's and the ruby's blaze
Diſputes the palm with beauty's queen
Nor beauty's queen commands ſuch praiſe,
Devoid of virtue if ſhe's ſeen

But the ſoft tear in Pity's eye
Ou ſhines the diamond's brighteſt beams,
But the ſweet bluſh of Modeſty
More beauteous than the ruby ſeems.

If we ſpeak of improvement, merciful Redeemer, how
edif ing to the ſoul is this generous ſenſibility! " It is bet-
" ter to go to the houſe of mourning, than to the houſe of
" feaſting, for that is the end of all men, and the living
" will lay it to heart Sorrow is better than laughter for
" by the ſadneſs of the countenance, the heart is made bet-
" ter The heart of the wiſe is in the houſe of mourning,
" but the heart of fools is in the houſe of mirth As the
" crackling of thorns under a pot, ſo is the laughter of the
" fool This alſo is vanity." You know who ſaid ſo—
The man who had ſpent many a day, and many a night,
in the bower of voluptuouſneſs, far from the cries of miſery, and the moans of complaint, who gat him " men-
" ſingers and women-ſingers, and the delights of the ſons
" of men,' who had, times without number, ſaid in his
heart, " Go to now, I will prove thee with mirth, there-
' fore enjoy pleaſure,' who ſought by a prudent uſe of
wine, to exalt his own ſpirits, and to promote the hilarity
of thoſe about him, in a word who kept not from his eyes
whatſoever they deſired, nor with-held his heart from any
joy This, I ſay, was the man whom experience, as well
as inſpira on, prompted to give the preference you have
juſt now heard There is—yes, there is attendant on virtuous ſadneſs, a ſenſation, which, in point of indulgence
and elevation, at once, is ſuperior to all that was ever felt
by a light mind, in the fluſh of feſtivity, or amidſt the triumph of wit

Having

Having mentioned Wit, let me to proceed to warn you againft the affectation and the abufe of it. Here our text from the Colloffians comes in with propriety, " Let your " Speech be always with Grace, feafoned with Salt " Thefe remarkable words were addreffed to chriftians in general They are confidered by the beft commentators, as an exhortation to that kind of converfe, which, both for matter and manner, fhall appear moft graceful, and prove moft acceptable, being tempered by courteoufnefs and modefty, and feafoned with wifdom and difcretion, that, like falt, will ferve, at the fame inftant, to prevent its corruption, and heighten its flavour. How beautiful this precept in itfelf ! How ufeful and pleafing in the practice ! How peculiarly fit to be practifed by you, my female friends, on the turn of whofe converfation and deportment fo much depends to yourfelves, and all about you! From what I have now to offer, it will be found likewife to come, with advantage, in aid of our leading doctrine; fince there are not perhaps many worfe foes to that Sobriety of fpirit, which we would ftill inculcate, than the abufe and affectation already mentioned

It is not my defign to gather up, if I could, the profufions of flowers that have been fcattered by innumerable hands on this tempting theme, and by which thofe very hands have, in their own cafe, fhown how difficult it is to refift the temptation I would only obferve, that the dangerous talent in queftion has been well compared to the dancing of a meteor, that blazes, allures, and mifleads Moft certainly it alone can never be a fteady light and too probably it is often a fatal one Of thofe who have refigned themfelves to its guidance, how few has it not betrayed into great indifcretions at leaft, by inflaming their thirft of applaufe; by rendering them little nice in their choice of company, by feducing them into ftrokes of fatire, too offenfive to the perfons againft whom they were levelled, not to be repel'ed upon the authors with full vengeance; and finally, by making them, in consequence of that heat which produces, and that vanity which fosters it, forgetful of those cool and moderate rules that ought to regulate their conduct?

A very few there may have been, endowed with judgment and temper, sufficient to restrain them from indulging " the rash dexterity of wit," and to direct it to purposes equally agreeable and beneficial But one thing is certain, that witty men for the most part have had few friends, though many admirers Their conversation has been courted, while their abilities have been feared, or their character hated, or both In truth the last have seldom merited affection, even when they first have excited esteem Sometimes their hearts have been so bad, as at length to bring their heads into disgrace At any rate, the faculty termed Wit, is commonly looked upon with a suspicious eye, as a two-edged sword, from which not even the sacredness of friendship can secure It is especially, I think, dreaded in women. In a Mrs Rowe, I dare say, it was not. To great brilliancy of imagination, that female angel joined yet greater goodness of disposition; and never wrote, nor, as I have been told, was ever supposed to have said, in her whole life, an ill-natured, or even an indelicate thing Of such a woman, with all her talents, none could be afraid In her company, it must have been impossible not to feel respect, but then it would be like that, which the pious man entertains for a ministring spirit from heaven, a respect full of confidence and joy If aught on earth can present the image of celestial excellence in its softest array, it is surely an Accomplished Woman, in whom purity and meekness, intelligence and modesty, mingle their charms. But when I speak on this subject, need I tell you, that men of the best sense have been usually averse to the thought of marrying a witty female?

You

You will probably tell me, they were afraid of being
outſhone, and ſome of them perhaps might be ſo But I
am apt to believe that many of them acted on different motives Men who underſtand the ſcience of domeſtic happineſs, know that its very firſt principle is eaſe, Of that
indeed we grow fonder, in whatever condition, as we advance in life, and as the heat of youth abates But we cannot be eaſy, where we are not ſafe We are never ſafe
in the company of a critic, and almoſt every wit is a critic
by profeſſion. In ſuch company we are not at liberty to
unbend ourſelves All muſt be the ſtraining of ſtudy, or
the anxiety of apprehenſion how painful! Where the
heart may not expand and open itſelf with freedom, farewell to real friendſhip, farewell to convivial delight! But
to ſuffer this reſtraint at home, what miſery! From the
brandiſhings of wit in the hands of ill-nature, of imperious
paſſion, or of unbounded vanity, who would not flee? But
when that weapon is pointed at a huſband, is it to be wondered if from his own houſe he takes ſhelter in the tavern?
He ſought a ſoft friend, he expected to be happy in a reaſonable companion He has found a perpetual ſatiriſt, or
a ſelf-ſufficient prattler How have I pitied ſuch a man,
when I have ſeen him in continual fear on his own account,
and that of his friends, and for the poor lady herſelf, leſt,
in the run of her diſcourſe, ſhe ſhould be guilty of ſome petulance, or ſome indiſcretion, that would expoſe her, and
hurt them all! But take the matter at the beſt; there is
ſtill all the difference in the world between the entertainer
of an evening, and a partner for life Of the latter a ſober
mind, ſteady attachment, and gentle maners, joined to a
good underſtanding, will ever be the chief recommendati-
ons, whereas the qualities that ſparkle, will be often ſuf-
ficient for the former.

As to the affectation of wit, one can hardly ſay, whether it be moſt ridiculous or hurtful The abuſe of it,
which

which we have been juft confidering, we are fometimes,
perhaps too often, inclined to forgive, for the fake of that
amufement, which, in fpite of all the improprieties mentioned, it yet affords   The other is univerfally contemptible and odious   Who is not fhocked by the flippant impertinence of a felf-conceited woman, that wants to dazzle
by the fuppofed fuperiority of her powers? If you, my
fair ones, have knowledge and capacity, let it be feen by
your not affecting to fhow them, that you have fomething
much more valuable, humility and wifdom.

> " Naked in nothing fhould a woman be,
> ' But veil her very wit with modefty
> ' Let man difcover, let not her difplay
> ' But veild her charms of mind with fweet delay "

Muft women then keep filence in the houfe, as well as
in the church? By no means There may indeed be many
cafes, in which it particularly becomes a young lady to obferve the apoftolic rule, "Be fwift to hear and flow to fpeak;"
but there are many too, wherein it will be no lefs fit, that
with an unaffuming air fhe fhould endeavour to fupport
and enliven the converfation It is the opinion of fome,
that girls fhould never fpeak before company, when their
parents are prefent, and parents there are, fo deficient in
underftanding, as to make this a rule How then fhall
thofe girls learn to acquit themfelves properly in their abfence? It is hard if you cannot diftinguifh, and teach your
daughters to diftinguifh between good breeding and pertnefs,
between an obliging ftudy to pleafe, and an indecent defire
to put themfelves forward, between a laudable inquifitive-
nefs, and an improper curiofity But this, I confefs, is
not the moft common miftake in the education of young
women, and they muft permit me to fay, that it were well
if the generality of mothers were careful, by prudent inftruction in private, to reprefs that talkative humour which runs
                                                    away

away with ſo many of them, and never quits them all their life after, for want of being curbed in their early years But what words can expreſs the impertinence of a female tongue, let looſe into boundleſs loquacity ? Nothing can be more ſtunning, except where a number of Fine Ladies open at once——Protect us, ye powers of gentleneſs and decorum, protect us from the diſguſt of ſuch a ſcene——Ah ! my dear hearers, if ye knew how terrible it appears to a male ear of the leaſt delicacy, I think you would take care never to practiſe it

For endleſs prattling, and loud diſcourſe, no degree of capacity can atone I join them together, becauſe in effect they are ſeldom ſeparate But the noiſy, empty, trivial chatter of everlaſting folly—it is too much for human patience to ſuſtain. How different from that playful ſpirit in converſation, ſpoken of before ; which, blended with good ſenſe, and kept within reaſonable bounds, contributes like the lighter and more careleſs touches in a picture, to give an air of eaſe and freedom to the whole ! This freedom and eaſe, when accompanied with decency and variety, a certain native prettineſs and unſtudied correctneſs, are among the moſt pleaſing characteriſtics of female ſociety in its beſt ſhape.

Your talking ſo much about dreſs, and faſhions, and faſhionable amuſements, as the far greater part of you are ever doing, in preference to better ſubjects, is, to ſay the ſofteſt thing of it, a weakneſs which cannot be juſtified, but which perhaps muſt, in ſome meaſure, be forgiven to your ſex As to the love of ſcandal and diſpute, which may be called the Acid of Speech, in contradiction to the Salt recommended by our apoſtle, it muſt be reſerved for a future conſideration. The men, indeed, are ready to triumph at the very mention of it Whether they have reaſon to triumph on the whole, may be a difficult queſtion The agreeable qualities named a moment ago, they muſt fairly

give

give up to the women How few of them in comparison, possess, or at least exercise the power of keeping discourse alive, without assistance from wine, from politics, from business, from the news of the day, and from another theme, for which their unrestrained and inextinguishable passion, in male company, argues a descent of soul, a degradation of thought, whereof men endowed with the least understanding, ought to be ashamed!

I just mentioned Unstudied Correctness as appropriated to the conversation of cultivated women I mean that easy elegance of speech, which results from clear and lively ideas, expressed with the simplicity of nature, somewhat aided by the knowledge of books To this the best scholars amongst the men, must seldom or never lay claim It is necessarily precluded by their profounder studies, and that scrupulous attention to the minutest rules of grammar, which is induced by the turn of their education, and which, though by practice it may become in a great degree habitual and mechanical, will yet appear deficient in the happy facility, wherewith so many females clothe their sentiments That they, who are naturally fond of ornament in every thing else, should show a certain honest neglect of it, where it is least requisite, where it is generally hurtful, by embarrassing and fettering that which ought to be free and unaffected, surely entitles them to some praise.

How often have we seen very ingenious men perplexed, when they have wished to explain themselves on some topic by no means abstruse, and which they perfectly understood! With how little grace have we heard them tell a story! In these, and such like points, women of any capacity excel To what can the difference be owing? I fancy to this, that the former, in their words and ideas, attend too sedulously to precision and embellishment, while the latter are content to speak just what they mean, and

to

to relate ſimply what they read or heard, as it riſes to their minds, without the labour of accuracy, which often hampers the faculties in their operation, and diſturbs the train of nature.

On this principle, I preſume, is founded that maxim, which makes the perfection of art to lie in concealing it; an attainment extremely uncommon, and which, where it has taken place, has been always conſidered as the moſt difficult, and the moſt beautiful, of any that can diſtinguiſh the productions of taſte From that it is, that the celebrated works of ancient genius have been judged to derive a large ſhare of the ſuperiority uſually aſcribed to them From the ſame ſource chiefly, to compare ſmall things with great, has probably ariſen that peculiar happineſs in letter-writing, which the men, I think, are willing to allow to your ſex Here, indeed, they comfort themſelves with their ſuperior ſtrength, and depth, and learned elegance in that, and other matters where intellect is concerned. Pretenſions to theſe, with a few exceptions, I believe, to ſay the truth, you had better reſign.

For my part, I could heartily wiſh to ſee the female world more accompliſhed than it is, but I do not wiſh to ſee it abound with metaphyſicians, hiſtorians, ſpeculative philoſophers, or Learned Ladies of any kind I ſhould be afraid, leſt the ſex ſhould loſe in ſoftneſs, what they gained in force; and leſt the purſuit of ſuch elevation ſhould interfere a little with the plain duties and humble virtues of life. Amiable inſtances of the contrary I know there are I think at this moment of one lady, in particular, who to an extenſive knowledge in philoſophy and languages ancient and modern, with ſome portion of poetical genius and a conſiderable degree of literary fame, has the ſenſe and worth to join every domeſtic quality that can adorn a woman in her ſituation

To

To inculcate fuch qualities, together with thofe elegant and intellectual improvements, which young ladies
would do well to acquire, with a view to fobriety, ufefulnefs, felf-enjoyment, and the powers of pleafing, will be
the bufinefs of fome fubfequent addreffes. What place religion ought to have in female difcourfe, muft be likewife a
fubject of enquiry under another head. In the mean while,
let me intreat you to recollect, that on cultivating a proper
fpirit of converfation will depend a great part of your proficiency and ours, of your future confequence and merit in
fociety; of your entertainment, fatisfaction, and, I may
add, fafety, through the fucceffive ftages of life Much
of that life is fpent in fcenes of focial intercourfe.   Important occafions arife but feldom A large proportion muft
be configned to trifles. Little things belong to little
mortals The virtue and happinefs of the fexes are principally affected by the daily indifcriminate tenor of their
commerce. What felicity, and what glory, may not you,
my friends, derive from thofe talents by which that is regulated and fweetened, refined and raifed!

SERMON

SERMON VI.

On Female Virtue, with Domestic and Elegant Accomplishments.

1 TIM ii 8, 9.

I will—that women adorn themselves with Sobriety.

PROV xxxi 10, 3t.

Who can find a Virtuous Woman? For her price is far above rubies ———Give her of the fruit of her hands, and let her Works praise her in the gates.

To divert fancy, to gratify desire, and in general to be a sort of better servants, are all the purposes for which some suppose your sex designed. A most illiberal supposition! The least degree of refinement or candour will dispose us to regard them in a far higher point of light. They were manifestly intended to be the mothers and formers of a rational and immortal off-spring, to be a kind of softer companions, who, by namelefs delightful sympathies and endearments, might improve our pleasures and soothe our pains: to lighten the load of domestic cares, and thereby leave us more at leisure for rougher labours, or severer studies, and finally, to spread a certain grace and embellishment over human life To wish to degrade them from so honourable a station, indicates a mixture of ignorance, groffnefs, and barbarity. But the men who think in this manner, do themselves irreparable wrong, by putting it out of their power ever to enjoy the tendereft sentiments, and moft delicious feelings of the heart. He that has a true taste of happinefs, will choose, for his own sake, to cherish the kindeft opinion of the female deftination

Yet what shall we say' Are there not many women who seem to have entirely forgotten it themselves, to have

relinquished

relinguifhed at leaft the moft valuable part of their claim,
and to have confpired with thofe male tyrants in finking
their own importance ? How often do we fee them disfigu-
red by affectation and caprice! How often difgraced and
ruined by imprudence! What fhameful inattention to the
culture of their minds, in numberlefs inftances! What
perverfion, in not a few, of excellent underftandings,
through a levity that paffes for innocent, becaufe not polluted by vice, nay for agreeable, becaufe accompanied with
youth! Who that is a well wifher to the fex, can forbear to be mortified on finding fuch multitudes fo ungainly
in their manners, fo unentertaining in their difcourfe, fo
deftitute of every folid and ufeful improvement, in a word
fo totally devoid of all that can confer fignificance, or
beget efteem, not to fpeak of downright worthleffnefs,
proceeding from bad principles or wicked company.

With refpect to thefe indeed, as well as the reft, I
am willing to believe, that they are frequently occafioned
by vacancy of thought, and want of occupation, which
expofe the mind to every fnare; and that, in many cafes
all this evil might, through God's bleffing, be happily prevented by an early and diligent application to Female Accomplifhments Such, therefore, I will proceed to recommend, as a farther means of maintaining the fobriety enjoined by our apoftle. Not that I propofe, to confine
myfelf to this fingle view. Every other laudable and
beneficial purpofe, which thofe accomplifhments are calculated to ferve, will concur to enforce them They may
be divided into three claffes, Domeftic, Elegant, and Intellectual

As to the firft, I muft remind you that, how much
foever they may be now neglected by many women as below their notice, no height of rank or affluence can juftify
fuch neglect The care of a houfhold all ages and nations
                                        have

have agreed to conſider as an indiſpenſible part of female
employment, in every ſituation that admits it   The paſſage from which I have taken one of my texts deſerves, on
this occaſion, your particular attention   As it exhibits,
perhaps, the moſt beautiful picture that was ever drawn
of the Virtuous Woman, in a ſphere of activity which
you all hope to fill, and for which you ought to qualify
yourſelves as much as poſſible in your preſent condition ;
I will read the whole, together with a ſhort paraphraſe, which
I have borrowed chiefly from the pious and learned biſhop
Patrick, but without adhering to his diction

Verſe 10 " Who can find a Virtuous Woman ? for
" her price is far above rubies ' Such a perſon, ſays the
mother of Lemuel (a young prince, for whoſe welfare ſhe
was moſt tenderly ſolicitous) ſuch a perſon as I would recommend for a wife is hard to be found , one endowed
with true worth and piety, who deems nothing beneath
her that can any way become her ſtation ; one, in ſhort,
poſſeſſed of thoſe various and excellent qualities that fit her
for adorning it, and render her infinitely more valuable
than all the pearls or precious ſtones, with which ſo many
women are fond of being decked

11 " The heart of her huſband doth ſafely truſt in her ,
" ſo that he ſhall have no need of ſpoil " In her perſonal
honour and fidelity, and alſo in her œconomy and prudence
with regard to all affairs at home, her huſband repoſes ſuch
perfect confidence, that he can go abroad, and attend to
public buſineſs, without the ſmalleſt anxiety about his
domeſtic concerns, or the leaſt temptation to enrich himſelf at the expence of other men.

12 " She will do him good, and not evil, all the days
" of his life " She will not only return his love with
equal affection, but endeavour to enſure and heighten his
esteem

efteem by every engaging and refpectable virtue She will not only avoid whatever might provoke or difpleafe, but ftudy to deferve well of him by promoting his intereft, and raifing his reputation, and that not merely by ftarts, or in tranfient fits of good humour, but uniformly and conftantly every day of her life.

13 " She feeketh wool and flax, and worketh willingly " with her hands " To Her, idlenefs is fo hateful, that her hufband has no occafion to excite her to induftry. Of her own accord fhe fets up a linen and woollen manufacture, to which fhe applies her hands fo readily, as well as fo dexteroufly, that it is apparent fhe delights in the work.

14. " Sne is like the merchants fhips fhe bringeth her " food from afar " Her application and ingenuity enable her to maintain her family without expence, by exchanging the product for foreign commodities, when neceffary, on terms no lefs advantageous, than if her hufband fitted out a fleet of merchant fhips, to fetch them directly from diftant countries.

15 " She rifeth alfo while it is yet night; and giveth " meat to her houfhold, and a portion to her maidens " With fuch fpirit and vigour does fhe proceed, that, inftead of indulging herfelf in over much fleep, fhe rifes before break of day, to make provifion for thofe who are to go abroad to work in the fields, and to fet her maidens their feveral tafks at home.

16 " She confidereth a field, and buyeth it : with the " fruit of her hands fhe planteth a vineyard." So far is fhe from wafting her hufband's eftate, that by her frugality and capacity fhe is continually improving it; firft purchafing a field fit for corn, when fhe meets with one that on due infpection, fhe finds worth the price, and then

from

from the fruit of her own labours, adding to it a vineyard, which ſhe takes care to have well planted.

17 " She girdeth her loins with ſtrength, and ſtrength-
" eneth her arms." As ſhe is quick in her orders to thoſe about her, ſo ſhe beſtirs herſelf with the utmoſt activity, declining no pains or exertion proportioned to her ſtrength, which is increaſed by conſtant exerciſe, and which, with the chearfulneſs, expedition, and utility that attend it, ſhe prefers to all the decorations and delicacy of indolent beauty.

18. " She perceiveth that her merchandize is good · her
" candle goeth not out by night." Her labour indeed ſhe finds ſo wholeſome, and her traffick ſo profitable, that ſhe does not always conclude her work with the day , but often continues it through as much of the night, as can be ſpared from neceſſary repoſe.

19. " She layeth her hand to the ſpindle, and her hands
" hold the diſtaff" Such manual operations as are ſuited to her ſex, ſhe reckons not any diſparagement to her quality. Her fingers ſhow a dexterity that is alike pleaſing in the performance, and beneficial in the effects.

20. " She ſtretcheth out her hand to the poor: yea,
" ſhe reacheth forth her hands to the needy." Thoſe hands, which ſhe employs with ſo much diligence, for the advantage of her family, ſhe fails not to ſtretch out with equal alacrity for the relief of the indigent She is not ſo engroſſed by the cares of her own houſhould, as to forget the claims of thoſe who have no habitation. In her, frugality never degenerates into parſimony, but always miniſters to munificence. The poor, whether nearer or more re-
mote, ſhare liberally in her bounty

21. " She is not afraid of the ſnow for her houſhold:

H   " for

" for all her houfhold are clothed with fcarlet." Her
bounty in the mean while is accompanied with fuch difcretion, that her own family and fervants are in no danger
of fuffering by it. They are provided againft the hardeft
winter, they have changes of raiment for the feveral feafons, and when they are to wait upon her, or to appear
on any particular occafion that requires it, fhe is careful
to have them clothed with a degree of fplendour

22 " She maketh herfelf coverings of tapeftry : her
" clothing is filk and purple " The furniture of her houfe
is noble Her own apparel correfponds with it. She is
not ignorant of what belongs to her rank, and fhe fupports
it with a magnificence fo much the more confpicuous for
being principally her own handiwork.

23. " Her nufband is known in the gates, when he fitteth
" among the elders of the land." Her attention to the appearance of her hufband is no lefs than to her own. When
he comes into the courts of judicature, and takes his place
amongft the fenators of the country, he is diftinguifhed
by the richnefs and elegance of the robes which fhe has
prepared for him The beholders pronounce him a happy
man, in having fuch a wife as does him honour in public
as well as private, and who, by eafing him of all leffer
cares, leaves him at full liberty to devote himfelf to the moft
important tranfactions.

24. " She maketh fine linen, and felleth it, and deliver-
" eth girdles unto the merchant " Her induftry to provide for her family is fuch, that fhe follows more arts than
one or two; making, for example, befide other articles
already named, fine linen, embroidered belts, and girdles
of different kinds curioufly wrought, which fhe fells at a
confiderable price to the Phœnician merchant.

25 " Strength and honour are her clothing ; and fhe
shall

shall rejoice in time to come." Although in every thing she makes, whether for sale or for use, she displays a just taste of what is both beautiful and splendid, still it must be remembered, that her chief ornaments are a firm and constant mind, a modest and becoming deportment, a manner of dealing with all, that is honourable, uniform, and generous, which, joined to her other qualities before-mentioned, free her from all fear about future events, and prepare her to meet affliction, decay, and even death itself, with serenity and hope.

26. " She openeth her mouth with wisdom, and in her " tongue is the law of kindness." Add to the rest this particular praise, that as she preserves the due mean between taciturnity and loquaciousness, so she loves not to talk on foolish and frivolous subjects, but on such as are serious and useful; on which, when she can introduce them with propriety, she is sure to deliver herself pertinently and gracefully. Her language on all occasions is soft and pleasing, expressive of a gentle mind, and a tender heart. From the same fund, she is led to embrace every opportunity of inculcating on all around her, kind affection and mutual concord.

27. " She looketh well to the ways of her houshold, " and eateth not the bread of idleness." In her own house most especially she is studious of conveying edification. She observes the motions, and inspects the manners of every one there, whom she neither suffers to go abroad at their pleasure, nor to labour at home without proper instruction a concern which might alone be thought sufficient to employ her; insomuch that if she did nothing else, she would yet deserve the bread she eats.

28 " Her children arise up, and call her blessed · her " husband also, and he praiseth her." Happy the children

of fuch a mother, whofe maternal care for their provifion,
but much more for their education, cannot fail of exciting
their love and gratitude very early, and of difpofing them
when grown up, to honour her perfon, and venerate her
virtues! Happy beyond expreffion the hufband of fuch a
wife! He can never commend her fufficiently While
he attempts the favourite fubject, he is fo ftruck with her
furpaffing worth, that he cannot reftrain himfelf from
crying out,

29 " Many daughters have done virtuoufly; but thou
excelleft them all " The number of thofe women who
have acted worthily, who have mightily advanced their
families, and nobly ferved the generations in which they
lived, is not fmall   They are well entitled to applaufe,
and I give it them with pleafure; but there was never
any comparable to Thee. Thy merits, thou beft of women, and moft beloved, thy merits far, far tranfcend
them all!

30. " Favour is deceitful, and beauty is vain. but a
" woman that feareth the Lord, fhe fhall be praifed." A
good complexion and fine fhape are, no doubt, engaging
A graceful mein and lovely features are yet more fo But
as the greateft beauty foon fades, and at laft vanifhes, fo,
alas! many ill qualities may lie concealed under all thefe
fair appearances, fuch, indeed, as utterly difappoint
every hope of happinefs from that quarter. A truly pious
woman, one who is governed throughout by a fenfe of
duty, and who, to all her other excellent qualities, adds
that reverence for God, which gives them at once elevation and ftability—fhe, and fhe alone, is the completely
amiable object, who will always impart delight, and always
deferve approbation.

31. " Give her of the fruit of her hands, and let her
" own works praife her in the gates " Let all confpire
                                                        to

to extol her character, for I cannot do it enough. Let
her never want her juſt tribute of commendation While
ſome are magnified for their high birth, ſome prized for
their great fortune, others admired for their ſingular beauty, and others cried up for attainments of no intrinſic, or
of no conſiderable value, let her perſonal conduct, and
her ſuperior qualities, be celebrated with peculiar honours
in the largeſt aſſemblies; where, indeed, if all men ſhould
be ſilent, that conduct and thoſe qualities would reſound
her praiſe.

What a deſcription is here! Can you attend to it without
emotion? Or have modern manners ſo warped your minds,
that the ſimplicity of ancient virtue, inſtead of appearing
to you an object of veneration, looks romantic and ridiculous? Tell me then in good earneſt, were the women
of thoſe days the leaſt eſtimable, or the leſs attractive, that
they did not waſte their lives in a round of diſſipation and
impertinence, but employed them in works of ingenuity
and uſefulneſs, of piety and mercy; that even women of
the firſt rank amongſt them, as we are informed by the
oldeſt and beſt authors, held it no diminution to apply
their hands to different kinds of manufacture, that they
took great delight in ſuch occupations; and finally, that
good houſewifery, in all its extent, was reckoned an eſſen-
tial qualification of every matron?

I am ſufficiently ſenſible of the influence that the cuſtoms
of different ages and nations have on the modes of thinking
that ſucceſſively obtain; nor do I expect, that in this land
called Chriſtian, which ought to be unequalled on account
of its attainments, as much as it is on that of its advantages,
our mothers or our daughters, in general, will be perſuaded by any thing preachers can ſay, to emulate the humble
grandeur of many a noble lady, of many a fair princeſs
in former generations Yet I am not without hope, that
                                                    ſome

fome of them may be induced to copy, though at a diftance, thofe modeft but exalted originals

I mentioned our daughters, as well as mothers, becaufe I would not have them think that they have nothing to learn from the picture we have laft furveyed. Would the Virtuous Woman, fo fweetly pourtrayed by Lemuel's mother, and fo particularly marked by the characters of married and maternal excellence, have been, what fhe was, if in her fingle ftate fhe had not ftudied the neceffary prin-ciples?

After looking at fo fublime a ftandard, I am well aware that any thing I can now offer on this part of my fubject will appear to fink. I am forry for it. But fince it muft be fo, let the mortifying fentiment be felt by all, as a juft fatire on the declenfion of this age. To fay the truth, the zeal of the preacher is too much depreffed by that con-fideration, to bear him out in urging our young women to a clofe imitation of what however he muft always admire. In fhort, when we fpeak of good houfewifery now a days, we muft fubmit to fpeak in a lower key. Would to heaven that of this fcience many mothers would teach their daugh-ters but the common rudiments, that they were unfafhio-nable enough to educate them to be fit for any thing beyond mere fhow!

What do not great families fuffer daily from the incapa-city, or inattention, of thofe miftreffes that leave all to houfe-keepers and other fervants! How many large eftates might be faved from ruin by a wifer conduct! I muft fay it once more, that no woman in the world ought to think it beneath her to be an œconomift. An œconomift is a cha-racter truly refpectable, in whatever ftation. To fee that time which fhould be laid out in examining the accounts, regulating the operations, and watching over the interefts

of

of perhaps a numerous family—to ſee it loſt, worſe than
loſt, in viſiting and gaming, " in chambering and wanton-
" neſs," is ſhocking   It is ſo, let the incomes be as certain, as conſiderable, or as immenſe as you will, though
by the way they are hardly ever ſo immenſe in reality, as
they often appear   But where, on the contrary they are
both moderate and precarious, a conduct of this kind, we
have no words to ſtigmatize, as it deſerves.

Merchants and tradeſmen that marry ſuch women are
ſurely objects of ſingular compaſſion, if indeed they were
deceived into an opinion, that the women they have choſen for their partners, were taught this neceſſary piece of
knowledge   But very ſeldom, as matters are managed at
preſent, have they ſuch deception to plead for their choice.
Is it poſſible they can be ignorant in what manner young
ladies are bred at moſt of our Boarding-ſchools? And do
they not ſee in what manner they generally behave on
coming home? Some of them, I acknowledged before,
when placed in houſes of their own, appear to much more
advantage than could be reaſonably expected   But I repeat the queſtion I then aſked, Is ſo great a chance, in an
affair of ſuch conſequence, to be relied upon ?

It muſt be owned alſo, that in this age, the order or
figure of a table is pretty well underſtood, as far as relates
to ſplendor and parade.   But would it not be worth your
while to improve upon the art, by learning to connect frugality with elegance, to produce a genteel, or however a
good appearance from things of leſs expence ? I know it is
difficult, eſpecially in great cities, but I am ſure it is laudable, and deſerves to be attempted   This you may depend upon, that moſt men are highly pleaſed to obſerve
ſuch œconomical talents in a young woman, and thoſe talents in one that is married will ſcarce ever fail to animate
the application, excite the generoſity, and heighten the
confidence

confidence of a hufband   The contrary difcourages and
difgufts beyond expreffion; I mean, where the hufband
has any fobriety, or any prudence.   The follies infepara-
ble from profufion, and the miferies daily produced by it,
I do not pretend to enumerate.   A moment's confideration
will convince you, that it is always unwife, and muft be
generally deftructive.

Next to direct profufion is that indifpofition to family
affairs, which too commonly follows on habits of diffipation
contracted early   A young woman who has turned her
thoughts to thofe matters in her father's houfe, or in any
other where Providence may have difpofed her lot, and
who has been accuftomed to acquit herfelf well in any leffer department entrufted to her care, will afterwards, when
her province is enlarged, flide into the duties of it with
readinefs and pleafure   The particulars have already paffed through her mind   The different fcenes, as they rife,
will not difconcert her.   Being acquainted with the leading rules, and having had fome opportunities of applying
them, or of feeing them applied, her own good fenfe will
dictate the reft, and render eafy and agreeable to her that
which, to a modifh lady, is all ftrange, perplexing, and
irkfome   How ftrong the contraft!   Who does not perceive, where the preference is due?

Hear what a mafterly writer, who feems to have been
well acquainted with the world, and particularly the com-
mercial part of it, has advanced on this head in his advice
to a fon, where he is directing him as to the choice of a wife.
" This bear always in mind, that if fhe is not frugal, if
" fhe is not what is called a Good Manager, if fhe does
" not pique herfelf on her knowledge of family affairs, and
" laying out her money to the beft advantage; let her be
" ever fo fweetly tempered, gracefully made, or elegant-
" ly, accomplifhed, fhe is no wife for a tradefman: and,"
he

he even adds, " all thoſe otherwiſe amiable talents will
" but open juſt ſo many ways to ruin." After relating a little ſtory, full of inſtruction, he thus goes on :. " In ſhort,
" remember your mother, who was ſo exquiſitely verſed
" in this art, that her dreſs, her table, and every other
" particular, appeared rather ſplendid than otherwiſe, and
" yet good houſewifery was the foundation of all. and her
" bills, to my certain knowledge, were a fourth leſs than
" moſt of her neighbours, who had hardly cleanlineſs to
" boaſt, in return for their awkward prodigality."

But perhaps you will tell me, that you may never have
occaſion to exert ſuch qualities in any ſphere of conſequence.
The anſwer is obvious. As the future is uncertain, you
ought to acquire them in caſe of need; beſides, in fact,
there is no ſituation, where the general principles of frugality are not neceſſary, on the ſcore both of diſcretion and
charity. In the mean while the acquiſition will be honourable, and the ſtudy uſeful. It not only becomes your ſex,
but will employ your minds innocently, and virtuouſly,
at hours which you might be tempted to ſpend in a very different manner   The ſubject is not intricate; yet it admits
of a conſiderable detail, and will take up ſome time   The
learning to write a fair hand, and to caſt accounts with facility, the looking into the diſpoſitions and practices of ſervants; the informing yourſelves about the prices of every
thing needful for a family, together with the beſt methods,
and propereſt ſeaſons for providing it; the obſerving whatever relates to cleanlineſs and neatneſs in the furniture and
apartments of a houſe   the underſtanding how to deal with
domeſtics, tradeſmen, and others; above all, the obtain-
ing every poſſible light with relation to the nurſing, management, and education of children—theſe and ſuch like articles will, if I miſtake not, furniſh ample ſcope for the exerciſe of your faculties, in the purſuit of what I have termed Domeſtic Accompliſhments. Nor would I have you deſpiſe

pife any one of them as trivial or dull If they fhould
feem either, you muft give me leave to fay the fault is in
you If on any pretence whatever you fhould affect to call
them fo, I fhould deem it a mark of—But I forbear, and,
for your encouragement to fuch application, would take
notice, that from what is thus neceffary and beneficial, you
may, time after time, pafs, with a tranfition often imperceptible, to what is alfo pretty, and entertaining Which
leads me to fpeak,

In the fecond place, of the Elegant Accomplifhments I
propofed to recommend Of thefe all will be found confiftent with Chriftian Sobriety, and feveral conducive to it
Where morals are not in fome meafure concerned, the peculiar modes of an age can occafion no material difference
Some particulars, I am now to touch upon, might not fuit
that unfettled and perfecuted ftate which the firft profeffors
of chriftianity were in, nor that diftinguifhed feverity of
manners which would naturally arife out of fuch a condition,
as well as out of their late feperation from paganifm, and
yet thofe things may be no way improper in a chriftian woman of thefe times, when religion is eftablifhed, when property is fecured, and when the prevalence of a fyftem fupremely benevolent has nothing to fear from a jealous poli-
cy, or a bigoted priefthood

To begin with that exercife which women appear almoft
univerfally fond of, but which fcrupulous minds have ufually thought exceptionable. For my own part, I muft acknowledge, I can fee no reafon for declamation againft the
moderate and difcreet ufe of Dancing " To every thing,"
fays Solomon, " there is a feafon, and a time to every pur-
" pofe under the heaven "—among the reft—" a time to
" dance" Even thofe purfuits which all approve, and
approve moft highly, may be abufed Nothing is exempt
from fnares, but one of the worft is a difpofition to be pee-
v.fh,

viſh, illiberal, and unſociable   In the Jewiſh inſtitution,
it is well known, the exerciſe in queſtion was adopted into
religious worſhip itſelf   It is yet more remarkable, that
in the parable of the prodigal ſon our Saviour mentions dancing, as making a part of the friendly and honeſt feſtivity
indulged on his return.   The ſingle inſtance recorded in
the New Teſtament, wherein it was perverted to a pernicious purpoſe, has been weakly urged againſt a practice
that, uſed with temperance, and prudence, is certainly
adapted to promote health and good humour, a ſocial ſpirit,
and kind affections between the ſexes, with that eaſy graceful carriage, to which Nature has annexed very pleaſing
perceptions in the beholders

With reſpect to this laſt, it ſeems to me, that there can
be no impropriety in it, any more than in modulating the
voice into the moſt agreeable tones in ſinging , to which
none, I think, will object   What is dancing, in the beſt
ſence, but the harmony of motion rendered more palpable? Aukwardneſs, ruſticity, ungraceful geſtures, can
never ſurely be meritorious   It is the obſervation of a
celebrated philoſopher, who was deeply ſkilled on moſt
ſubjects, that " the principal part of beauty is in decent
" and gracious motion " [f] And here one cannot help regret-
ting that this, which may be conſidered in ſome meaſure
the virtue of the body, is not oftener ſeen in our country,
as if the ſole deſign of dancing were to ſupply the amuſement of the hour   A modeſt but animated mien, an air
at once unaffected and noble, are doubtleſs circumſtances
of great attraction and delight

I ſaid a Modeſt mien, for that muſt never be given up
And on this account, I own, I cannot much approve of a
young lady's dancing often in public aſſemblies, which,
without a ſingular guard, muſt gradually wear off that
lovely baſhfulneſs ſo largely inculcated in a former diſcourſe.

Private

Private circles confiſting chiefly of friends and relations, and where perſons of more years than the younger performers are preſent, I ſhould eſteem in every reſpect the moſt eligible Where ſuch precautions are obſerved, and this diverſion is not ſuffered to interfere with health, regularity, modeſt apparel, and prudent expence, I freely confeſs, that I am one of thoſe who can look on with a very ſenſible ſatisfaction, well pleaſed to ſee a company of young people joyful with innocence, and happy in each other. If an exerciſe ſo ſociable, and ſo enlivening, were to occupy ſome part of that time which is laviſhed on cards, would the youth of either ſex be loſers by it? I think not

Having mentioned cards, I will uſe the freedom, unpleaſing as it may prove, or ill bred as it may ſeem, to offer a few plain remarks on the paſſion for them, which is now become ſo ſtrangely predominant, as to take the lead of every thing elſe in almoſt every company of every rank With many indeed it ſeems to be a calling, and, as a witty author has obſerved, " a laborious one too, ſuch as they " toil night and day at, nay do not allow themſelves that " remiſſion which the laws both of God and man have " provided for the meaneſt mechanic The ſabbath is to " them no day of reſt, but this trade goes on when all " ſhops are ſhut. I know not," continues he, " how they " ſatisfy themſelves in ſuch an habitual waſte of their time, " but I much doubt that plea, whatſoever it is, which paſ- " ſeth with them, will ſcarce hold weight at his tribunal " who hath commanded us to redeem, not fling away our ‛ time "

To the ſame occupation what numbers ſacrifice their health and ſpirits, with every natural pleaſure that depends on theſe, not excepting the comforts of freſh air, purſuing it in the country with the ſame unabating ardour as in

town, and to all the beauty and fweetnefs of rural fcenes
in the fineft feafon, preferring the fuffocating atmofphere
of perhaps a fmall apartment, where they regularly, every
day if poffible, crowd round the card-table for hours together! What neglect of bufinefs and ftudy, what ruin of
credit, of fortune, of families, of connexions, of all that
is valuable in this world, often follows the frenzy I fpeak
of, who can exprefs?

I will fuppofe, my fair hearers, nay I do hope, that
the demon of Avarice has not yet taken poffeffion of your
hearts. But do ye know any thing fo likely to introduce
him, as the fpirit of Gaming? Is not this laft a kindred
fiend, and does not he, like moft other tempters, advance by flow fteps, and with a fmiling afpect? Tell me
in fober fadnefs, what fecurity can you have, that the
love of play will not lead you to the love of gaming?

Between thefe I know there is a diftinction. But is it
not a diftinction, at beft, refembling that between twi-
light and darknefs, and does not one fucceed the other almoft as naturally? The former at firft is chearful and ferene, retaining fome rays of pleafantry and good humour,
but by little and little thefe difappear. A deepening fhade
takes place, till at laft, every emanation of mirth and
good nature dying away, all is involved in the gloom of
anxiety, fufpicion, envy, difguft, and every dreadful paffion that lours in the train of Covetoufnefs. I fay not,
that this always happens, but I afk again, what fecurity
is there that it will not happen to you? Did not every
gamefter in the world, whether male or female, begin juft
where you do? And is it not probable, that many of that
infamous tribe had once as little apprehenfion as you can
have, of proceeding thofe lengths to which they have fince
run, through the natural progrefs of vice, no where more
infatuating or more rapid than in this execrable one?

But

But let us suppose the desire of winning should in you
never rise to that rage, which agitates the breast of many
a fine lady, discompofes those features, and inflames those
eyes, where nothing should be seen but soft illumination.
Are there not lower degrees in the thirst of gain, which a
liberal mind would ever carefully avoid? and pray consider
when either by superior skill, or what is called better luck,
you happen to strip of her money, of that money which
it is very possible she can ill spare, an acquaintance, a
companion, a friend, one whom you profess at least to love
and honour, perhaps at the very moment to entertain
with all the sacred rites of hospitality—is there nothing unkind, nothing sordid, in giving way to that which draw⁻
after it such consequences? Is this the spirit of friendship
or humanity? Blessed God! how does the passion I condemn, deprave the worthiest affections of nature, and how
does that bewitching power the Fashion of the times, per
vert even the best understandings, when resigned to its
impostures!

Nor is it the laws of humanity and friendship only, that
are transgressed by the lust of gaming. The sweet emotions of love and tenderness between the sexes, are often
swallowed up by this all-devouring appetite, an appetite.
which, perhaps, beyond any thing else, tends to harden
and contract the heart, at the same time that the immoderate indulgence of it, excludes a thousand little reciprocations of sentiments and joy, which would serve to kin-
dle and feed the flame of virtuous affection ——How much
conversation suffers from it, who does not perceive?

Here indeed you will tell me with an air of triumph,
that it prevents a great deal of scandal. What, then, are
your minds so unfurnished, so vacant, that without cards,
you must necessarily fly to that wretched resource? Creation, providence, religion, books, observation, fancy;

do

do thefe prefent fo narrow a field of entertainment, as to
force you on the alternative of preying either on the reputation, or on the property of others?——But, now I
recollect, while you poffefs an art of fuch utility as this
laft, for filling up the blanks of difcourfe, as well as for
repairing the waftes of extravagance, why fhould you give
yourfelves any trouble to read or think, to enlarge your
ideas or improve your faculties, beyond the ufual ftandard
Surely the knowledge of the moft fafhionable games, of
the moft remarkable characters, of the reigning modes and
amufements of the feafon, with a few common-place compliments, remarks, and matters of fact, but efpecially
fome paffages of private hiftory, told by way of fecret to
all the world, is quite fufficient, by the help of a little vivacity which Nature will fupply, to accomplifh you for
every purpofe of modern fociety ———Alas, how poor
is all this! How unworthy the principal attention of being
made " but a little lower than the angels," and profeffing
to believe in the communion of faints!

But are there not many general companies, in which
it were impoffible to fpend a long evening with any tolerable eafe, or propriety, but by borrowing affiftance from
the card-table? I grant it, as things are now, and, when
you are fo fituated, your complying with the occafion may
be both allowable and proper, provided the ftakes are but
trifling, your tempers not ruffled, and what you win or
lofe, is agreed to be given away in charity. By this means,
perhaps you may " make to yourfelves friends of the mam-
" mon of unrighteoufnefs"

But tell me, I befeech you, where is the neceffity of
being very often in general companies? Are thefe the
fcenes of true enjoyment? What, where the heart cannot
be unfolded, where the underftanding has little or no play
where all is referve, ceremony, fhow, where the fmile

of

of complaisance is frequently put on to deceive, and even the warmest professions of regard are sometimes made the "cloak of maliciousness!"

There is not, methinks, any thing more contemptible or more to be pitied, than that turn of mind, which finding no entertainment in itself, none at home, none in books, none in rational conversation, nor in the intercourses of real friendship, nor in ingenious works of any kind, is continually seeking to stifle reflexion in a tumult of pleasures, and to divert weariness in a crowd.

' But can it be supposed, that even in more private meet-' ings, people should be always able to pass the time with-' out cards?' You ought to speak more plainly, and say, to kill the time; for that is commonly the case. By the most favourable reckoning, the greatest part of those hours that are devoted to play, is lost. That which was begun for amusement, is lengthened out to fatigue. No one improving or generous idea is circulated; no one happy or solacing recollection is secured The whole is to be set down as a large portion of the span of life cut off without advantage and without satisfaction, as far as virtue or reason is concerned

' What then shall we do when together?' Do! Why, converse, or hold your tongues, as good sense and unaffected nature prompt to either Do! Why, work, read, sing, dance, laugh, and look grave by turns, as occasion serves, any thing in the world that is innocent, rather than eternal play. For persons in all the gaiety of health, and sprightliness of youth; persons not relaxed by infirmity, or exhausted by business; persons with numberless sources of delight laid open to them, and every natural relish lively and strong—for them to be at a loss how to spend a single evening without cards, what a degradation of the human mind!

Willing

Willing to corroborate an argument which to me appears of ſuch importance, I will avail myſelf of the words of a writer now living, who is not leſs reſpectable for the force, than for the morality of his pen   Complaining of the fatal paſſion for play, he mentions, amongſt other miſchiefs to which it leads, its tendency " to deſtroy all diſtinctions " both of rank and ſex ; to cruſh all emulation, but that " of fraud, to confound the world in a chaos of folly ; to " with-hold youth from its natural pleaſures, deprive wit " of its influence, and beauty of its charms ; to extinguiſh " the flames of the lover, as well as of the patriot ; to ſink " life into a tedious uniformity, and to allow it no other " hopes or fears, but thoſe of robbing and being robbed." He adds, in the ſame animated ſtyle, " That if thoſe of " your ſex who have minds capable of nobler ſentiments, " will unite in vindication of their pleaſures and their pre- " rogatives, they may fix a time at which cards ſhall ceaſe " to be in faſhion, or be left only to thoſe who have neither " beauty to be loved, nor ſpirit to be feared ; neither " knowledge to teach, nor modeſty to learn, and who, " having paſſed their youth in vice, are juſtly condemned " to ſpend their age in folly."

But I proceed to a more agreeable taſk, that of recommending, in the next place, thoſe ingenious works mentioned a little while ago.

As to needle-work in particular, we find it ſpoken of in ſcripture with commendation   Its beauty and advantages are univerſally apparent.   It was practiſed by ladies formerly, and ladies of the firſt rank, much more than it is at preſent   They indeed had much more leiſure than moſt of their poſterity.   They were ſimple enough, I ſuppoſe, to be in love with home, and to ſeek their happineſs in their duty.   Of that duty they conſidered diligence as a part nor does it appear to have in the leaſt cramped their imaginations.   Of their ſkill in this way we have ſeen very lau-

I   dable

dable monuments They only wanted inftruction in the
principles of the Fine Arts, to give their performances a
a jufter title At any rate, their time would by fuch
means pafs away more pleafantly. They would be under
little temptation of wandering abroad, confequently they
would efcape infinite fnares and inconveniences Then,
too, private converfation would be cultivated on a much
more rational footing, and many a pleafing difcuffion
would arife on the fubject of their various productions.
Their fancies, called forth by a thoufand prettineffes, and
kept up by the fpirit of elegant emulation, would of courfe
be polifhed and exalted This, I believe, will be found
true, that thofe females of the prefent age, who have refo-
lut on enough to copy fo antiquated an example, feldom
fail to prove the moft entertaining companions.

I once knew a lady, noble by her birth, but more noble by her virtues, who never fat idle in company, unlefs
when compelled to it by the punctilio of ceremony, which
fhe took care fhould happen as rarely as poffible Being a
perfect miftrefs of her needle, and having an excellent tafte
in that, as in many other things, her manner, whether at
home, or abroad with her friends (for friends fhe had,
though a woman of fafhion and bred at court) was to be
conftantly engaged in working fomething ufeful, or fomething beautiful, at the fame time that fhe affifted in fupporting the converfation, with an attention and capacity
which I have never feen exceeded For the fake of variety
and improvement, when in her own houfe, fome one of the
company would often read aloud, while fhe and her female
vifitants were thus employed. I muft add, that during an
intimate acquaintance of feveral years, I do not remember
to have feen her once driven to the polite neceffity of either
winning or lofing money at play, and making her guefts
defray the expence of the entertainment.

Permit

Permit me, before I diſmiſs this article, to offer a hint or two, that may not be unworthy your obſervation. Inſtead of that minute and laborious kind of work, which is often practiſed by young ladies, I ſhould think that ſlighter and freer patterns would, for the moſt part, be greatly preferable The ſight would be in no danger of being ſtrained; much leſs time would be required to finiſh them, and, when finiſhed, they would produce a much better effect. They would give, beyond compariſon, more ſcope to the imagination, they would exhibit an eaſe, a gracefulneſs, and a flow, that ought to enter, as much as poſſible, into all works of taſte; and as they would admit a far greater multiplicity of ornament, ſo likewiſe the purport of utility would be promoted in a far higher degree.

The buſineſs of ſhading with the needle is now, comparatively, ſeldom thought of but at ſchool, where it is frequently taught in a paltry, and always in a defective manner, though certainly deſerving a particular attention The diſpoſition, harmony, and melting of colours in this way, afford one of the fineſt exerciſes to female genius, and one of the moſt amuſing that can be imagined, beſide that ſuch productions are the moſt permament.

But the truth is, nothing complete or diſtinguiſhed in thoſe attempts can be expected, while the proper foundation is ſo generally omitted to be laid; I mean Drawing, which is

The third accompliſhment I would take the liberty to inculcate. That many more young ladies would be found qualified for ſuch a ſtudy than is uſually apprehended, I cannot doubt. Several, I am certain, have applied to it with the greateſt ſucceſs and pleaſure, who, before they began, did not promiſe themſelves the leaſt It is truly ſurpriſing, that ſo few of our more intelligent females

males should shew a desire of being instructed in so pleasing an art, at a time when it is to be learned with such advantage and encouragement.

None can be ignorant, that the principles and practice of drawing were never understood amongst us to the height they are at present; owing chiefly to the patronage of a society, that reflects the greatest credit on this country, and on this age. But here, justice to your sex demands an acknowledgment which we joyfully make, that several honorary rewards have been most deservedly gained by young ladies of rank and character, for specimens of ingenuity, which it is to be hoped their grand children will one day mention and emulate with honest pride.

If such of you, my amiable hearers, as are in a situation to try whether Nature has given you talents for this beautiful accomplishment, would fairly make the essay, you might very probably open to yourselves, and to your friends, a spring of entertainment that would never run dry; that would contribute to improve while it delighted you, by adding to your ideas of elegance and grace; that would prevent many a folly, and many a sin, which proceed from idleness, and, be not hurt if I add, that would prove the means of future support, should it please the Supreme Wisdom to reduce you to a state of dependance.

There are other pretty works, extremely proper for female hands, which I need not specify here, since several of the remarks already made, will, I presume, be applicable to them. Let it suffice to say in general, that whatever is genteel, and whatever is useful, in such occupations, should always claim your regard, when you have leisure and capacity. The former you will seldom want, if you have learnt to portion out your time with judgment, and

in

in the latter you ought never to pronounce yourſelves defective, before you have honeſtly tried

The laſt accompliſhment of the elegant kind, which I
ſhall mention, is Muſic This, I conceive, is to be recommended with more diſcrimination than the reſt, how
much ſoever ſuch a notion may contradict the prevailing
opinion. It is very true, there are young ladies who,
without any particular advantage of a natural ear or good
voice, have, by means of circumſtances peculiarly favourable, made great proficiency in muſic. but it is as true,
that they have made it at a vaſt expence of time and application, ſuch as no woman ought to beſtow upon an object, to which ſhe is not carried by the irreſiſtible impulſe
of genius.

In many other arts it is poſſible for original talents to lie
dormant, till called up by aſſiduity or accident, but where
there is a ſtrong propenſion to this, it will, I imagine,
hardly forbear to burſt out, by means of the tranſcendent
pleaſure derived from it on all occaſions. If it do not, if
even the beſt muſic can be heard without a degree of delight, bordering on tranſport, either the practice will never reward the pains neceſſary for acquiring it, or, there
being no native vein of excellence in that way, it will, as
has been commonly obſerved, be diſcontinued on a change
of condition; in which caſe you loſe the labour of years,
that might have been directed with laſting benefit into ſome
other channel.

Be this as it may, you will readily allow, that for a
young perſon who has no turn for the ſtudy I am ſpeaking
of, to be condemned both to mortify herſelf, and to pu-
niſh her acquaintance, by murdering every leſſon put into
her hands, is a very aukward ſituation, however much
her maſter may, for the ſake of his craft, flatter her and
her friends, aſſuring them, perhaps with an air of great
ſolemnity,

folemnity, that he never had a better fcholar in his whole
life   If fhe whofe attainments in this kind are but indifferent, could be contented to amufe herfelf, and thofe of her
own family, now and then, with an air that happened to
pleafe them, it were well   but how does a judicious hearer
blufh for the poor beginner, when fet down by the command of a fond parent, to entertain perhaps a large company, as we have often feen, with performing that of
wh ch fhe fcarce knows the very rudiments, while all is
difappointment on their part, and, if fhe have any underftanding, confufion on hers!

Is the preacher then an enemy to mufic? Much the reverfe   Where there is real genius for it, improved by art,
and regulated by fentiment, nothing furely can be more
charming, or more affecting   Its importance in the ancient Jewifh worfhip, is well known. Of its beauty and
ufefulrefs in our churches, when conducted in a manner
fuitable to its facred purpofe, and not proftituted to levity,
or perverted by oftentation, I am not infenfible. Its influence in all ages and nations ftands univerfally confefled
It is founded in fome of the ftrongeft perceptions of Nature, wherever fhe has feen fit to confer a lively fenfibility
to the melody of founds

But how much is it to be regretted, that this wonderful
charm of melody properly fo called, together with the
whole merit of expreffion, fhould be facrificed, as we frequently find, to the proud but poor affectation of mere
trick and execution, that, inftead of rendering the various
combinations of founds a powerful inftrument of touching
the heart, exciting agreeable emotions, or allaying uneafy
fenfations, as in the days of old, it fhould be generally de-
graded into an idle amufement, devoid of dignity, devoid
of meaning, abfolutely devoid of any one ingredient that
can infpire delightful ideas, or engage unaffected applaufe!
                                                        With

What lover of this enchanting art but muſt lament, that the moſt inſipid ſong which can diſgrace it is no ſooner heard in places of public entertainment, than every young lady who has learnt the common notes, is immediately taught to repeat it in a manner ſtill more inſipid, while the moſt ſublime and intereſting compoſitions, where ſimplicity and greatneſs unite, are ſeldom or never thought of in her caſe, as if the female mind were incapable of reliſhing any thing grave, pathetic, or exalted !

Let me here call on every muſical ſpirit of your ſex, to aſſert the rights of good ſenſe ; and to inſiſt that thoſe, who are entruſted with this branch of their education, ſhall not fail to introduce them, as early as poſſible, into an acquaintance with whatever is moſt beautiful and noble in the article of melody   The more thorough knowledge of harmony may come afterwards, if you be ambitious of advancing ſo far   In the mean time you will have the ſatisfaction of pleaſing the beſt judges, and of entertaining yourſelves with ſuch pieces as, while the words to which they are ſet convey no ſentiments but what are elevated or virtuous, ſhall ſerve to refine and enliven your thoughts, to raiſe your ſpirits into joy, or compoſe them into ſweetneſs, and on choſen occaſions, by the diviner ſtrains of ſolemn muſic, to lift your hearts to heaven, prove a kind of prelude to the airs of paradiſe, and prepare you for joining the choir of angels.

SERMON

SERMON VII.

ON FEMALE VIRTUE, WITH INTELLECTUAL AC-
COMPLISHMENTS

1 TIM II 8, 9

I will—that women adorn themselves with Sobriety.

PROV IV 5, 6, 8, 9

*Get Wisdom, get Understanding —Forsake her not, and she
shall preserve thee love her, and she shall keep thee.—
Exalt her and she shall promote thee.—She shall give to thy
head an ornament of grace · a crown of glory shall she deliver to thee*

IN a country like this, where there is certainly a native
fund of good sense, where sciences and arts are widely cultivated, where works of genius and taste in every kind are
allowed to abound, is it not somewhat strange, that the
common style of conversation should be so little instruc-
tive or entertaining? How seldom do we fall into a company, in which we learn any thing useful, or hear any
thing whatever above the rate of the multitude, such as
low jests, vulgar conceits, incoherent disputation, or im-
pertinent tattle! How very seldom does a thinking man
come away from the visit of an evening, delighted with
his manner of spending it! One who has conversed only
with a small circle of ingenious friends, will hardly conceive what a frivolous, what a piteous thing, the ordinary
strain of company appears to an intelligent by-stander

The favourite communications of men of pleasure are
beyond description corrupt and grovelling, with scarce any
diversity. Those of gay assemblies are the quintessence of
dulness

dulnefs and diffimulation; except only that the firft is
fometimes tinctured with a few fprinklings of fmartnefs, and
the laft always concealed under the fpacious colours of civility   As to the bufy, the learned, and the grave, the
greater part are no fooner releafed from their refpective purfuits, than they throw themfelves loofe into a liftleffnefs
of difpofition, that wanders with impatience in queft of
public diverfion, or diffufes itfelf in private through the
vacuity of idle talk   as if there were no medium between
ferioufnefs and folly, or as if people could not find relief
from the ftretch of application, in the agreeable unbendings
of moderate amufement and rational difcourfe.   In fhort,
if we want to find a converfation enlivened with variety and
fpirit, enlightened by intelligence, and tempered by politenefs, we muft feek for it amongft a few men who join fentiment to knowledge, and a few women who join knowledge to vivacity.

That the number of thefe fhould be fo fmall, compared
with the untaught and the ungoverned Many, is furely
matter of lamentation.   To what fhall we chiefly impute
it ? To what elfe, but to that whirl of diffipation, which,
like fome mighty vortex, has fwallowed up in a manner all
conditions and characters ? That the young indeed fhould
be often carried down the ftream, till they fink into infignificance, is not much to be wondered at, how much foever it is to be regretted.   But, alas! they do not always
ftop there.   From what is trivial, how eafy the tranfition
to what is mean ! How quick the defcent from thoughtlefs-
nefs to vice ! Nothing, perhaps, requires better fenfe, or
a ftricter guard, than to trifle without being foolifh, or to
be frolickfome without fin   They that would hold faft
their righteoufnefs, and not depart from the decorum of
their character, cannot be too careful to regulate their converfation, as well as their conduct, by the great law of reflection,

flection, and in the hour of gaiety itself, not to lose sight of Wisdom. But how should this be expected, where the mind is wholly unimproved, where no internal resources are secured in the days of youth, but all is left to nature, neglected by education, and warped by fashion, or to the scanty supplies which company, news, and accidents afford.

What I would therefore now labour is, with the help of God, to persuade you, my fair auditory, to enrich and adorn your understandings with such attainments, as shall render you not only less dependant on external amusements and empty gratifications, but more superior to every thing corrupting and dangerous, such as shall entertain and edify you at the same time, enable you to enjoy solitude, and qualify you to shine in conversation even without designing it, to inspire a mixture of complacence and respect, in fine, to unite decency and sense with mirth and joy. Thus would I still endeavour to promote that spirit of Christian Sobriety which our apostle inculcates, and by the same means contribute to the felicity and dignity of your sex.

The passage from the Proverbs, which I have read to you, by way of a second text, requires no commentary; and in truth I know not any that could do it justice. As it is, it must strike you at once with its simplicity, tenderness and sublimity. The Wisdom or Understanding, so beautifully personified by Solomon, is doubtless to be considered chiefly as representing Religion, which is certainly the highest exercise of our rational powers. But I see no reason for conceiving it to represent that only. In many parts of his writings it is manifestly used to signify Mental Improvements, in the proper sense of the phrase, nor is there any thing said of it here, which will not in one degree or another hold true of these, when under right direction, besides, in fact, the cultivation of those powers to every

valuable

valuable purpofe is unqueftionably a duty which we owe to
their author   That the exhortation is addreffed by our
infpired writer to a male fcholar, whom in the manner
of eaftern teachers he calls his fon, makes no effential difference in the fpirit of his doctrine, as I hope will appear
from the fequel. '

The degree of thofe Intellectual Accomplifhments which
your fex fhould aim at, I pretend not to determine.   That
muft depend on the capacities, opportunities, and encouragements, which you feverally enjoy   With regard to
all thefe however, this may be faid in general, that they
are better, and more than many of you feem folicitous to
improve

As to the firft indeed, I fcruple not to declare my opinion, that Nature appears to have formed the faculties of your
fex for the moft part with lefs vigour than thofe of ours;
obferving the fame diftinction here, as in the more delicate
frame of your bodies   Exceptions we readily admit, and
fuch as do the individuals great honour in thofe particular
walks of excellence, wherein they have been diftinguifhed.
But you yourfelves, I think, will allow that war, commerce, politics, exercifes of ftrength and dexterity, abftract philofophy, and all the abftrufer fciences, are moft
properly the province of men.   I am fure thofe mafculine
women, that would plead for your fharing any part of this
province equally with us, do not underftand your true interefts   There is an influence, there is an empire which
belongs to you, and which I wifh you ever to poffefs. I
mean that which has the heart for its object, and is fecured by meeknefs and modefty, by foft attraction and virtuous love

But now I muft add, that your power in this way will
receive a large acceffion from the culture of your minds, in
the

the more elegant and polifhed branches of knowledge
When I fay fo, I would by no means infinuate, that you
are not capable of the judicious and the folid, in fuch proportion as is fuited to your deftination in life. This, I
apprehend, does not require reafoning or accuracy, fo
much as obfervation and difcernment. Your bufinefs chiefly is to read Men, in order to make yourfelves agreeable
and ufeful It is not the argumentative but the fentimental talents, which give you that infight and thofe openings
into the human heart, that lead to your principal ends as
Women Neverthelefs, in this ftudy you may derive
great afutance from books. Without them, in effect,
your progrefs here will be partial and confined Neither
are you to attach yourfelves wholly to this ftudy, important as it is, and grateful as you may find it. Whatever
kind of reading may contribute to your general improvement and fatisfaction, as reafonable beings defigned for
fociety, virtue, and religion, will deferve your attentive
regard Suffer me to enter a little into the detail And

Firft, I would obferve, that Hiftory, in which I include
Biography and Memoirs, ought to employ a confiderable
fhare of your leifure Thofe pictures which it exhibits, of
the paffions operating in real life and genuine characters,
of virtues to be imitated, and of vices to be fhunned; of
the effects of both on fociety and individuals; of the mutability of human affairs, of the conduct of divine providence, of the great confequences that often arife from little
events, of the weaknefs of power, and the wanderings of
prudence, in mortal men, with the fudden, unexpected,
ar frequently unaccountable revolutions, that dafh triumphant wickednefs, or difappoint prefumptuous hope,—the
pictures, I fay, which Hiftory exhibits of all thefe, have
been ever reckoned by the beft judges, among the richeft
fources of inftruction and entertainment

On both accounts, we would also recommend books of Voyages and Travels, a favourite study of the celebrated Mr Locke. How amusing to curiosity! How enlarging to our prospects of mankind! How conducive to cure the contracted prepossessions of national pride, and withal to inspire gratitude for the peculiar blessings bestowed upon our country, to excite on one side pity towards the many millions of human beings, left by mysterious heaven in ignorance and barbarity, and to beget on the other, admiration of the virtues and abilities displayed by numbers of these under all the disadvantages that tend to darken and overwhelm them .

Here too we would mention Geography, as closely connected with both the former, as often useful in conversation; and in which a competent skill may be acquired with little application, but much amusement.

These several studies, to which may be added the principal facts, or great out-lines of Astronomy, are beautiful, and they are improving. Some of them present the most interesting scenes; all contain the most pleasing discoveries. They open and enlarge the mind, they dilate and humanize the heart, they remind us that we are citizens of the universe; they shew us how small the part that we fill in the immense orb of being. Amidst the amplitude of such contemplations, superfluous trifles shrink away, wealth and grandeur " hide their diminished heads," a generous ambition rises in the thoughtful mind, to approve itself to the all-inspecting eye of Him to whom none of his works are indifferent, but to whom those only can be acceptable, that, under the uncertainty and imperfection of sublunary things, seek their security, happiness, and glory, in doing well

Permit me to ask, whence it proceeds that studies like
                                                            these

thefe are neglected by the generality of your fex ? Is it becaufe they are not calculated to inflame the fancy and flatter
the paffions , or becaufe to relifh them to purpofe, requires
fome degree of folidity and judgment ?—But did not the
preacher fay, that there were women who are no way
deficient in thefe latter qualities ? He did, and therefore
pleafes himfelf with the hope, that the hints now offered, may imprint conviction on fuch, where there has
been an omiffion, and encourage perfeverance where there
has not

As to works of imagination, it is allowed on all hands, that
the female mind is difpofed to be peculiarly fond of them,
and furely when blended with inftruction, fo as to be rendered more immediately fubfervient to it, they have a particular claim to your attention   In this view, we muft not
forget to recommend Fables, Vifions, Allegories, and fuch
like compofitions, where Fancy fports under the controul
of Reafon ; Dramatic Writings alfo, where truth of
character, and purity of thought are preferved ;
(of thefe laft, how confiderable the number !) Poetry
of all kinds, where a ftrict regard is paid to decorum,
but chiefly of the fublimer forms, where Nature, Virtue,
Religion, painted and embellifhed with all the beauty of a
chafte, yet elevated imagination —What a field is here
opened within the reach, and adapted to the turn of female
faculties ! What a profufion of intellectual ornament is
fpread before you, for memory to collect, and for reflexion
to work upon ! How many fprightly, delightful, and lofty
ideas do here pafs before the mental eye, all dreffed in the
brighteft colours ! How ftrangely inexcufable muft thofe
be, who complain at any time of want of amufement,
when the genus and invention of every illuminated age,
have taken fuch happy pains to fupply the nobleft !

I fay nothing now of Novels and Romances, having had
occafion to fpake of them fo largely in a former
                                        difcourfe.

difcourfe   But I muft not omit to recommend thofe
admirable productions of the prefent century, which turn
principally on the two great hinges of fentiment and
character, joining defcription to precept, and prefenting in
particular the moft animated fketches of modern manners,
where the likenefs is caught warm from life, while the
powers of fancy, wit and judgment, combine to expofe vice
and folly, to enforce reformation, and in fhort, but fpirited effays, to convey the rules of domeftic wifdom and
daily conduct   I need not here name the Spectator, or
thofe who have followed him with various fuccefs in the
fame track ; many of them ingenious, fome of them mafterly writers   How much are both fexes indebted to their
elegant pens, for a fpecies of inftruction better fitted perhaps than moft others of human device, to delight and improve at the fame moment, fuch is its extent, its diverfity
its familiarity, its cafe, its playful manner, its immediate
reference to fcenes and circumftances with which we are
every day converfant !

Works of this kind are peculiarly calculated to allure
the lively and the gay, who are not yet delivered over to
licentioufnefs.   Hardly indeed will girls, for inftance, who
mean no ill, but whofe fancies are all alive and reftlefs,
fubmit to have their underftanding attired at Wifdom's
glafs ; if lovely forms and fmiling images be not often
reflected from thence, to detain the eye, and captivate the
heart.   In reality, none of you, my dear hearers, can be
too well acquainted with thofe approved mafters of life,
thofe able teachers of decorum, thofe fingular fuccefsful
painters of truth and morality   Let me advife you to
dwell on their pictures, to imbibe their fentiments, to
replenifh your minds with that inexhaufted fund of ftories
and examples which they have furnifhed   You cannot fail
of improving under fuch tutors   They too will provide
you with a touch-ftone, by which to judge of other
writings, and while you are fearching " for knowledge as
for

for hid treasures," to seperate between the pure ore and the alloy.

I should not on this occasion do justice to your sex, if I did not say, that such books as those last-mentioned are, in a particular degree, proportioned to the scope of your capacities. Of this I am certain, that amongst women of sense, I have discovered an uncommon penetration in what relates to characters, an uncommon dexterity in hitting them off through their several specific distinctions, and even nice discriminations, together with a race of fancy, and a fund of what may be strictly termed Sentiment, or a pathetic manner of thinking, which I have not so frequently met with in men. It should seem that Nature, by her liberality to the female mind in these respect, has seen fit to compensate what has been judged a defect in point of depth and force; and a real defect, I believe, it is, if estimated absolutely. If estimated with a due regard to the design and formation of the sex, it ought to be considered as no defect at all.

I have already hinted, that to men and women the Almighty has allotted very different provinces, on the filling of which with suitable kinds of ability and excellence depends, under his conduct, the proper perfection and welfare of each. In all I have said therefore, or may yet say, concerning Female Accomplishments, I would be still understood, as recommending what is refined in study, and useful in the milder modes of life; not what is profound in the former, or of no material advantage in the latter. This hinders not, however, but that those ladies, whom Nature, not confining herself to her customary operations, has endowed with any signal strength of genius, may, if favoured also by their situation, give way to that original bent, by prosecuting severer studies to every prudent length. I say, to every Prudent Length. For should they push their application so far as to hurt their more tender
der

der health, to hinder thofe family duties for which the fex
are chiefly intended, or to impair thofe fofter graces that
give them their higheft luftre; nothing, I think, can be
more apparent than that, in fuch cafes, they would relin-
quifh their juft fphere, for one much lefs amiable, and
much lefs beneficial But neither from this, nor from
what was advanced immediately before, does it follow,
that, in what relates to the acquifitions of the mind, women in general may not purfue ftudies that are folid, as
well as entertaining ; which leads me to add,

In the next place, that the moft obvious branches both
of Natural and Moral Philofophy fhould engage fome portion of your time.   That they are fo feldom, and fo flight-
ly thought of, you muft allow me to fay, is a melancholy
reflexion.   Does Creation through her infinitely extended,
and infinitely diverfified fcenery, difplay innumerable
wonders ? Have thefe been traced with fkill and accuracy,
by many learned, and many laborious hands? Are they
laid open to you, and almoft preffed upon you, from every quarter? For of Natural Philofophy, I confider Natural Hiftory as a part —And can ye with a giddy eye turn
away from this glorious fpectacle, to gaze on the meaneft
ornament of beauty, or the fillieft pageant of vanity;
thus poorly, not to fay impioufly, proftituting that admiration which ought to be confecrated chiefly to the works
of your all-perfect Creator ?

Are the great and eternal obligations of Confcience, the
maxims of a wife and worthy behaviour, the duties you
owe to the Supreme of Beings, to your fellow-creatures,
and yourfelves , the rules neceffary for the government of
your own minds in particular, or for the management of
thofe that may be hereafter committed to your care, are
thefe mighty confiderations, unfolded and enforced as they
have been with equal clearnefs and eloquence by various

K   writers—

writers—are these, I say, matters of so little concern with
you, that the business of contriving some petty circumstance of dress, or the care of settling some foolish party of
pleasure, shall be preferred in almost every case of competition?

Here, I must confess, it is difficult to repress the risings
of indignation Here I cannot deny, but the feelings of
contempt, mixed with those of compassion, are in some
danger of banishing the favourable ideas we entertain of
your sex, when seen in happier points of light —For
shame, Ladies, let not this reproach rest on you any longer Hasten to vindicate your reputation from the infamy
of impertinence and nonsense Be ambitious to demonstrate, by the most substantial proofs, that you are capable
of better things than the placing of a ribbon, or adjusting
an head-dress, than the glittering in an assembly-room, or
prattling at a tea-table Be all ardour to emulate those excellent ones of your sex, who, without affecting to despise
any thing that is innocently female, discover in their conversation among their friends, a mind devoted to wisdom,
and ennobled by knowledge.

The duty and advantage of reading the Scriptures, with
a few books of the most serious and devotional strain, I will
take another occasion to consider,—But, I think, I hear
you exclaiming that, though God has given you the capacities of intellectual improvement, men have denied you
the Opportunities of it. Let us therefore proceed to examine how this matter stands, which was

Our second point. If your complaint be well founded,
you are certainly objects of pity, instead of blame If the
men, jealous of dominion, do really seek to depress the women, by keeping them in a state of ignorance, they are
surely guilty of equal cruelty and meanness But though
the complaint be a very common one, and very popular
with

with your fex, I muft take the liberty of faying, that it appears to me without any foundation, adequate to the bit-
ter_nefs with which it has been made, or to the keennefs
with which it has been propagated

That your minds are often much neglected at home,
that they are neglected perhaps yet more at many Boarding-
fchools, we readily admit, and heartily regret   But are
you neverthelefs defirous of knowledge ?   Then, what
fhall hinder you from attaining it ?   Is there any law or
ftatute by which you are prohibited, under fevere pains and
penalties, to read or to think, if you be fo minded ? Books
you have, or may have, on every fubject that is proper
for you   This is not a country where thefe are fcarce ;
where friendfhip, if permitted, will not fupply, or where
Benevolence, if afked, will not lend them.   You will be
pleafed to remember too, that the price of one expenfive
gown, or of one fhining toy, will at any time furnifh a
little library of the beft authors   Nor does it appear, that
you are at a lofs to find as many plays and novels, as the
moft infatiable avidity can devour   But in fact there are
few young ladies, who are not tolerably provided with
books ufeful as well as amufing   and in thofe who are not
under the neceffity of earning their bread, it is both an
idle and unthankful pretence, to plead that they want either opportunity or leifure for any one ftudy befitting
their fex.

Not to fpeak of the time that with fo much propriety
they might, and that, for fo many reafons, they ought to
redeem from endlefs vifitings and other follies , what is
there to prevent their reading alternately to one another,
when cuftom or conveniency engages them at work together ? Such an exercife would not only enlarge the ftock
of ideas in each individual, but alfo prefent materials on
which their minds might operate, with an energy quick-

ened

ened by mutual exertion, "As iron sharpeneth iron, so
"doth the face of a woman her friend." You, my fair
pupils, cannot be offended, that to suit the quotation to
the argument, I should here read Woman for Man. How
smoothly have I seen those hours steal away, which were
thus employed in a little ring of intelligent females, all
sweetly solicitous to improve and be improved by each
other!

By this means too, may be acquired a very valuable
and pleasing accomplishment, that of reading well; and to
this cause, I presume, it is to be ascribed, at least in part,
that there are not a few women who possess it in no contemptible degree, and that there are some who read delightfully. It is likewise probable, in some measure, owing
to that fine feeling of nature and of sentiment, which
may be supposed to result from the delicacy of their or-
gans. If, in the exercise I speak of, they are often deficient, where force and vehemence are requisite, to that
very delicacy it is obvious to impute it; and also perhaps
to their running too commonly into a monotony, which
their teachers have not taken sufficient pains to correct.

Having touched on this head, I will take leave to remark
by the way, that nothing, as I apprehend, can be more
erroneous, than to begin the study of what may be termed
the Art of Reading, with poetry chiefly. For by the
flow and harmony of the numbers, a learner is carried
insensibly into the repetition of those musical tones,
that chance to seize the ear with particular delight; from
which the voice, once got into the same strain, cannot
without a struggle persuade itself to break away: a principal source of the evil of monotony, where it has not been
contracted by bad example, and where the sense of an
author is understood or attended to. Where it is not, the
proper emphasis cannot be expected.

Now

Now to prevent or remedy this prevailing evil, the most likely method, I conceive, would be to begin with frequently reading aloud those productions in prose of which the style is plain and easy, such as unadorned Narrative, short Stories, Familiar Epistles ; but principally those that approach nearest to the language of conversation, such as Dialogues, and the best Dramatic Writings ; mixing for a considerable time, nothing that is versified, and endeavouring to support the voice with firmness and simplicity till you have formed a habit of so doing. Then by slow and almost imperceptible progression, you should advance to what is more varied, rhetorical, and raised ; such as Allegories, Orations, Moral and Religious Discourses, and Essays of the pathetic kind, together with the most beautiful and elevated parts of Holy Writ, keeping to these, till your voice has acquired flexibility, expression, and energy. After repeated and patient efforts in this way, you may proceed with success to reading and reciting pieces of poetry, in different styles ; setting out with those where there is least, and rising gradually to those where there is most of the tender, the impassioned, and the sublime. Need I add, that all this should be practised in the frequent hearing, and under the kind animadversion, of an experienced judge ?

But perhaps you think the practice too laborious and troublesome Do ye ? **Go**, thou trifler, and be ashamed of thy folly —To neglect the study of thy native English, the skilful use of which, joined to sentiment and knowledge, would render thy conversation charming ; and yet contentedly to puzzle thy silly head, with learning a little imperfect French, which it is, a hundred to one if ever thou shalt have occasion to use—how preposterous and futile ! To the language last named, I am no enemy : I only blame its occupying so large a place in the female education of this country For women of rank, the fashion has

made

made it neceſſary   But what can be more ridiculous than
to ſee our city girls, not excepting the daughters of plain
tradeſmen and honeſt mechanics, taught for years together,
at great expence, a ſmattering of that which ſoon after they
leave the Boarding-ſchool is generally forgotten, while
they are left ignorant of the ſuperior beauties, and juſt pro-
nunciation of their mother-tongue?

I mentioned the exerciſe of Reciting verſes   With relation to this, I would only ſay, that I do not wiſh a young
woman to indulge it in any company, that is not very
private and choſen indeed, how much ſoever it is to be
deſired, that ſhe ſhould ſtore her memory with ſome of
the moſt ſelect ſentiments, and ſtriking deſcriptions, from
the beſt writers botn in verſe and proſe.

On this laſt particular I am led to obſerve, that, for a
unſengaged hour, there can be few occupations of greater
entertainment or utility, than that of imprinting on the
mind thoſe paſſages from any good author, which happen
to pleaſe and affect more than ordinary, either by repea-
ting them often at the time, till they are got by heart, or
by writing them down, or ſometimes by doing both   The
advantages of ſuch a practiſe are ſufficiently apparent
Would it be one of the leaſt, think ye, that the attention
of her who was thus employed, would be often turned
from viewing and admiring her perſon or dreſs in the mirror, to tne contemplation of Truth and Virtue, and fixing
their fair and venerable image in her ſoul?

Beſide the ſeveral opportunities of mental culture now
enumerated, I muſt not forget to add, that in all probability
there are few young women who are not, or who may not
be, acquainted with ſome perſons of both ſexes, endowed
alike with worth and capacity, that would take the higheſt
pleaſure, by their converſation and counſel, to aid them
in the purſuit of knowledge, which brings me to conſider,
- In

In the laft place, your complaints of want of Encouragement to that purfuit Who are they then that feek to difcourage you; I have read of foolifh mothers, that would not fuffer their daughters to read, left they fhould dim the luftre of their eyes, or fpoil the bloom of their complexions. But I have never met with one, that ferioufly carried her folly fo far. On the other hand, I have known parents not a few, who, though they had no tafte for knowledge themfelves, would yet fpeak with the utmoft fatisfaction of a girl that was fond of her books.

But perhaps my little friend is afraid, left the men fhould fufpect her of being what the world ftyles in derifion, a Learned Lady Indeed ? Is this then a character fo very eafily acquired, that you are in danger of it the moment you emerge from the depth of ignorance, and begin to think and fpeak like a reafonable being ? You are over hafty in your apprehenfion. A Learned Lady is by no means a creature that we run the rifk of being often fhocked with. For my own part, I have never, ftrictly fpeaking, feen fuch a one, and when at any time I have met with what approached to that character, I muft profefs, I found nothing to excite terror But poffibly you mean a fmatterer in learning There, indeed, I join with you in wifhing you may never incur the imputation.

That men are frighted at Female pedantry, is very certain A woman that affects to difpute, to decide, to dictate on every fubject , that watches or makes opportunities of throwing out fcraps of literature, or fhreds of philofophy, in every company , that engroffes the converfation, as if fhe alone were qualified to entertain, that betrays, in fhort, a boundlefs intemperance of tongue, together with an inextinguifhable paffion for fhining by the fplendor of

her

her fuppofed talents; fuch a woman is truly infufferable.
At firft, perhaps, fhe may be confidered merely as an object of ridicule , but fhe foon grows into an object of
averfion Be affured however, that, where a character
fo unnatural appears, it is not the effect of too much
knowledge, but of too little. The deep river flows on
with a noble ftillnefs, while the fhallow ftream runs bab-
bling along Sufpicious of her own deficiency, the Pedant
we defcribe, fufpects left you fhould difcover it; but inftead
of learning caution from that confcioufnefs, fhe ftrives to
dazzle you with the little fhe does know: Or elfe, what
is more probable, elated with that which to her circumfcribed view appears great, fhe cannot reftrain herfelf from
difplaying it on all occafions; when farther progrefs, and
higher ground, would have taught her modefty, by fhowing her immenfe regions of truth yet untravelled, of which
fhe had no conception before.

In fact, we find that the beft fcholars of either fex are
the leaft oftentatious It will ever be fo, where erudition
is accompanied with judgment, and matured by reflexion
Take care to preferve fober fenfe, and unaffuming manners
far from giving difguft by literary attainments, to any perfon whofe regard is of moment, you will give pleafure to
every thinking man and woman of your acquaintance.
I am even inclined to believe that, when in converfation
you claim no kind of pre-eminence, but inftead of pretending to teach are willing to learn, inftead of courting applaufe, are ready to confer it, inftead of proudly directing
are content quietly to follow the current of difcourfe,
every creature living will be delighted with your deportment, will liften with attention, and even deference, to
one who has thus learnt, that the nobleft improvement of
fuperior knowledge is fuperior humility.

Now and then, indeed, there may be an invidious female, who cannot bear to fee herfelf outdone But that
is

is a circumstance, which will only add to your exaltation;
while every one else will be tempted, for the sake of mortifying her, to pay the more respect to you Be this as it
may, the notion that letters are apt to generate self-con-
ceit, because it cannot be denied, that the abuse of them
has often done so, will in those of the least candour or
discernment, serve to heighten esteem for her, who considers an excellent understanding, as only next in value to
an excellent temper. If on an any occasion it should happen, that the foolish or the worthless of one sex, or of the
other, are prejudiced against a young woman for discove-
ring, though without parade, a cultivated mind, what
then ? Is not the single plaudit of a real judge sufficient to
outweigh a whole theatre of others

But you will ask, Do we not often see handsome idiots
complimented and caressed by those men, from whom better things might be expected, while the most accomplished women in the same company, shall be overlooked, if
destitute of personal charms ? The fact cannot be dissem-
bled, and far be it from me to justify such partiality.
There is in beauty a magic, which certainly does enchant
for a time the generality of beholders. But this will by no
means excuse the injustice of neglecting merit in those who
want that advantage Let it be remembered, however,
that the triumph of their rivals is commonly, like that of
the wicked, short The spell on which it is founded, is
soon broke. Men, at least of any significance, are seldom
long in recovering their senses The admiration raised
by " a set of features, or the tincture of a skin," is often
by the witlessness of the possessor, thrown down in an instant The witchcraft of a fair outside, is always dispelled
by familiarity. Nothing can detain affection or fix esteem,
but that kind of beauty, which depends not on flesh and
blood The least degree of understanding, will be disgusted
at petulance, caprice, or nonsense, even in the fairest
                                                    form.

form. External allurements are continually lofing, internal atractions are continually gaining A beautiful character " is as the morning light, that fhineth more and more
unto the perfect day ' Senfe, fpirit, fweetnefs, are immortal All befide " withers like the grafs" The power of a
face to pleafe, or indeed to difpleafe, is diminifhed every
time it is feen When appetite does not predominate, and
appetite cannot predominate always, the foul will feek a
foul, it will refufe to be fatisfied with any thing lefs If
it find none, in vain fhall the brighteft eye fparkle, in vain
fhall the fofteft finile entice But if a mind appear, and,
wherever it refides, a mind will appear, it is recognized,
admired, and embraced, even though the eye fhould poffefs
no luftre, and finiles fhould at the moment be banifhed by
forrow.

> " Mind, mind alone, bear witnefs earth and heaven,
> " The living fountain in itfelf contains
> " Of beauteous and fublime! Here hand in hand
> " Sit paramount the Graces————"

I cannot conclude this difcourfe, without taking fo fair
an opportunity of addreffing myfelf to fuch of the men as,
by directing their praifes of young women wholly or chiefly
to an outward appearance, turn the attention and folicitude
of the little idols fo ftrongly that way, as often to occafion
the neglect of thofe inward perfections which can alone
give them value Have you forgotten, Sirs, that what
they fee you admire, and hear you applaud, they will be
induced to think moft worthy of admiration and applaufe,
and that on it of courfe they will beftow their whole or their
chief care? If you, who ought to affift their judgments,
and animate their refolutions, in what relates to the conduct of life, be accuftomed to pay your main homage to
their perfons, their perfons they likewife will adore. Beauty with them will conftitute Merit, and every other endowment will be employed as a handmaid to drefs that, if
                                                          not

not as a pandar to fell it. Accordingly I fear, that to your
fcore muft be charged many errors of the fex, often lefs
juftly imputed to them Thofe errors, I am fure, it would
become you to prevent, or to correct at the fource, by
pointing out to them what, in your wifer hours, you want
and wifh them to be, and what, when they are, will not
fail to captivate love, to command veneration, and to add
permanence to both.

Confider, I befeech you, how honourable it will be
for you, inftead of corrupting the fair, to mend them, inftead
of perverting their ideas, to lead their tafte to knowledge
and elegance, to worth and delicacy, to humility and
meeknefs, things which in your inmoft fouls you cannot
but prize, whenever you meet with them in an amiable
woman, and of which you are fecretly convinced the abfence
cannot be compenfated by any advantages of form or feature, any decoration of fafhion or fhow How much nobler the power to fave, than the power to deftroy! How
much fweeter the praife of being efteemed men of virtue
and fentiment, the friends and patrons of the fex, advocates
for their true intereft, and zealous to promote it, than that
of being looked upon as fmooth-tongued courtiers, or good-
natured triflers! To flatter a giddy girl into good humour,
or even tendernefs, by telling her perpetually how handfome or how fine fhe is, requires no capacity Every
empty fellow, every frivolous dangler, every wretch of a
parafite can do the fame But to engage the efteem of a
woman of principle and difcernment, to preferve that efteem
and even to enfure in her breaft a filent teftimony, that you
have contributed to eftablifh this principle, and to improve
this difcernment—is triumph indeed! Thofe coxcombs that
in truth make no diftinction, but yet would perfuade every
young thing they fee, that her face, her fhape, her drefs,
her air, furpafs thofe of all her fex, and after throwing
her into ecftafies of felf-complacence, go away and laugh
to their companions—are a deteftable race

Concerning

Concerning many of you, my friends, I hope, better
things. Nor do I mean by aught I have faid, rigidly to
preclude every degree of compliment in converfation with
the fair fex. I am for commending with moderation, what
is commendable; for acknowledging with prudence, what
is pleafing. Young minds ought to be encouraged. In
every young mind there is fomething good. An agreeable
appearance is certainly engaging. Truth will never deny
it: courtefy will readily own it. But then under the fhelter of kind approbation, falutary counfel may be admitted.
Wifdom may be found a welcome gueft, when introduced
by affection—I was going to fay, that vanity may be fuccefsfully turned againft itfelf. But why fhould the love of
honeft praife be deemed vanity? Even tell your female friends
that you do efteem them for whatever in their charaĉters is
eftimable Tell them without exaggeration, but generoufly at the fame time, what that is. Defcribe with complacence the qualities and accomplifhments, which you
have ever held moft truly attractive, which it is in their
power to acquire, and which it will be their glory to poffefs.
If they have beauty, be not afraid to add how alluring it
appears, when illuminated by fenfe, and arrayed by virtue.
If they have none, remind them freely that fenfe, and virtue have often borne away the palm from the fineft figure
that ever Flattery deified, if deftitute of thofe living and
lafting graces

SERMON

SERMON VIII.

ON FEMALE VIRTUE, WITH INTELLECTUAL AC-
COMPLISHMENTS.

1 TIM. II. 8, 9.

I will—that women adorn themselves with Sobriety.

PROV. IV. 5, 6, 8, 9.

Get Wisdom, get Understanding.—Forsake her not, and she
shall preserve thee: love her, and she shall keep thee.—
Exalt her, and she shall promote thee.—She shall give to thy
head an ornament of grace: a crown of glory shall she de-
liver to thee.

ON the subject of Intellectual Accomplishments much
remains to be said. At a time when they are neglected by
so many women, who, if they read at all, read only for a
little transient amusement, they cannot sure, considering
their importance, be inculcated too strongly. They may,
it is true, be perverted. What is there of the greatest
moment, that may not? Because works fit only for the
veil of darkness have been wrought in the face of day,
does it follow that " light is not sweet, or that it is not a
pleasant thing " for the eyes to behold the sun;" or that
benefits innumerable are not derived to mankind from the
resplendent luminaries of Nature? Were these extinguished
what were this world? And what, think ye, must be that
mind, where all is enveloped in a night of ignorance?
" For the soul," says Solomon, " to be without knowledge
is not good." Of so great a defect do we not see every day
the unhappy consequences in the conduct of both sexes?

With regard to yours, my beloved sisters, I am willing
to

to impute much of the folly and mifery that involve multitudes of women, not to their being altogether unacquainted with the main outlines of their duty, traced by the hand of GOD on every heart a little more or a little lefs clearly, but to their want of that relifh for knowledge, and of thofe attainments in it, which certainly tend to exclude many temptations, and to fortify againft the influence of others. On this account, I muft again and again urge the Culture of your minds. Your Virtue, your Sobriety is intimately concerned in it. That fhall be my firft argument. its connexion with your dignity or figure in life fhall be my fecond, and my third fhall turn on its ufefulnefs to promote your comfort and felicity, confiderations furely that merit your attention. I pray GOD to blefs them for your improvement.

I beg in with fhewing, that the Intellectual Accomplifhments briefly delineated in the preceding difcourfe will have a tendency to exclude many temptations. To what dangerous refources are the generality of young women driven by the love of pleafure and amufement, ill directed! Having formed no tafte for thofe that arife from reading, writing, agreeable reflections, and rational converfation, their paffions, naturally ardent, fly without previous examination to every object which flatters that ardour by promifing all the vivacity of joy. In this career, it is not difficult to conceive what fnares may entrap beauty, and what habits may corrupt innocence. When firft entered on, it is very poffible that no evil is intended. For that very reafon none is fufpected, and this confidence betrays. When Vice begins to unveil her daring front, Confcience is alarmed, and fhrinks from the monfter. But curiofity, opportunity, importunity, the flatteries of felf-deceit, the dreams of youthful fancy, the bias of fafhion, the fear of being ridiculed that venture to oppofe; all thefe concur with the powers of darknefs in mifleading the poor unexperienced

rienced adventurers, and so courses, of which the bare
'idea filled them at a distance with horror, familiarity at last
reconciles them; if not so far as to procure real or thorough approbation, 'far enough however to engage perseverance, attended with a feeling of remorse that gradually
abates, till they are often inextricably entangled in a thick-
et of guilt and wretchedness

What numbers of miserable beings are now lost there,
whose first deviations were occasioned by nothing more
than a desire of escaping from inactivity or dulness to something that might divert or employ! But had an early love
of books prevented this languor, by furnishing at home a
harmless and varied entertainment, such as was adapted to
give play even to the liveliest imagination, there had been
evidently much less inducement to seek it abroad, and many a soul that is at this day hurrying on to destruction,
might probably, in that case, have been walking with
Wisdom and Happiness Nor would I have you think,
that I speak of those only, who have broke through all the
restraints of decorum There are a thousand tracks leading
to sin and woe, beside that infamous road to which the hand
of public censure is pointed

The supposing, indeed, so wide a distance between the
extremities of guilt and its intermediate stages, is among
the most natural mistakes of a mind destitute of knowledge.
Of this internal light one of the greatest advantages is, to
throw such illumination on virtue and vice through all their
essential, and even many of their minute distinctions,
as to make them be discerned with clearness, and felt with
conviction; while there rise up to view nameless beauties
in holiness, and nameless deformities in sin, that pass un-
heeded by the dim inattentive eye of an understanding unin-
formed. This delicacy of perception alone, in a breast
not yet corrupted by evil custom, will create a salutary
dread

dread of many purfuits and connexions that often prove exceedingly hurtful   In general, it feems obvious, that by
how much more we are acquainted with our duty, by fo
much the jufter apprehenfions we fhall have of its importance, and by fo much the greater capacity for performing
it.

But the grand ufe of an affection for knowledge, as to
the point before us, is that of preventing idlenefs and diffipation, which it certainly does where fuch affection is
properly regulated, and this cannot be repeated too frequently, nor preffed too powerfully   The human mind
was made for action   In virtuous action confifts its higheft enjoyment   It will not, it cannot continue long unem-
ployed, efpecially during the fprightly feafon of youth.
Even feeble age find its principle delight in recollecting the
days of juvenile activity, and rehearfing the enterprifes
which diftinguifhed that happy period.   But now there are
many young ladies whofe fituation does not fupply a fphere
of domeftic excercife fufficient to fill up that part of their
time, which is not neceffarily appropriated to female occupations and innocent amufements.   What then fhall they
do with it, or with themfelves, if books be not called in
to their affiftance?   Purfue the enquiry in you own minds.
Many of you, alas! are but too well qualified to purfue it,
can but too well imagine the infipid, foolifh, and even
pernicious expedients, which under thofe circumftances
are early practifed for killing time and thought.

In truth, it cannot appear furprifing to fee thofe who
have no notion of internal entertainment, hunting after fa-
fionable diverfions.   For my part, I am only furprifed
when thofe who from a better education have had opportunities of knowing what an extent and diverfity of ideas
and imagery, of information the moft grateful to the mind,
and of defcription the moft affecting to the heart, may be
found

found in a well chosen library · when such, I say, do yet prefer to all this the hollowness and dulness, which infeparably attend a perpetual train of public amufements, or private vifiting.

But I am inclined to hope, that a preference fo unjuft and unwife, is feldom made by thofe laft mentioned, that *they who have tafted the pleafure of converfing intimately with the beft authors living and dead,* and from this happy commerce have contracted an intellectual turn, will not be often tempted to mingle with the unthinking crowd. When, for the fake of unbending the mind more entirely, and avoiding any unneceffary air of fingularity, they do at any time join it, the fame turn will contribute to preferve them from the feduction of vice and folly.

It is not to be denied, that from the head to the heart the diftance, in a moral reckoning, is often immenfe, that between fublimity of idea and elevation of conduct there is no neceffary connexion   that the fineft fentiment, and the groffeft paffions have, been obferved to meet in the fame mind; that our Firft Mother was betrayed by the pride of knowing, and that the height of capacity in Lucifer, only increafed the fall of that fon of the morning.   All this is true   But fhall we hence infer, that the defire of knowledge well directed, and wifely applied, is not likely to produce any worthy impreffions?

Imagine two young ladies, of whom one delights in elegant and virtuous ftudies, the other in fafhionable idlenefs. Will you fay, that the former is equally in danger with the latter of defcending to vulgar, or to vicious pleafures?   As familiarity with perfons of refined manners may be expected to communicate a correfponding refinement   is it not probable, that intimacy with the moft beautiful compofitions will, in the fame way, impart a beauty to the foul?

L   And

And is there not ground to believe, that this will make her
who is possessed of it, ashamed to allow herself in any thing
unhandsome, even as it is reasonable to suppose, that
she who has been genteely bred, will disdain the thought
of a low behaviour? Or, because the natural tendency
of things is sometimes crossed, will ye say that it is therefore destroyed? Have ye not heard, that a rule is not over-
thrown, but rather confirmed, by exceptions? Young
people, we know, are often corrupted by bad books. and
have we not likewise known them improved by good ones?
She must be depraved and sunk indeed, who from contemplating the majesty and happiness of Virtue in the best
examples, together with the meanness and misery of Vice
in the worst, that history or poetry holds up to view, can
go away, and in her own deportment counteract immediately the feelings of love and admiration for the one, of
contempt and abhorrence for the other, which objects of
this kind must unavoidably awaken. She again, who
should not perceive herself prompted to a prudent and amiable demeanour, or guarded against the contrary, by those
pictures of discretion and excellence on one hand, of levity
and worthlessness on the other, with which sentimental
and moral writers abound, must be absolutely void of decency, or of reflexion To instance but in one subject
more, she must be wholly given up to trifles that can pursue them with the same fondness, after having her imagination raised, and all her faculties expanded, by those wonderful representations of the works of GOD, which are
contained in many books of Philosophy and Geography,
Voyages and Travels

  But now represent to yourselves a young lady, whose
understanding is utterly uncultivated What is there to
correct her passions, or to govern her practise? What is there
to direct her in her choice of companions, and diversions;
to guard her against the follies of her own sex, and the arts
of ours, in short, to prevent her falling into any or every
                                                    snare

snare, that is or may be laid for her? Suppose her to
have received from nature the seeds of common sense.
Do these require no attention to raise them? or is this most
useful plant to be reared without the aid of experience?
But where, or how, is that to be obtained by a girl? Must
she discover the wiles and wickedness of libertines by con-
versing with them? Must she learn how to defend against
danger by having run into it; or how to avoid the blandishments of pleasure by having felt its bitterness? By men the
knowledge of the world is commonly gathered in it   Very
different from the situation of women is theirs in this respect, and they, it is to be apprehended, often purchase a
little wisdom at a great expence.   By entering into any
company that tempts, engaging in any friendship that offers, or accepting of almost any creature that happens to
court them, it is but too well known what mischiefs a
number of our young gentlemen incur   A female that acts
upon the same plan is lost, and she who would effectually
escape dishonour and remorse, reproach and ridicule, must
endeavour to know the world from books, to collect experience from those who have bought it, and to shun mif-
conduct herself by observing the calamities it has occasioned
to others.   But I said,

Secondly, That Mental Acquisitions were of importance
to your dignity and figure in life.   Consider, my dear sif-
ters, how many women are, in a discerning eye, lessened
by their extravagant attachment to dress and toys, to equipage and ostentation, in a word, to all the gaudy apparatus
of female vanity, together with the endlessly ridiculous, no
less than frequently fatal consequences, which these draw
after them.   Consider how trite and childish, men of sense
must necessarily deem those arts, that are daily practised
on our sex by multitudes of yours, not to speak now of
worse enticements.   Consider the emptiness, insipidity,
and inelegance of their conversation—how contemptible!

Above

Above all the reft, confider the jealoufy and envy, the mean fufpicion and fhameful malignity, to which we have feen the female breaft enflaved, and frequently on the flight-eft foundation, frequently on no foundation at all—how debafing! Now from thefe evils the love of letters, with that liberal caft of thought which they are naturally calcula-ted to give, would I am perfuaded, be one powerful pre-fervative

A young woman fo worthily, and fo happily engaged, will not find leifure for unneceffary trifles and idle parade: or if it were poffible fhe fhould, a confcious fuperiority will enable her very much. to defpife them Endowed with her powers of pleafing, fhe will not find herfelf redu-ced to the little tricks played off by many of her fex: In the company of her friends, fhe muft ever appear with pe-culiar advantage In other companies, where fhe leaft thinks of appearing, an agreeable tincture of intelligence, an eafy correctnefs of expreffion, if it fhould be proper for her to take any part in the difcourfe, will ftill diffufe themfelves Perhaps too fhe will deliver herfelf with a graceful, though modeft freedom. Her letters, or any other compofition that may fall from her pen, will be read with particular eagernefs and approbation, her corref-pondence wil be prized as an honour, and her acquaintance courted as a privilege, attention will hang upon her words, and refpect follow in her train. Such a woman will know how to entertain and charm, beyond the duration of an hour Is it carrying our ideas too far to fay, that, in all probability, an emanation of fentiment and fpirit will be vifible in her air and manner, that her mind will radiate in her eyes? It may not always, but it will often. With regard to thofe vile paffions before mentioned, which arife from rivalfhip in drefs, beauty and the like, as fhe has learnt to value herfelf on better things than the laft, the firft

by

by confequence will not have the fame hold of her foul befides, I fuppofe her to have acquired an enlargement and generofity, which nothing but books, or knowledge of the world, or the principles of genuine piety, can infpire.

Of the two latter the operation is in fome refpects defective, without the concurrence of the former How improving foever an acquaintance with life may be found on fome accounts, there are inftances, in which it will hurt the feelings of the heart, if thefe be not from time to time foftened and cherifhed, by the more foothing reprefentations of men and things fupplied by authors of a candid ftrain. It is alfo to be remembered, that in matters of religion, a zeal without knowledge has been often deftructive, and is always hurtful. But fuppofe no fuch zeal to take place fuppofe that meeknefs, as it certainly ought, makes a part, and a large one too, of the pious character in any woman, yet without the feafonings of a good underftanding, without fomething of that falt and poignancy which are derived from writers of tafte and learning, there will arife, in repeated intercourfe, a famenefs and a flatnefs that muft diminifh efteem though they may not deftroy affection. Add to this, that, on a variety of fubjects, ignorance will inevitably produce a poornefs and vulgarity of thinking, which, to perfons whofe views are nobler, will be rather difguftful.

In truth, the acquifitions we recommend would prevent or cure moft of thofe little prejudices, and little paffions, which often hurt the fex in the opinion of their beft friends Not to infift on what has been mentioned more than once, their aftonifhing prepoffeffion in favour of public places, greatly owing to their want of fomething rational and agreeable to employ them at home, what fhall we fay of that abfurd partiality, which we frequently fhow for well dreffed fops, who pretend indeed to admire them,

but

but are too frivolous and conceited to admire any, in good earneft, but themfelves? Surely a well informed underftanding would enable women to defpife fuch infignificance, and to give the preference to merit, and modefty, in a plain habit

To what fhall we chiefly impute that female curiofity, which has been fo long, and in moft inftances, fo juftly a topic of fatire? Is it poffible, that women could fhow fuch amazing eagernefs to be acquainted with every minute particular in the life, character, drefs, fortune, and circumftances of others, did they poffefs a fund of domeftic entertainment and liberal converfation? The original principle, by receiving a right direction, might certainly be turned into a rich fource of improvement, that would fpread increafing luftre around you.

That aptnefs alfo to be aftonifhed, alarmed, affrighted at trifling accidents, imaginary evils, or natural events ever fo little unufual, which, when carried far, and frequently recurring, makes a young woman appear quite filly, is often the effect of fhallownefs Ignorance is prone to admire, and admiration readily fwells into a paffion, or finks into a panick whereas an enlightened mind is feldom wrought up to ecftafy, and feldom overwhelmed by terror.

The fame reafoning will hold in relation to the incapacity of keeping a fecret, with which your fex have been fo often reproached Thofe infignificant females, who are deftitute of better ideas, will be naturally tempted to give themfelves an air of confequence, by communicating every piece of information which they happen to receive under the notion of fecrefy But the acquifition of valuable knowledge helps to remove this temptation, by conferring real importance, as well as by fupplying fitter converfation

Again

Again, were women to contemplate the fatal confequences of avarice, ambition, vanity, luxury, the violence of love, and the fury of revenge, as appearing in the
ruin of families, the devaftation of provinces, and the fall
of empires, is there not reafon to hope, they would be lefs
dazzled with thofe objects, and lefs affected by thofe occafions, that are apt to foment fuch propenfities,—propenfities which, though in their cafe not fo confequential to
others, are yet many times extremely degrading, as well as
pernicious, to themfelves

And with regard to that ignoble difpofition to fcandal,
by many deemed one of the characteriftic blemifhes of your
fex, you could not poffibly indulge it fo often, were you
furnifhed with a fufficient compafs of obfervation and fentiment, on fubjects much more innocent, and furely not
lefs interefting —Not lefs interefting, did I fay? How, in
the name of God, are you concerned with the faults of
thofe with whom you have no connexion? or what call
have you to remark upon them, farther than may be neceffary to guard yourfelves or others againft their contagion,
or, their confequences? Are you vain of the wit and vivacity which you difplay, or fancy you difplay, on fuch
occafions? Ah, what fuperior honour would ye acquire
from candour, fweetnefs, and felf-correction! But thofe
qualities are the offspring of felf-knowledge, and a comprehenfion of what is truly beautiful and becoming in life.
Let me perfuade you, my beloved pupils, with all your improvements, " with all your gettings, to get thefe two
" effential parts of Underftanding " From them will refult benefits innumerable this among the reft, they will
prevent I know not what affectations, by which many a
pretty fool of your fex is daily expofed

But why be at all this pains? On thefe points you are
under no kind of apprehenfion, confident that, wherever
you

you appear, you cannot fail of commanding regard, sure
that, whenever you are pleased to open those lips, which
you have heard so frequently praised, every ear will be attentive, and every heart allured. Indeed? Are ye very
confident, very sure?——Take care you be not disappointed It is my duty to tell you, whether you will believe it or no, that I have known many a man, who, in
the company of women, has applauded that which he in-
wardly despised, and with hypocritical rapture listened to
nonsense, where the speaker was handsome. Obsequiousness and adulation will attend on youth and beauty But
can you be contented with an incense so cheap, an incense
offered to a face or to a shape alone, an incense that does
not rise from the altar of the heart, an incense, in fine,
that is lavished, with an undistinguishing hand, on every
insignificant image that happens to be cast in a regular
mould, and coloured with a mixture of white and red?
Where, alas! is your delicacy? Have you no ingenuous
pride? Are you so very vain, (pride and vanity are different things) so very ignorant, after all the admonitions you
have received, as still to construe flattery into approbation,
and smiles into attachment? But I intreat you, reflect
When beauty and youth are gone, and go they will—what
then? Why, then, all this adulation and obsequiousness
will vanish with them, and if you be not adorned with
attractions more substantial and durable, into what neglected things will you have the mortification to sink.

An Accomplished Woman can never become an object
of neglect· she must always remain an object of distinction
amongst her acquaintance. When she was young, she
might please more, but as even then she pleased chiefly
by her mind, she will therefore continue to please still
The discerning Few at least will discover in her, beauties
which neither the inroads of age, nor the ravage of sick-
ness, can deface. When "declined into the vale of years,"
she

she will still, from the superiority of her character, stand forth an exalted figure. Sense and capacity, joined to worth and sweetness, are exempted from the condition of all things else, which is to lose their influence, when they lose their novelty "The ornament of grace which Wis- "dom shall give to thy head," will not appear with less real lustre, when infirmity shall cause that head to shake "The crown of glory which she shall deliver to thee," will in Reason's eye receive new dignity from grey hairs, or rather, according to our inspired author, those "grey "hairs are" themselves ' a crown of glory, being found "in the way of righteousness "

Do ye know a woman far advanced in life, but yet farther in virtue and understanding, who with mild insinuation employs them to render wise and happy those about her, especially the young, who for such in particular makes every kind allowance, not forgetting those early days, when she stood in need of indulgence, who when her health will permit, takes pleasure in seeing herself surrounded by a circle of youth innocently gay, condescending even to mix in their little sports, and by a graceful complacency of look, and pleasing remainder of ancient humour, to encourage and promote their harmless amusement —Do ye know such a woman? Then speak your opinion freely Will this youthful circle be in any danger of despising her, because she is old? On the contrary, will they not contend with one another, who shall pay her most veneration, who shall stand highest in her affection? Can you conceive a character more respectable, and at the same time more amiable? What is there good or excellent, to which she will not have it in her power to win them?

And now think of a decayed beauty, who in the height of her bloom, and the career of her conquests, trusted solely to that bloom, and never dreamt of securing those con-
                                                    quests,

quefts, fuch as they were, by any thing more folid and
abiding Inexpreffibly mortified that both are at an end, fhe
would fain, if poffible, keep up the appearance of them ftill
How ? By a conftrained vivacity, by a juvenile drefs, by
that affectation of allurement and importance, which we
fo readily pardon to the prime of life, but which in its decline is univerfally condemned as aukward and unnatural
Place her in the young affembly we have juft fuppofed.
There let her endeavour to fparkle, as in the days of old,
there let her lay traps for admiration amidft the wrinkles
of age   How ludicrous, and how melancholy at the fame
moment ! What girl or what boy of them all, will not be
ftruck with the impropriety ? Every mark of decay, every
fymptom of change, will be traced and examined with
acutenefs   No part of her figure will be overlooked, not
a fingle flip in her behaviour forgiven whereas, if warned
by the effects of time, fhe prudently gave up to her juniors
all competition of looks and fhow, and ftudied only to make
herfelf agreeable by her converfation and manners, there
is fcarcely one of thofe little critics that would ever reflect
upon her years, or that would not be delighted with her
good fenfe, and obliging deportment —No, my young
friends, nothing can fave you from contempt at that period,
if during this you be not at pains to improve your minds
She who is, fhall in one fenfe, and that the beft, be always
young

   If fhe fhould continue fingle, and her fituation. or her
choice, fhould lead her to cultivate but few acquaintance,
amongft them fhe muft ever be loved and valued   If fhe
fhould be married, and to a man of tolerable judgment, with a tolerable temper, he will count himfelf happy in fuch an affociate, he will even be
proud of thofe talents in her which do honour to his
election   I have always remarked, that women of capacity
and elegance have poffeffed the hearts of their hufbands in
a degree which is not common , I mean, where thofe
                                        hufbands

husbands had any worth or difcernment   You will eafily
imagine, that I fuppofe the women in queftion too wife and
too excellent, to affect fuperiority, or not to give their
partners all the credit and confequence poffible, on every
occafion   Between men and women there is feldom any
ravalfhip in what relates merely to intellect, nor are the
former ever much hurt by any confcious inferiority in that
refpect, where the latter do not fhow themfelves,
efpecially before company, arrogant or pretending

I muft not forget to fubjoin how much the Mental Improvements, now enforced, will contribute to adorn and
animate the companion, to direct and dignify the miftrefs,
to accomplifh the mother and the friend, to fpread a charm
over the whole matrimonial ftate, and to relieve thofe duller
hours that are apt to fteal on the moft delightful condition
of humanity

Nor can I difmifs this part of the argument, without men-
tioning what has often appeared to me one very remarkable inftance, amongft many that hiftory records, of the
tranfcendant power to captivate and preferve efteem, which
Intellectual Accomplifhments worthily exerted, confer upon a woman   It is that of Madam Maintenon, the celebrated favourite and wife of Lewis the Fourteenth

This monarch, born with ftrong propenfities to pleafure,
bred in its very lap, indulged from the beginning in all his
paffions, early poffeffed of unlimited power, conftantly accuftomed to the moft exquifite flattery, formerly drunk
with fuccefs and glory, always courted by the female fex
with every art that beauty, wit, or ambition could employ
in his intercourfe with them, ftill addicted to novelty and
change—this very monarch, not yet arrived at the age of
fifty, in full health, environed with all the fplendor of a
                                                        moft

moſt brilliant court, read in little elſe beſides comedies and novels, finds in the converſation of that lady, whoſe origin was not high, whoſe fortunes had been always low, and who was now older than himſelf by ſeveral years—finds, I ſay, in her converſation ſuch innocence, ſuch ſweetneſs, ſuch unequalled charms of taſte and intelligence, as induced him to break off every engagement of a voluptuous kind, and to enter with her into the moſt honourable of all connexions, in which he appears to have maintained his fidelity to the laſt. Madam Maintenon had from her youth improved herſelf by reading, and the beſt company, whom her beauty and talents drew about her, in a country where the ſociety of the women is much more regarded than in this. Lewis was firſt attracted by the extraordinary ſpirit and elegance of her letters, and then abſolutely fixed by her ſentiments, her attention, and her ſubmiſſion. Theſe were a balm to his ſoul, tormented by domeſtic, perſonal and political chagrins. In theſe he obtained a relief from that wearineſs and wretchedneſs, which the pomps and pleaſures of the world have ſerved only to increaſe, while they promiſed to prevent or cure them. We do not find, that this illuſtrious lady was fond of faſhionable diverſions: her books and her work were the principal amuſements of her leiſure.

But it is time to proceed to our laſt point, namely, the uſefulneſs of Mental Acquiſitions to your comfort and felicity. And here it is worthy your obſervation, that the moſt High, having formed his rational offspring for a happineſs more refined and noble than the indulgence of the ſenſes alone, has wiſely made the gratifications thence ariſing in a great meaſure momentary. To prolong theſe inferior enjoyments, is the laborious taſk of the ſlaves of appetite and fancy in league with each other. But as it is undertaken in oppoſition to the deſign of the Almighty, and proſecuted in defiance of his laws, it muſt ever be vain

They

They only fatigue themselves in the attempt   From efforts beyond her scope and powers, Nature will always recoil   Satiated with external pleasures, she turns inward
Experiencing there a void, which the whole system of
matter cannot fill, she is prompted by innate ambition to
aspire after higher objects   Her spiritual faculties, and divine extraction, point her to the world of ideas   From that,
and from what may be called the Commerce of Minds,
she wishes to derive her chief satisfaction   But you will
easily conceive, that such commerce cannot be carried on
to any extent, nor with any variety, without a competent
store of the goods proper to it: those, I mean, which experience and reflexion, genius and reasoning, discourse and
memory, have accumulated and laid up in the writings of
different ages, as in so many convenient repositories for
the use of all those who are willing to avail themselves of
this better wealth.   They who are not, must necessarily
labour under much internal poverty.   Accordingly, how
do they strain to supply the needful demands of conversation, when in company, and when alone, how do they
struggle to elude, because they cannot content, the cravings
of the immortal mind!   To the want of this provision, and
the incapacity of sustaining the weight of their own spirits
pressing upon them in solitude, must we not principally
impute their impatience for all manner of entertainments,
that may help to fill up the painful blanks of time, without any considerable expence of that which they can least
afford—thought? But this expedient is merely temporary,
and extremely imperfect.   Diversion long continued is
drudgery, and still the soul falls back upon herself.

Now, if in the intervals of leisure you can with relish
repair to books, you need never be at a loss.   You may
happily avoid, if you will, the toils of restless amusement,
and the sighs of immoderate mirth.   Excuse this last expression.   Have you not sometimes proved the truth of Solomon's

mon's remark, that " even in laughter the heart is for-
" rowful " Have you not now and then perceived a figh
to steal from you, when oppreffed and exhaufted by frequent burfts of merriment ?—If fhe who is in love with reading fhould, on particular occafions, be led into fcenes of
that kind, with what redoubled ardour will fhe return to
filence and ftudy ! From the noife, buftle, and barrennefs
of modern converfation, with what exalted pleafure will
fhe betake herfelf to the fociety of the celebrated dead,
or of admired authors yet alive, where all is ftill, ferene,
and delightful ! After being difgufted with the naufeous,
or the meagre diet, ferved up in moft companies, where
low fcandal, or mere town-talk, fupply the place of urbanity and fenfe; how rich and regaling will fhe find that
repaft, which her library is always ready to furnifh !

There fhe will not fail of meeting with food of every
different flavour, whether of a lighter or more folid fubftance, agreable to her prefent inclination, at the fame
time that nothing is forced upon her, and fhe is left at liberty, not only to vary the entertainment as often and as
much as fhe pleafes, but alfo to rife from it whenever fhe
will Hiftorians, Philofophers, Orators, and Poets, the
beft writers of every clafs, within her compafs, are ever
prepared to gratify without conftraint or ceremony her intellectual tafte Nor will they take offence at any preference, which at any time fhe may be difpofed to make
She can never intrude upon them at an improper feafon,
nor appear to leave them, with abruptnefs And when
fhe does leave them, inftead of room for uneafy retrofpect,
the manner in which fhe has been employed will be productive of felf-approbation. She will feel her foul nourifhed and ftrengthened, her fpirits cheared and elevated, or
collected and compofed The duties of life fhe will go about
with frefh refolution, and a quicker comprehenfion of
what becomes her To congenial minds her attachment
will

will be increafed. With them fhe will enjoy, as often as
fhe has opportunity, fentimental and friendly delight, the
circulation of thought, the reciprocation of confidence,

" The feaft of reafon, and the flow of foul "

And thefe, my friends, are fatisfactions which depend not
on youth, nor on the advantages peculiar to it fatisfactions
which, in fome refpects at leaft, will grow with your growing years , and which, in every cafe, will furvive the tranfient flower of beauty Let me again remind you of the
period of its decay. Of that period you cannot be reminded
too often

When it arrives, thofe hollow-hearted men, that for
their own ends now fwarm about you with every femblance
of love or admiration, will difperfe like flies at the approach
of winter. In a little time they will forget you, as if you
had never been ; or remember you only to fay, to every
one they meet, how much you are altered But what
words can paint the defolation of her, who finds herfelf
thus forfaken and defpifed, without any refource in her
own breaft ?

I think I fee her flying to her glafs, day after day, to obferve whether that flatterer will prove more conftant At
firft fhe is aftonifhed, fhe is fhocked, at the ftupidity of
thofe men, who can become infenfible to a face or a form
like hers ? But in a little time that once foothing glafs,
which was wont to tranfport her with the reflected image of
herfelf, begins to withdraw its flatteries too. _ She
is alarmed and depreffed.   She   feeks confolation
from fome low dependant, who, with a grave face
and glozing accent, affures her fhe is handfomer than
ever, while the mercenary wretch fecretly laughs her to
fcorn Every artifice of drefs, all the feduction of ornament, is ftudied and practifed with more exquifite folicitude   She views herfelf on every fide : the waift feems re-
paired,

pared Her spirits rise, she is overjoyed With renew-
ed expectation she sallies forth she dances her usual round -
some one in pity tells her how she looks · the evening is
past in triumph She returns home exhausted with the flutter. Next morning the mirror is consulted again She is
pale, sickly, faint, her eyes are sunk, the wrinkles appear—more than ever. Again she is startled, terrified,
falls into a rage The storm bursts on her domestics, spends
itself, subsides. The usual methods are tortured, to make
her up, and if some new expedient is suggested, that can
better disguise nature, and deceive the beholder—what a
discovery! Thus between the vicissitudes of hope and
fear, of exultation and despondence, on a subject to her
weak and unfurnished mind the most interesting of all others,
she is miserably tossed, till by such repeated and violent
perturbation, conspiring with the addition of years, she
is consigned over to despair, the heart overwhelming despair, of being ever praised more for those unhappy charms,
which she at length perceives are beyond recovery lost —
What young woman of reflection would not prevent such
ridiculous distress? But can you think of any way to prevent it, so efficacious, as turning betimes your principal
attention to your better part? That even in this way you
shall become wholly indifferent, about the decline of an
appearance which used to give your friends as well as yourselves pleasure, I will not affirm. But if so high a strain
of philosophy, be hardly practicable, still however I think
you must acknowledge, that the advances of age will be
supported much the more easily for such preparation. In
the mean while, how many vexations that harrass and
distract the greater part of your sex, will be thus obviated
by you!

In truth, most of the grievances complained of by mortals are self-created They proceed from that fondness of
fancy, which gives consequence to trifles, or from those
gusts

gufts of paffion, which produce agitation without caufe
But next to the power of religion, can you imagine any
means of avoiding both fo probable, as the wife and calm
purfuits to which I would now perfuade you? Permit me,
my much loved hearers, to fucceed Defer not, by the
cultivation of your minds, as well as hearts, to lay in a
ftore of enjoyment and comfort, fuch as you can repair to
in fecret, when all abroad is unfolacing and infipid.

Every thing external is haftening to change and diffolu-
tion. You yourfelves are gliding infenfibly down the current of time. You are on your paffage-to eternity , and
can you bear the thoughts of refigning a paffage as important
as it is fhort, to the blind impulfe of chance, caprice and
ignorance? Or fuppofe you are fo far careful of confequences
as to fecure a fafe arrival, can ye, like illiterate and incu-
rious mariners, failing by fome beautiful coaft, be fatisfied to hurry along, without attending to the various
profpects and numerous objects, which Nature and Art
have fpread out before you, or without taking advantage
of the beft affiftance you can find on your voyage, to improve in whatever is inftructive, ornamental, and praife-
worthy? Have ye forgotten, that, when landed on the
blifsful fhore, your felicity will bear no inconfiderable proportion to your prefent attainments in knowledge; that
the moft enlarged underftandings, where the difpofitions
have been of a piece, will be rewarded by the nobleft difcoveries, in fhort, that they who fhine now with the
faireft lights of wifdom fhall, like the more diftinguifhed
ftars of heaven, be crowned hereafter with fuperior fplendour?

M   SERMON

SERMON IX.

On Female Piety.

I TIM II. 10.

—Which becometh women profeffing Godlinefs.

PROV XXXI 30

Favour is deceitful, aad beauty is vain · but a woman that feareth the Lord, She fhall be praifed

THE frailty of women has been frequently a topic of triumphant declamation. On this fubject much unkind wit has been difplayed, and many a dull farcafm is daily added, and widely circulated, with an air of confcious fatis-faction Hardly can one go into a company of men, where licentioufnefs of tongue paffes for freedom of conver-fation, without hearing the poor women abufed for their worthleffnefs or weaknefs, or both. But fuppofing them particularly frail, is it noble to exult over them on that account, and in their abfence too, when they have not an opportunity of defending themfelves? Should not the ftrong rather pity and fupport the weak? Yet after all, how does it appear that any fingular ftrength of refolution belongs to our fex, or that yours ftand chargeable with pe-culiar infirmity?

The lofs of virtue is, no doubt, often followed with ex-treme depravity in women. But is not the fame thing to be feen amongft men, although it is not remarked with the fame attention, or cenfured with equal rigour? If many unhappy females run into fuch " excefs of riot, and fuper-fluity of raughtinefs," as feem to juftify the obfervation, that there is nothing fo profligate as a vicious woman, may

it

it not be frequently imputed to their being driven almoft to a ftate of defpair ? Forfaken as they are by the wretches that ruined them, abandoned by their relations, if any they have, commonly dreading the fcorn of their own fex, and often too little confidered by the virtuous part of ours, what can be expected, in general, from creatures who have put off the modefty of nature, and are propelled by evil habits, co-operating often with bafe affociates, and bitter poverty ?—Do I then plead the caufe of vice ? God forbid But I cannot endure that want of candour, which would aggravate the guilt and mifery of beings, who to us fhould be objects of fo much compaffion, I fay to Us, of whom many are the firft authors of this very guilt and mifery, while the reft are all likewife fubject to go aftray

Here I fhall probably be afked, Does not the apoftle Peter exprefly ftyle the woman the weaker veffel, he does, but in the fame fenfe that thofe veffels are fo ftyled, which being of finer materials, or more delicate conftruction, and therefore eafily broken or hurt, are for that reafon, and for the regard alfo which people have for them, ufed with particular tendernefs That this is his meaning is manifeft from the paffage referred to, where he fays, " Give ho-" nour unto the wife as unto the weaker veffel " Why honour on that fcore, if the epithet Weaker is not to be underftood as I have now, according to the beft interpret-ers, explained it ?

But does not St Paul, fome verfes after the text from Timothy, obferve, that " Adam was not deceived, but " the woman being deceived, was in the tranfgreffion ?" True. it does appear from the hiftory, that " the ferpent," as our apoftle fays elfewhere, " beguiled Eve through his " fubtilty," and that the man, though aware of the deceit, was, by his fondnefs for his deluded yet ftill lovely partner, drawn into the fame tranfgreffion. But what was it that

M 2   expofed

expofed the woman to that fnare by which fhe was feduced?
Paffions, it muft be owned, extremely culpable in their
nature, and fatal in their confequences; but not the paffions for which her daughters have been indifcriminately
blamed In reality, the refolute fpirit and perfevering vigilance, with which great numbers of women preferve
their honour, while fo few men in comparifon are reftrained by the laws of continence, feem to me no flight proof
that the former poffefs a degree of fortitude well worthy of
praife

But what is all this to the purpofe of our prefent meditation? Much every way I meant it as my firft argument
in behalf of Female Piety, and on what footing it ftands I
will proceed to fhow, after remarking that the perfons to
whom our text from St. Paul is addreffed, are by him fuppofed to profefs a refpect for religion,—" As becometh
" women profeffing Godlinefs:" a fuppofition we are willing to make in your favour, my beloved hearers; fo far,
I mean, as to render it unneceffary to inculcate that profeffion from thofe general notions of truth and duty, which,
with a few exceptions, I do hope you readily acknowledge.
Inftead of this, our reafoning and exhortations will turn
chiefly on fuch principles and facts as relate more immediately to your fex, fituation, and time of life, confidered
in conjunction with the character and manners of the
age

And now for the argument already fuggefted, you will
be more fenfible of its force by attending to the following
obfervations, That the firmnefs, with which fo many of
you guard your virtue, being transferred to the practice of
Piety at large, will, by God's affiftance, contribute to
render it eafy and delightful; that the confiderations of
Religion will, in their turn, fupport and chear you under
the reftraints of confcience and decorum; that you will
hence

hence derive the mighty fatisfaction of the divine approbation amidft the cenfures of the uncharitable, and the divine protection againft the machinations of the ungodly; and, in the laft place, that the injuftice, unkindnefs, and treachery of the world, fhould engage you to greater prudence, purity, and devotion.

As to the firft, it is certain that the practice of real Piety requires no fmall refolution and perfeverance Is it not likewife certain that in what concerns their reputation, many young women poffefs a large fhare of thefe? Let them but apply this to the difcharge of their duty as chriftians, and the happieft effects will enfue; uniformity, facility, and joy in religion, What cannot courage and conftancy atchieve? In the point to which I allude, you are often heroines. Your life is a feries of felf-denial. But felf-denial from right principles is the perfection of chriftianity. Do but act on thefe principles throughout, and you fhall one day walk with our SAVIOUR in white, he will confefs your names as worthy before his FATHER and before his angels; you fhall follow the Lamb whitherfoever he goeth, finging to your golden harps a new fong, expreffive of fignal triumph and praife.

It has been faid of women, and I believe with truth, that they are remarkably fteady to their purpofe. Let it be feen that you are fo in what is good. And "let not "your good be evil fpoken of," on account of any thing that might give ground to fufpect you controul your paffions in one way only, and that too from no higher principle than the fear of fhame. By a noble command of yourfelves in other points, where this confideration cannot be fuppofed to operate fo ftrongly, make it appear that you are governed by religious as well as prudential motives.

We would not leffen the influence of any one wife, or

ufeful

useful confideration, from the fide of this world· but we wifh your minds to lie more open to the efficacy of the next So far as mere reputation goes, it is much the fame to a woman, whether the regularity of her conduct be the refult of pious or of political maxims But in the fight of God, and at the bar of confcience, how vaft the difference. In that day when the fecrets of all hearts fhall be laid open what will it avail you, if the decency of your behaviour fhould be found to have proceeded from no nobler fpring than the defire of faving appearances ; Who can exprefs the horror of a female hypocrite at that all-revealing period when, ftript of every difguife, fhe fhall be pointed out to the congregated univerfe as an infamous creature, whofe foul was enflaved to fenfuality, at the very time that fhe affected the ftricteft virtue, treated indifcretion in others with the feverity due to vice alone, had no allowances to make for human frailty, and with fupercilious difdain looked down on many of her fex not half fo wicked as herfelf?

Let it be carefully remembered, that as, in what regards outward trials, the gofpel is literally the doctrine of the crofs ; fo, with refpect to inward conflicts, it is properly the difcipline of the paffions. Here, in truth, the religion of a chriftian muft begin and end What pity, my honoured pupils, if you who have that amazing power over the exterior of your deportment, if you who offer to a fpotlefs name thofe continual facrifices which your greateft enemies cannot deny, fhould after all lofe the reward of undiffembled fanctity, by being excluded from that vifion of God, which Jefus has promifed to the pure in heart ! What pity, in the mean while, that fuch power is not more generally allowed to exert itfelf on the ample theatre of a life truly virtuous, and that fuch facrifices fhould not, by the confolations of devotion, be fweetened, confecrated, and turned into fo many fources of fublime enjoyment !

But

But this reminds me of having likewife faid, that the confiderations of Religion will conduce mightily to fupport and chear you under the reftraints of fobriety and decorum. In proportion as thofe confiderations are made more familiar, will thefe reftraints become lefs painful, till at length they in a manner change their nature, and feem like filken bands, that even while they confine you, are as eafy as they are ornamental

Between all other philofophy and the philofophy of Jefus one glorious diftinction is this, that the latter not only difplays a higher ftandard of moral excellence, but alfo communicates fuperior powers of virtuous action. To the fainter conclufions of Reafon it fuperadds the bright difcoveries of Faith The Future world, with the great tranfactions of the fupreme adminiftration, which are introductory to it, are there unveiled. There the vanity, and withal the importance of the prefent ftate, is unfolded. There divine pardon and eternal life, as " the gift of " God through Jefus Chrift," are enfured and afcertained to obedient believers. The hiftory of the Redeemer is there exhibited with all the beauty of fimplicity, and energy of truth: a hiftory, my dear hearers, equally important to all that read it, and to thofe that read it with a ferious unprejudiced difpofition, unfpeakably affecting; a hiftory, which involves the moft extenfive and lafting interefts of human nature, and to fuch as view it in that light carries with it, beyond all other writings, a vital, home-felt, and heart-awakening influence The ingenious breaft, inflamed by the friendfhip, and penetrated by the fpirit of Jefus, burns with the love of virtue, and heaves with the hope of falvation. Jefus is the pattern of virtue. gratitude is one of the worthieft incentives, and faith, which is the fundamental principle of the whole fyftem, faith in the mercy and acceptance of the Univerfal Father, through the mediation of his meritorious Son, by whom he is car-

rving

rying on a fcheme of grace, that comprehends all fincere penitents of whatever name or nation, throughout all fucceffive ages—this faith, I fay, imparts to feeble and defponding creatures a ftrength and encouragement that no other fyftem could ever infpire.

Nor are thefe ideas beyond the ordinary reach of female underftanding They depend not on a nice chain of reafoning, nor on the abftrufe refearches of fcience. How much foever they may have been difguifed by the dreams of the fchools, to conceive them as they are fet forth in fcripture, mafculine intellects are by no means neceffary. Connected with Facts the moft aftonifhing to the imagination, and Sentiments the moft touching to the heart, they feem to lie particularly level to the beft characters among your fex In fhort, to feel their tendency, and experience their operation, a modeft, fufceptible, and affectionate mind is chiefly required.

Permit me to afk you, as in the prefence of God, do ye in good earneft believe in the Holy Ghoft, in the catholic church, in the communion of faints, in the forgivenefs of fins, in the refurrection of the body, in the life everlafting, in Him who is the refurrection and the life, the all-fufficient facrifice, the all-prevailing advocate, the meek, the lowly, and the loving mafter, as well as the awful and impartial judge? Do ye often by devout contemplation realize thefe, and the other wonderful objects of chriftianity, together with the grand principles of natural religion? To both do you frequently join the heaven-moving force of fervent prayer, the powerfully combined influences of public worfhip, and the fweetly fupporting communications of holy friendfhip? Then fay, whether you can ever be at a lofs for motives to animate, or for aids to fecond your endeavours after wifdom and virtue? Surely no.

Wifdom

Wifdom and virtue are beautiful forms, and for their own intrinfic worth unqueftionably entitled to all poffible love and veneration. But little acquainted with the human heart are they, who would build the morals of mankind on this fingle bafis Decency of chara&er, dignity of condu&, the honours due to temperance, integrity, benevolence, magnanimity, and other qualities of that order, are ideas as folid as they are refined, and which ought certainly to be cherifhed by all who are capable of comprehending their moment. To offer to depreciate them is vile, and not more repugnant to reafon than to fcripture, where the beauties of holinefs are exprefsly named, and " whatfoever things are venerable, lovely and of good report," are, as mentioned in a former difcourfe, recommended in fo many words. But yet, on the other hand, confidering the paffions, diforders, and debility of beings, fituated as we are, to truft the caufe of righteoufnefs and truth to the fole ftrength of fuch arguments—what is it, but hazarding the moft valuable interefts in the world on a bottom utterly unequal to fo precious a freight?

A few fele& fpirits, more liberal and elevated than ufual, may in their progrefs towards perfe&ion, derive fome extraordinary affiftance from their fublimer fpeculations, at leaft when not under very difficult or delicate circumftances of temptation. But what, think ye, would become even of Them, much more, what would become of the far greater part, when immediately under fuch circumftances, did not religion ftep in to their aid with her more forcible and ftriking fan&ions, founded on their hopes and fears for futurity, as thefe are conne&ed with a fenfe of the Almighty's infpe&ion, and a faith in the illuftrious fa&s of revelation? How little in general were the philofophers of antiquity themfelves influenced by the fyftem in queftion, with whatever pomp they profeffed,

or

or with whatever eloquence they displayed it? Some of
them, it is true, were men of great virtues, as well as
great conceptions while the rest were striking examples
how much easier it is to talk than to act well, and that to
reform the world there is wanted a diviner power than reason alone

With regard to the case now before us, it may be observed that those young persons, who have had the misfortune to be in a great measure left to the common notices
of nature, go astray much more frequently, than others
on whom the principles of Piety have been early and judiciously impressed.

When I say judiciously impressed, I mean to insinuate
that many hopeful children have been lost, through the
imprudent efforts of their well meaning, but ill informed
parents, to make them good by severe confinement and
constant admonition. Those children alone will be truly
good, and are likely to continue so, who are at once ena-
moured of their duty, awed by their Maker, and devoted
to the securing of that " life and immortality which are
" brought to light through the gospel "

Here I cannot help recollecting a most memorable instance, wherein a much celebrated youth was guarded
against the indulgence of appetite by the power of religion.
I speak of Joseph, when tempted by the wife of Potaphar.
Consider the complicated snare that was laid for his innocence, probably the blandishments of beauty; certainly
the repeated, pressing, and passionate solicitations of an
artful woman, of his mistress, who if she pleased could
evil, procure his farther advancement, the opportunities
of privacy . the prospect of close concealment, his time of
life; his plentiful condition, those warm affections, that
strong sensibility, which the sequel of his story shows to
have

have been natural to him, the extreme danger manifeſtly
attending his refuſal, I mean all the miſchiefs to be dreaded from the reſentment and violence of a proud but fond
female reſiſted, diſappointed, enraged, who would not
fail, however falſely, to repreſent the unbounded confidence
of a generous maſter abuſed, and, finally, thoſe miſchiefs
falling at one blow upon a dependant and a ſtranger, whoſe
proſperity in that family had no doubt rendered him the
object of envy to ſome, and whoſe proteſtations in his own
favour would never be believed by others to the diſadvan-
tage of a woman of her rank and fortune. Such was the
ſnare   And what was it that enabled our amiable hero to
to conquer it? The hiſtory will inform you.   " He refuſed,
" and ſaid unto his maſter's wife, Behold, my maſter wot-
" teth not what is with me in the houſe, and he hath com-
" mitted all that he hath to my hand. There is none grea-
" ter in this houſe than I, neither hath he kept back any
" thing from me but thee, becauſe thou art his wife how
" then can I do this wickedneſs and ſin againſt God?" Excellent young man! From a crime, to which ſo many
allurements concurred to incite him, he ſtarts back with
horror. ſo ſtrongly are his natural feelings of gratitude and
probity ſeconded by a reverence for the Omniſcient! " How
" then can I do this great wickedneſs, and ſin againſt
" God?"—No, my ſiſters, there is not in the world ſuch a
preſervative from vice as the fear of God   Temptations,
by which human reſolutions alone have been frequently
foiled, are often overcome by the ſame reſolutions when
enforced by religious faith.

From theſe remarks you will plainly perceive, that what
we wiſh for you is not a victory over your paſſions hardly
gained, and at the expence of your tranquillity ; but a ſacred
ſelf-poſſeſſion, a certain diviner controul of your own wills
that ſhall diſtinguiſh you in the ſight of him who " de-
ſireth truth in the inward parts " A ſentiment this, that ſeems
conformable

conformable to the beſt conceptions of nature ; ſince we
find the power, which according to the pagan creed repreſented both Wiſdom and Fortitude, was ſuppoſed to be of
your ſex   On the ſame principle does the wiſeſt of men
ſpeak ſo often of the former in the feminine gender.   Thus
at leaſt did ancient genius treat the women with reſpect.
It is particularly obſervable that of republican ſtates, where
that genius commonly appeared moſt eminent, the ſage
legiſlators preſcribed to females a peculiar gravity and ſimplicity of manners ; ſo different were their ideas of what was
becoming from thoſe of modern times !

But I add farther that, from the ſtudy of inward purity
as well as outward decorum, even that purity which the goſpel ſo ſtrongly enforces, you will reap the mighty ſatisfaction of the Divine Approbation amidſt the cenſures of the
uncharitable, and the Divine Protection againſt the machinations of the ungodly   Hard enough, it muſt be
owned, is the caſe of women, as to the general reflections
made on their deportment   If they behave with reſerve,
they are pronounced prudiſh , if with franknefs, bold ; if
with that juſt temperament of both which is the proper medium, capricious and uncertain   What ſhall they do ?
What can they do, but hold the middle way, with that
attention to the rules of caution on one ſide, and of affability on the other, which times, places, and perſons ſeem
to require · " committing their cauſe to him that judgeth
" righteouſly," and truſting their ſafety to him that never
forſakes the virtuous ?

Such a reſpect for human judgment, as avoids giving
occaſion of cenſure, is undoubtedly right in every individual of ſociety   of your ſex eſpecially, whoſe reputation
is of ſo nice a contexture   But while for this purpoſe a
chriſtian woman purſues, as nearly as ſhe can, the path
of prudence, what internal ſerenity does ſhe enjoy, by
                                                        following

following at the fame time the direction of a principle,
that higheft and happieft guide of life ! To fay the truth,
there may be fituations, wherein the latter appears to be
left the fole guide, fo impoffible is it for the former to find
a way through the labyrinth In this cafe, you can have
but one reafonable care ; which is, to do what confcience
charges as your duty In every cafe, that muft be your
principal care. In making it fo, there will be this great
advantage amongft many others, that you will every day
grow lefs anxious about any thing elfe.   The eafe of
mind, the gaiety of heart refulting from fuch a conduct,
are not to be expreffed.

If the world fhould approve, it is well.   The approbation
of the beft people, at leaft, will give you real pleafure ;
and the beft people are naturally candid. If the world
fhould condemn, and even the candid Few, which is by no
means impoffible, fhould be led by mifreprefentation, or by
miftake, to join in the fentence; ftill however you will
have the comfort of not having deferved it.   And from this
inferior tribunal you will alfo have the felicity of appealing
to that which is fupreme and infallible, with the humble
affurance of being juftified there through the powerful interpofition of an advocate, whom no paffion or mifap-
prehenfion can bias   At the fame time too you will have
the confolation to hope, that fooner or later he in whom
you truft " will bring forth your righteoufnefs as the light,
" and your judgment as the noon-day " Seldom or never,
I think, does a perfevering virtue fail of breaking out with
frefh beauty, and augmented luftre, from thofe clouds with
which calumny may have obfcured it , even as the vernal
fun by purfuing his career, fhines forth at laft with a kind
of victorious fplendor, that difpels the remaining damps
of winter, delights the eye, and infpires the heart of every
beholder.

But

But suppose the worst, that the erroneous multitude should continue to load you with unmerited reproach, I am not afraid to say you are happy still, if you know how to avail yourselves of the supports of religion, particularly a sense of the Almighty's Approbation What ought to discourage her who can triumph in this, and likewise in that which is immediately connected with it, an assurance of the Almighty's Protection?

Nothing can be more certain than that your sex is, on every account, entitled to the shelter of ours? Your softness, weakness, timidity, and tender reliance on man, your helpless condition in yourselves, and his superior strength for labour, ability for defence, and fortitude in trial; your tacit acknowledgment of these, and frequent application for his aid in so many winning ways, concur to form a plea, which nothing can disallow or withstand but brutality Appetite indeed is naturally brutal: untamed by religion, unchained by reason, what havock does it not commit? Nothing can be more wild or ferocious than lawless desire How often, alas, does it disfigure and degrade minds otherwise adorned with very valuable qualities! Have we not seen men, who in a sober mood were open to the tenderest feelings of humanity, incapable of any thing unjust or dishonourable, calm, and pliant to good advice; who yet in the rebellion of their blood, were as ungovernable and fierce as any beast of the forest, broke through all restraint, and to gratify the passion that impelled them, rushed on crimes utterly repugnant to the best sentiments of their own hearts! Need I tell you that from such men your virtue is in danger, and by so much the more by how much the qualities just named are, when allowed to operate, particularly engaging? But the fact is that, being inlaid in the constitution, they do operate frequently, and never perhaps more than immediately after those unhappy deviations, for which something within whispers the necessity of
making

making every poffible atonement. It is in this way that thofe good-natured but unhappy men keep themfelves and one another in countenance, and often fteal into your affection   Yet are thefe by no means the worft enemies of woman-kind.

It is your fmooth, cool, complimental libertines, who have fteeled their breafts 'by a fyftem whom the boafted principles or rather no principles of infidelity, have raifed to a glorious contempt of all laws human and divine, delivered from the vulgar conceit of immortality, and enabled to conquer the little weakneffes of nature, with the ignoble prejudices of education, which happened to be on the fide of juftice, honour, fympathy,—it is fuch men, my fair ones, fuch flagitious and obdurate wretches, whofe wiles, fhould you chance to be thrown in their way, you have moft reafon to dread   And believe me, they abound every where. From you indeed they will carefully conceal the enormity of their characters, and the blacknefs of their opinions; till by gaining your confidence they can infinuate the laft with advantage, fo as to take off your apprehenfions of the firft, and blunt the edge of your refolutions   A fenfe of piety, the love of virtue, a regard to reputation, the fear of confequences, every principle borrowed from this world and the next, they are well aware would be alarmed and excited, were they to difclofe their defigns, or explain their ideas at once, without preparation or preface —But I will not attempt to unfold the myftery of iniquity, in which they wrap themfelves, and work unfufpected   Let it remain involved in its native darknefs and horror ? which cannot however hide it from the eye of heaven, whofe hotteft vengeance fhall one day overtake and blaft it.

Your fafety, I faid before, lies in retreat and vigilance, in fobriety and prudence, in virtuous friendfhip, and rational converfation, in domeftic, elegant, and intellectual
accomplifhments,

accomplifhments; I add now, in the Guardianfhip of Omnipotence, as that which muft give efficacy to all the reft; but which can only be obtained by fomething more and better than them all, I mean, True Religion. What reafon have you to hope for a privilege fo great, if you do not afk it? What caufe could you have to complain, if your righteous CREATOR, on whom every confideration ought to teach you dependance, were to leave you to yourfelves amidft thofe dangerous attacks, or artful fnares, which you prefumptuoufly imagine you could refift by your own ftrength, or elude by your caution? That humility which does not deprefs, as chriftian humility never can, is the beft means of fecurity. She who is moft fenfible of her hazard, is moft likely to be on her guard. She who perceives her own imbecility, will be glad to invoke a higher power Nor will the parent of all be deaf to one of his reafonable offspring, who apprehenfive of the difficulties to which her frame and fituation expofe her, heartily implores his help

Vain very often is the help of man, even when afforded in its utmoft extent What then muft be the cafe, when it is not only not afforded, but when he who ought to protect is bent to deftroy? To whom fhall young creatures of your fex, little lambs, innocent, gentle, fearful, undefended, befet by ravenous lions, or " by wolves in fheeps- " cloathing,"—to whom fhall they flee, but to the Shepherd of Ifrael? And will he, think ye, reject or abandon them; he who has promifed to " gather the lambs " with his arm, and to carry them in his bofom." he who has always fhown himfelf more efpecially concerned for objects of diftrefs and deftitution, the poor, the prifoner, the ftranger, the oppreffed, the widow and fatherlefs, and fuch as have none to help them, in a word, he whofe providence is then neareft, and whofe affiftance is then readieft, when his creatures are moft forfaken by others?

To

To obtain the divine interpofition, it is urged by the Pfalmift as a prevailing argument, that he was unprotected and defolate "O be not far from me, for trouble is "nigh at hand, and there is none to help me I looked "on my right-hand, and beheld, but there was no man "that would know me; refuge failed me, no man cared "for my foul I cried unto thee, O LORD · I faid, "Thou art my refuge." The common FATHER "hears "the young ravens when they cry unto him," and are early left by their hard-hearted dams. Are not ye better than many ravens? "Can a woman forget her fucking child, "that fhe fhould not have compaffion on the fon of her "womb?" fays GOD by the prophet He fpeaks of it as a monftrous thing, and fcarce credible in any. Can fhe forget—She, in the fingular number. The anfwer is remarkable: "Yea, they may forget" They, in the plural, confeffing it poffible that more than one fuch wretch may be found amongft the dregs of nature. "Can a wo- "man forget her fucking child? Yea, They may forget, yet I will not forget thee." Can you figure any thing more tender and foothing? Can you hefitate a moment to throw yourfelves on "the everlafting arms, on his "right-hand, who rides on the heavens for your help, on "his excellency in the fky?" Or having fo done, can you harbour a doubt of your fafety, while "your place of de- "fence is the munition of rocks?"

But to proceed to our laft argument · let the injuftice, unkindnefs, and treachery of the world, engage you to greater Prudence, Purity, and Devotion Any natural or any amiable tye by which you are or may be bound, GOD forbid that I fhould feek to flacken. Moderate affections for proper objects you are allowed, you are called to indulge. By fuch means you will fill your places in fociety, or be in the way to fill them, at the fame time that you will enjoy the beft thing in human life, the friendly feelings

of the heart   But fhall I repeat once more, what has in
one fhape or another been faid fo often, that whenever
thefe are ill directed, or carried too far, they are fure to en-
tangle in guilt and difquietude ?   Now to prevent, as much
as poffible, the wandering of your paffions, the Almighty
makes ufe of the paffions of others.   To bring good out of
evil is the glory of his government.   The worthleffnefs of
thofe who have abufed their freedom, he permits as a warning to you, no lefs than a punifhment to them.

If men will endeavour to defpoil that virtue which they
fhould cherifh, to corrupt thofe minds which they fhould
improve, in a word, to ruin that fex whofe honour and
welfare are in a great meafure entrufted with Them; fhould
not fuch bafenefs fill you with difdain and abhorrence?
Can any of you be fo mean, fo furpaffing mean, as to doat
on the traitors?   Even where their aim is not deftruction,
where merely for amufement they flatter or foothe, fhould
ye fuffer yourfelves to be feduced into fondnefs?   How
foolifh to be taken with thofe little fuperficial attentions,
that are fo eafily learnt in the fchool of fafhion, and fo frequently practifed to hide a hollow, or difguife an unfeeling
foul!

Are ye ignorant of its being an eftablifhed fyftem amongft
men of gaiety and pleafure, that your fex have no principles, that you are defigned only to ferve their purpofes;
and that, when you refufe to do fo, it is mere pride or
grofs diffimulation?   Can ye think of this, and not be offended?   Will ye continue to prefer fuch characters to the
fober, fedate, and fentimental?

You often behold the wrecks of beauty that has been
blafted, and of innocence that has been betrayed.   Providence allows thofe miferable beings to carry their effrontery fo far as to appear without fhame in every public place,
the monuments of male falfhood as well as female infatua-
tion;

tion , and can ye fail of being impreſſed with ſalutary terror?

Can ye reſtrain the ſpirit of indignant virtue from darting out on thoſe men that, in your company, dare to ſpeak a language unfit for you to hear? Should not your eyes at leaſt make them ſenſible of the affront offered to your ears? and if they are hardened enough not to be aſhamed, does it not become you ever after to ſhun their ſight as you would ſhun a bear or a ſatyr? I am ſure you will think ſo, if you conſult either the dignity of your ſex, or the purity of your minds.

Love grafted on eſteem, or fed by it, is a juſt and noble principle But how has it been diſgraced by worthleſs pretenders! Join, my ſiſters, with all your power, to vindicate its honours. Let the ſanctity of your conduct ſerve, as much as poſſible, to recall the paſſion from empty form and criminal indulgence, from the blind admiration of an outſide, and the ſhort-lived gratification of youthful deſire, to a genuine, holy, and enlightened affection, ſuch as ſpringing chiefly from a ſympathy of honeſt and generous hearts, ſhall flouriſh when fancy, youth, and beauty, are no more.

If women will marry men of bad morals, if from whatever motive, they will manifeſtly endanger their own ſalvation, by forming ſo intimate a connexion with thoſe who betray a total neglect of theirs, what can we ſay either for religion or the ſex, that will make any impreſſion on thoſe who are prejudiced againſt both? What can ſhe plead that accepts without ſcruple the hand of a man, who is ſeldom or ever ſeen in a place of worſhip, and whoſe companions are known to be profane or licentious? Is this to act, in the greateſt concern of life, like a perſon of principle?

It

It is a common complaint, nor can the fact be denied, that moft of our young gentlemen now a days entirely difregard religious inftitutions But how can it be expected they fhould do otherwife, fo long as they find themfelves, in general, no way the lefs acceptable to the ladies, for fuch fafhionable impiety? What a fcandal in " women profeffing Godlinefs!"

Amidft fo much diforder and fo many fnares on all hands what can be fo wife for you, my chriftian friends, as to take refuge more and more in the fanctuary of devotion?— Let us not diffemble the truth. The greater part of either fex ftudy to prey on one another The world, in too many inftances, is a theatre of war between men and women. Every ftratagem is tried, and every advantage taken, on the fide of both On the fide of the former, ftrength and daring are joined to art and ambition, in which the latter abound To make a truce they often meet Even preliminaries towards a peace are often propofed. Individuals pafs over to the camp of the enemy, and are reconciled But what fhall we fay of the contending powers at large? Methinks they refemble this and a neighbouring kingdom, between which a general truce is always fhort, and a national peace never fecure.

To many young women the preacher will feem as one that mocks. The men they confider as their beft friends, and a lafting union is what they long for as the height of happinefs An union by fome means or other, will probably take place And if it fhall, to know that it proved lafting, entire, and happy, as happy as the prefent ftate permits, would, you may be well affured, give the preacher pleafure But if from this, or any imaginable connexion upon earth, you hope for compleat felicity, your hopes will be vain Imperfect yourfelves, you have no right to expect perfection from men In the moft agreeable
ble

ble attachments, you will ftill find a mixture. The beft
charaƈters will fometimes fay, or do that, which fhall
occafion pain, daily intercourfe will dull the relifh of delight;
and difagreeable accidents, but efpecially fevere diftrefs,
will not improve the tafte for it. Devotion, dearly beloved, Devotion will ever be your fureft and fweeteft refource " Acquaint yourfelves therefore now with God,
" and be at peace."

Even now, I doubt not, fome of you perceive that all
befide is uncertain and unfatisfaƈtory. Your father and
mother have forfaken you by death; or, which is far worfe,
by unnatural cruelty, or horrible felfifhnefs. You have
not perhaps in the world a friend to fupply their place Or
if you have, you cannot but know that human friendfhips
are often fallacious, and like other human comforts always
precarious. Every thing in nature is fubjeƈt to viciffitude;
and nothing more ufual than for men to adopt a different
deportment as their circumftances or interefts, their opinions or humours, vary. There is but one immutable friend,
" a friend that fticks clofer than brother," a lover, or a
parent " He is the fame yefterday, and to day, and for
" ever. He will never forfake you." He has engaged
himfelf by his promife, and " he is not man that he fhould
" lie, neithei the fon of man that he fhould repent."

I have often thought that, in fome refpeƈts, there is not
any creature fo forlorn or expofed, as a young woman,
beautiful, unexperienced, fingle, almoft wholly friendlefs,
bred to affluence, left in dependance, perhaps in indigence,
of which fome wretch curft with wealth is willing to avail
himfelf for the vileft ends. While I paint fuch a fituation,
who does not fee the need of Piety ? What remains for this
pretty fufferer, but to hold faft her innocence at all adventures, and look up to him " with whom the fatherlefs
" find mercy "——'Proteƈt me, O my heavenly Father,
' my

' my only fure and never failing friend; protect thy poor
' dependant, helplefs creature From this wildernefs of
' life I lift up my eyes to thee; to thy throne of pity I
' ftretch out my arms for fuccour Behold, I am needy, and
' feeble, and full of affliction I tread among fnares,
' I tremble for fear. But thou art good and merciful
' Save me O Lord, moft mighty, fave me from evil men,
' from vain companions, from folly, from myfelf. My
' wants fupply, moft gracious my weaknefs ftrengthen.
' for ever guard the virtue by thee implanted. Thou art
' the guide of my youth; lead me in a plain path, be-
' caufe of my enemies. Let none have power to hurt me,
' may fome have the goodnefs to fupport my fteps. Send
' down Wifdom from thy holy heavens, that fhe may la-
' bour with me continually, and fweetly counfel me in all my
' doings In thee, O God, in Thee alone have I put
' my truft let me never be confounded. Be my God for
' ever and ever, and my guide even unto death I afk it
' for the fake of my Divine Redeemer Amen.'

SERMON

SERMON X.

On Female Piety.

1 TIM. ii. 10

——Which becometh women professing Godliness.

PROV xxxi 30.

Favour is deceitful, and beauty is vain · but a woman that feareth the Lord, She shall be praised

DEVOTION, my beloved hearers, is a business of too much importance and dignity to be yet dismissed from our meditation   What has been already offered on this head, is but a small part of that which I would recommend to your attention.   From a former hint you will readily conceive, that to present you here with a regular system of piety is not my design.   Such an attempt were superfluous. Of the spiritual kind there are books innumerable, in which you will meet with all that can be said on the subject in general.   The inducements to Religion which are more immediately derived from your sex and situation, together with those Exercises and those Effects of it, that concern you more particularly, are the points to which my plan properly confines me

I will begin this discourse by removing a bar which has been thrown in our way by such as have appeared fond of every opportunity to depreciate the better half of the human species.   The devotion of women has been considered as nothing more than the passion of love directed to a divine object, when in reality they longed for an inferior one, or happened to be disappointed in their wishes . an opinion which has given occasion to some wit and more ridicule.

It

It feems to have proceeded chiefly from two caufes, the amorous ftyle which has by too many female pens been adopted into devotional writings, and the multitudes of young women who, denied originally the opportunity of indulging their natural inclinations, or afterwards croff-ed in the purfuit of them, have flung themfelves headlong into the gloomy retreats of a miftaken piety, where they have been taught to offer at a heavenly fhrine, thofe fires which were not fuffered to burn freely elfewhere

But now on the former circumftance I would obferve, that the language of love has not, fo far as I know, been admitted into books of devotion by female more frequent-ly than by male authors, and that, in this practice, both have probably thought themfelves warranted by the exam-ple of Solomon in his well-known fong: a compofition, of which I muft needs fay, that how naturally foever it came from a monarch of his character, in thofe earlier days of eaftern imagination and eaftern ardour, it fhould by no means be made a model for chriftian writers   In the New Teftament, although produced from the fame region, we find very little of this fort, and that little in the chafteft and pureft ftrain, at the fame time that there we are exprefsly required, and taught, " to worfhip God who is a fpirit in " fpirit and in truth ' But when we difapprove of the practice as indifcreet, muft we condemn it too as fenfual; or becaufe in fome it may have been the ebullition of a lafcivious fancy, fhall we pronounce it to be fo in all? Cer-tain it is, that among fuch as have ufed it, there have been not a few eminently diftinguifhed by the purity of their manners

In the cafe of thofe numerous votaries to the church of Rome, who by violence or craft, defpondence or fuperfti-tion, are immured in convents, what can be more natural, more reafonable, or in truth more neceffary, than that being

ing deprived of the pleasures of this world, they should ask confolation from the next ? Or if finding it impoffible to cultivate one of the strongeft propenfities of the human heart, by that kind of commerce which Nature intended, can they be juftly blamed for turning to an object, whofe infinite excellence shall furnish endlefs fcope for the beft fentiments and nobleft affections of the foul, thofe that are immediately connected with piety ? Will not the fame way of reafoning be applicable to women living in the world? I apprehend, it will.

But, in reality, the opinion we now examine would reflect no difhonour on feminine devotion, did not thofe who entertain it preceed upon a low idea of the paffion referred to   Whatever hold that paffion, for purpofes apparently wife, may take at firft of the animal part of our frame, they are utter ftrangers to its genuine character, who do not know that it is capable of rifing to the utmoft refinement By pleading the caufe of Virtuous Love, I fhall be able to prove its connexion with that which is Divine to be founded in nature ; I mean in cultivated nature, where a fenfe of the divinity obtains   As virtuous love operates on both the fexes pretty nearly alike, what I am going to obferve of its effects on the men may, I believe, be juftly applied to the impreffions produced by it on the women

A man fees in fome public place a great number of young perfons to whom he never fpoke   He furveys them all He is ftruck with one, who is really lefs beautiful than feveral others prefent, and who is fo even in his eyes   in her favour he decides at once   It is a common cafe : how fhall we account for it ? I conceive, thus   Every countenance expreffes, or is thought to exprefs, a character peculiar to itfelf , and that which correfponds moft with our particular tafte in the way of temper, behaviour, underftanding, we neceffarily and fpontaneoufly prefer   By
                                                                    this

this character therefore, whether real or imaginary, we
are determined   As we hinted in a former difcourfe, it is
the foul we feek.   With mind only can mind unite   That
which is prefented to our eyes attracts us merely as an
image of that which they cannot perceive   Our fenfes may
be faid to tie the knot; but, ftrictly fpeaking, the knot is
formed in the foul.   Our fenfes are properly the vehicles
of our affection; but to that affection they ftill act in fub-
ordination.   It is fupreme.   Its power is indeed fo great,
that were the gratification of the fenfes, in the paffion we
are now confidering, to interfere with the intereft of our
nobler part, or with this exalted fentiment which confti-
tutes its joy, they would be facrificed without hefitation.
To virtuous love the fpirit of facrifice is effential.   What
hazards, hardfhips, loffes, pains, has not this generous
attachment encountered, with pleafure and even with
extafy, happy in manifefting its zeal by the moft arduous
proofs! To mention but one inftance amongft ten thoufand, and that recorded in Holy Writ; we are told, that
" Jacob ferved feven years for Rachel, and that they feem-
" ed to him but a few days "—" Why! For the love he
" had to her."

But now fuppofe the man we have juft imagined, *to*
cherifh with fondnefs the fudden impreffion made upon
him by a certain appearance, to be introduced to the lady,
and to admire her more and more for thofe internal qualities, which from that appearance he prefumes her to poffefs   With her looks too he is every day more deeply
fmitten, but ftill as they are the fancied picture of her
mind   This ideal form follows him every where.   Bufinefs, company, amufement, he could not endure but for
the thoughts of her, which are for ever intermingling.
Her converfation, her fmiles, her approbation, even the
flighteft marks of her regard, are to him happinefs unequalled, and fuch as can only be excelled by the entire
                                        poffeffion

poffeffion of the endearing object. He purfues, he obtains
it. And now fuppofe him to difcover, that the character
he ufed to contemplate with tranfport was merely imaginary, that fhe is abfolutely deftitute of the difpofitions, the
fentiments, in one word, the foul which he had fondly figured——Need I fpeak the reft? Ah, what difappointment and mifery! Where now is his love? Where the
facred, fervent, elevated paffion, he fo lately foftered as
the felicity of his life! Intellectual and moral beauty he
chiefly fought. He finds it not; and becaufe he does not
find it, what happens? His very fenfes, though remaining conftitutionally the fame, revolt, are difgufted, and
chilled The enchanting face enchants no more and why?
Becaufe it no longer reflects the image that inflamed his
breaft A fool or a tyrant ftarts up there, where fenfe and
foftnefs feemed to refide.

But now let us reverfe this unhappy part of the fcene,
and fuppofe that the lady's real character anfwers to her
appearance; that, inftead of lofing, fhe gains by a more
intimate acquaintance; in fhort, that certain hidden graces,
which no feature, form, or air could fully exprefs,
difplay themfelves as circumftances rife to call them forth;
what will be the confequence? That the youthful ardour
of our lover will increafe? No, but a better ardour will;
that of rational efteem, fentimental complaifance, and felf-
congratulation The other, as he advances in life, will
gradually abate, and at length vanifh What then? Will
this tendernefs vanifh, or his affections abate? By no
means We have feen that from the beginning it was the
love of her mind principally. It is fo now more than ever.
It has lefs emotion. it has more folidity, it is lefs earthly:
it is more divine It is love mellowed into friendfhip
What fhall I fay? It is the fineft feeling of the human
heart And the attraction grows, partly by habit, partly
by the encreafe of thofe qualities that caufed it on her fide,
                                                        and

and partly by the improvement of good difpofitions on his.
The tumultuous and irregular pleafures to which perhaps
before he knew her, he was addicted, have now loft their
relifh. The calm, yet interefting joys, he taftes in her fociety, occupy all his leifure From every engagement,
whether of the bufy or idle kind, he returns to her with
new delight, glad to fhake off the interrupting world, and
impatient when it compels him to any long abfence. By
the lovely fympathies of her gentle bofom, his cares are
foothed, his labours foftened, and his loffes rendered eafy
Is he fuccefsful? His fuccefs is triumph, from this thought,
'I fhall be able to make her more happy whom my foul
'loveth' Is fhe in pain or ficknefs? Does her health decline? Will this man look on unconcerned? Ah! no
he will hang over her bed of diftrefs with augmented fondnefs, with an anguifh more charming than all the luxury
of fenfual indulgence Is her bloom withered? Are the
allurements of youth gone? Will he grow indifferent?
No, no! in his eye fhe is handfome ftill In all fhe fays,
and does, and looks, he ftill beholds, and ftill admires, the
unfaded and unfading beauties of her foul

If any profane or infenfible wretch, prone "to fpeak
"evil of the things which he knows not," and which he
cannot know, fhould affect to treat this reprefentation
with ridicule, as vifionary and unnatural, I can only pity
him You who are difpofed to be ingenuous and candid,
may reft affured that it is taken from life Thofe whom it
refembles will own it true, while they find it imperfect
But imperfect as it is, it will, if I miftake not, be fufficient
to prove the point for which I have produced it

Abftract, my fifters, from that regard to perfon, which
in the pureft paffion between the fexes we have acknowledged to be an original ingredient, but which we have
found to be only an inferior ingredient, and one whofe
                                    operation

operation is soon diminished; abstract from this, and what
is there in all the rest, that may not be traced to the love of
excellence? But what else, I would gladly know, is the
leading idea in the love of GOD? Between that first of
Beings, and the most accomplished of his creatures, the
distance is indeed infinite   The fairest virtues we see
around us are at best but faint emanations from him, who
is " the perfection of beauty " But from these, and from
the admiration they inspire, it is, that we are led up to
him, as by so many pleasing though scattered streams to
their fountain.

And now suppose that a young woman, possessed with
the belief of this highest excellence, is disappointed in her
prospects of an agreeable union with one of our sex   she
turns her thoughts to heaven   She contemplates truth and
rectitude, wisdom and goodness, power, mercy, and faithfulness, in their source.   She considers them as all working together for her good.   she sees them shining through
the cloud of disappointment.   From this cloud she hears,
as it were, her Maker thus addressing her, ' My daugh-
' ter, give me thy heart   Thy supreme affection none
' upon earth can deserve   Human attainments are all de-
' fective, human regards are often insincere   Put not
' your trust in the son of man   he may deceive, or he
' may change, or he may not be able to protect you   But
' of this kind you have nothing to fear from your creator.
' Throw thyself, my child, on my friendship '—She is not
disobedient to the heavenly call.   She prostrates herself in
the presence of the Most High.   To him she devotes
that heart which he formed, to him she pours it out with
freedom.   She adores the perfections of his nature   the
frailties of her own, with all the failings of her life past,
she penitently confesses   her tears flow.   Her mind is relieved; consolation pervades her soul, out of weakness
she waxes strong   Virtue never appeared to her half so fair,

Religion

Religion rises before her in full majesty; everlasting objects open to her view, solitude and silence begin to charm. Converse with her GOD, with her SAVIOUR, with her BIBLE, with HERSELF, yields a pleasure hitherto unknown In the midst of society she longs for its return; from the dissipation of amusements she retreats with joy, self-denial for the sake of GOD, and goodness, loses its name; her duty is her delight; the spirit of sacrifice is felt in all its nobleness She is great, and she is happy.—Say, ye sons of raillery; ye scoffers at female devotion, declare; what is there in all this unnatural, irrational, or in any respect unsuitable to the best conceptions of the human mind.

From what I have said let none imagine, that I mean to insinuate female devotion may not be found in married as well as single life; or that a woman will not have recourse to piety, unless she be driven to it by disappointed love. This, like every other distress, and more perhaps than any other, will prompt a young person of reflection to turn to the ALMIGHTY. But of worth or ingenuity those surely have no true feeling, who think that the character of the SUPREME cannot from a heart well disposed command an affectionate veneration in any condition, or under any circumstance whatever.

That in Female nature there are certain Qualities, which seem peculiarly calculated, by the grace of GOD, to dispose it for the reception and culture of this divine principle, I will proceed in the next place to demonstrate.

That your sex are, in a particular degree, susceptible of all the tender affections, will, I presume, be allowed by most Their propensity to those, with which the passion of love is more immediately complicated, has been charged upon them by many as matter of reproach. What to me appears in general to do them honour, is the warmth
of

of their attachments, and their aptitude to be affected with whatever has a tendency to touch the heart. But I have always thought that the fpirit of devotion depends on fentiment, rather than ratiocination; on the feelings of gratitude and wonder, joy and forrow, triumph and contrition, hope and fear, rather than on theological difquifition however profound, or pious fpeculation however exalted. Religion, it is certain, has been often mazed and loft in the labyrinth of fchool-divinity. Although, in " contending " for the faith once delivered to the faints," againft the the attacks of unbelievers, found criticifm and difpaffionate arguments be undoubtedly the proper weapons, and although to thinking minds they be alfo the natural inftruments of information and conviction; yet is it not by them that the devotional principle is awakened and kept alive ?

For unintelligible impreffions, or wild enthufiafm, I am not an advocate. He that is, expofes religion to difgrace. Common fenfe, calm reflection, univerfal righteoufnefs, a humanity unlimited by party, a moderation that can applaud virtue in an enemy; thefe my dear charge, never be given up on any pretence, or for any perfuafion. A faith without morality, a devotion repugnant to reafon, are not chriftianity; but hypocrify, or fuperftition. Beware of fuch as under the mafk of zeal would feek to remove you from the only ground which, by God's bleffing, can fecure your ftedfaftnefs, improvement, and comfort; I mean a fober evangelical piety.

In the days of the apoftles there were thofe that " lay " in wait to deceive, that crept into widows houfes, and " led captive filly women," In our days their fucceffors are numerous. I fay again, Of fuch beware, " left by " any means, as the ferpent beguiled Eve through his fub- " tilty, fo your minds be corrupted from the fimplicity " that is in Chrift" Remember always, that whatever

teacher

teacher or teachers would avail themfelves of the warmth of your paffions, or the vivacity of your imaginations, to feduce you into any fyftem unfriendly to a good temper and a good life, do either miftake the true defign of the gofpel, or have an ill defign on you. But then on the other hand you may be equally affured, that whatever teacher or teachers would attempt by dry difputation, or cold enquiry, to convert or edify fouls, are ftrangers alike to nature and to chriftianity What in truth is the latter, but an affectionate and powerful addrefs to the former, divinely adapted to take hold not of the underftanding only, but of the confcience, the will, and the paffions, that is of the moft vital and operative principles of the heart?

Among the reft I mentioned the paffion of Fear We are told by an apoftle, that " perfect love cafteth out " fear" But perfect love, in matters of religion, cannot, ftrictly underftood, be fuppofed compatible with human frailty To that is the fyftem of Jefus gracioufly proportioned There the paffion I fpeak of is applied to, in a manner the moft ftriking that can be conceived. For what purpofe? To damp refolution, or difhearten hope? No; but to reftrain the impetuofity of defire, and to prevent the mifery of diforder, not to frighten you from the mercy-feat, but to fhow you the neceffity of taking fhelter there. You, my female friends, are naturally fearful A confcious weaknefs prompts you continually to feek protection Feeling yourfelves, and knowing your fex to be helplefs, you flee to men for fafety. But do you always find it in them?—Need I point you to a fure refuge? I have done it already Are you mortified at the timidity of your nature? Are you depreffed by the feeblenefs of your frame? I know not that you have caufe I am certain you have not, if a fenfe of your condition have induced you put yourfelves under the guardianfhip of Omnipotence. Many of you it is evident, have the art of turning your infirmities to

your

your own advantage, fo far as concerns your influence with our fex But that power, which you thus extract from imbecility, is often, alas! by the unhappinefs of your paffions, only rendered productive of new and greater weakneffes , whereas, if you were wife, you might on your natural frailty build an invincible ftrength, by fecuring the protection of the Almighty

Your Encouragements to do this, by the practice of fuch a piety as I am now recommending, I will confider in the next place, thofe encouragements, I mean, which both Providence and Scripture prefent to your fex with an appropriation as obfervable in itfelf, as it is merciful to you.

Nothing can be more plain, than that Providence has placed you moft commonly in circumftances peculiarly advantageous for the exercifes of devotion, and for the prefervation of that virtue, without which every profeffion of godlinefs muft be regarded as an impudent pretence The fituation of men lays them open to a variety of temptations, that lie out of your road The buftle of life, in which they are generally engaged, leaves them often but little leifure for holy offices. Their paffions are daily fubject to be heated by the ferment of bufinefs; and how hard is it for them to avoid being importuned to excefs, while fometimes a prefent intereft, frequently a preffing appetite, and yet more frequently the fear of ridicule, ftimulates them to comply! How very hard for a young man to withftand

> " The world's dread laugh,
> " Which fcarce the firm philofopher can fcorn!"

In the cafe of our fex, do we not often fee ranked on the fide of licentioufnefs that reputation which ought to attend on fobriety alone? Is not the laft openly laughed at by thofe

O   to

to whose opinion giddy young men will pay most respect,
their own companions? is not its contrary cried up as a
mark of spirit? And if, in their unreftrained conversation
amongst a diversity of humours, they meet with affronts,
are they not constantly told, that the maxims of honour
require them to take revenge? Is not all this extremely
unfavourable to the religious life, of which so great a part
consists in purity and prayer, in regularity and coolness,
in self-command and mild affections? But from such snares
your sex are happily exempted.

In many instances men are attacked by folly, before they
furrender, whereas women must generally invite it by art,
or rather indeed take it by violence, ere they can possess
themselves of its guilty pleasures So far the Almighty,
in consideration of their debility, and from a regard to
their innocence, has raised a kind of fence about them, to
prevent those wilder excursions into which the other sex
are frequently carried, with a freedom unchecked by fear,
and favoured by custom

Corrupt as the world is, it certainly does expect from
young women a strict decorum; nor, as we have seen
before, does it easily forgive them the least deviation Add
that, while you remain without families of your own, few
of you are necessarily so engaged, as not to have a large
portion of time, with daily opportunities for recollection, if
you be inclined to improve them I go farther and subjoin
that your improving them by a piety the most regular and
avowed, if withal unaffected and liberal, will be no sort
of objection to the men, but much the reverse.

A bigoted woman every man of fense will carefully shun
as a most disagreeable and even dangerous companion.
But the secret reverence, which that majestic form, Religion, imprints on the hearts of all, is such, that even they
who

who will not fubmit to its dictates themfelves, do yet wifh
it to be regarded by thofe with whom they are connected
in the neareft relations. The verieft infidel of them all,
I am apt to believe, would be forry to find his fifter, daughter, or wife, under no reftraint from religious principle.
Thus it is, that even the greateft libertines are forced to
pay, at the fame inftant, a kind of implicit refpect to the
two main objects of their profligate fatire, Piety and Women, while they confider thefe as formed for each other,
and tacitly acknowledge that the firft is the only effectual
means of enfuring the good behaviour of the laft Let
them talk as long, and as contemptuoufly as they will,
about that eafiy credulity, and thofe fuperftitious terrors,
which they pretend to be the foundation of your religion;
fomething within will always give them the lie, fo long
as they perceive that your religion renders you more ftea-
dily virtuous, and more truly lovely

But let us turn to Scripture, and fee what peculiar in-
citement you have from thence to the profeffion and practice of godlinefs How encouraging to reflect, that the
very firft promife made to the human race diftinguifhed
your fex with a mark of honour, as fignal as it was unex-
ampled! Need I explain myfelf by faying, that the greateft perfonage who ever vifited our world, he who came
on the important defign, and who executed it in the moft
wonderful manner, none other and none lefs than " the
" fon of God, who was manifefted to deftroy the works
" of the devil," and on their ruins to raife an empire of
righteoufnefs and happinefs, elevated as heaven, and lafting
as eternity—that He, I fay, was from the beginning pre-
dicted under the fingular and interefting character of " the
feed of the woman?" How exalting a circumftance for your
whole fex, that the Saviour of men, the admiration of
angels, and the prince of heaven, was accordingly " in
" the fulnefs of time made of a woman!" And, oh, my

O 2   young

young friends, what dignity will it for ever reflect on maiden virtue, that " a virgin conceived and bore a son, the " only begotten of the Father, full of grace and truth?" Where is the religion, or the philosophy, that has lifted your nature so high, or placed the beauty of female purity and excellence in a light so conspicuous and noble ?

Nor must we forget to take notice of the particular honours, with which individuals of your sex have had their memories transmitted to posterity by the sacred records. Not to insist on the females of the Old Testament, that " through faith have obtained a good report;" it merits your observation how many we read of in the New, who for the duties of devotedness to their Saviour, the liberalities of respect to his person, and even the heroism of zeal in his cause, are marked out with a pre-eminence perfectly distinguishable

When of his apostles the most sanguine had denied, had even forsworn, and all the rest had forsaken him and fled, we find those faithful and gentle creatures surrounding his cross with lamentations, which they were neither ashamed nor afraid to avow   Never sure did female tears appear more graceful   Nor were they merely that transient flow of mechanical grief, so easily furnished by too many eyes, where the heart has little or no share in the soft effusion. The love which those devout daughters of Jerusalem bore to their master, nothing could extinguish.   Who has not read that affecting story of the visit to the sepulchre, paid by the pious Marys and their little company, together with the kind, generous, and as it might have proved, very hazardous purpose which produced it ?   Their setting out alone, at so early an hour, while it was yet dark, to engage in so solemn a scene, afforded a striking proof of the courage and constancy with which their piety had inspired them, amidst all that spirits like theirs must have

suffered

suffered from so many circumstances of sorrow In their
countenances, words, and gestures on that occasion, I
think I read the painful, yet amiable emotions, that wrought
in their tender throbbing hearts   I am particularly charmed
with the eager anxiety, and beautiful distress of Mary
Magdalene, whose gratitude for the transcendent mercies
she had received, did then flame out with such uncommon
fervour   While I contemplate the whole transaction,
with the conduct that preceded it, I cannot but admire
that justice which, in preference to all others, honoured
those excellent women with being the first witnesses and
publishers of Christ's resurrection, or, as an ancient writer
has expressed it, Apostles to the Apostles themselves   A
very natural, as it is in effect a most memorable attestation
to their superior attachment, and unconquerable fidelity !
Surely it was not in vain, that the annals of inspiration
have registered those pleasing facts with such particularity.
There they stand, and will for ever stand, illustrious monuments of female worth, in a conjuncture most peculiarly
trying, and of the extraordinary approbation it met with
from him, in whose sight devotion and perseverance, affection and faith, will always outshine the more showy
qualities that fill the world with history and wonder

I should have mentioned before this, the friendship of
Jesus to the sisters of Lazarus, his applause to the woman
of Canaan, and his pathetic address to the women who
followed him weeping, while he carried his cross   It is
likewise worthy of remark, that of all the disciples, he
who seems, in a certain divine sweetness of disposition, to
have resembled him most, directed one of those Epistles
which make a part of our scriptures to a lady, a person
of distinction much respected by him and all the believers
of that time for her eminent piety, and that of her children

And

And now if, with encouragements like thefe to the love
of God and our Saviour, any of you, my fair auditory,
fhould live in forgetfulnefs of both , what fhall we fay of
fuch, but that they are deftitute of true ambition, and totally
infenfible to the moft diftinguifhing favours of heaven?

But perhaps we fhall be told, that the perpetual flatteries
which many of you meet with from men on account of
its inferior gifts, fuch as youth, beauty, fancy, fprightlinefs,
prevent or deftroy thofe better fentiments which you might
be otherwife difpofed to cultivate. I doubt it not But do
you plead this is an excufe ? Your fituation, we have granted all along, fubjects you to temptations in particular inftances But we have feen, that it frees you from other very dangerous fnares, and includes the moft powerful attractives to
your duty What are you to infer from the whole, but
that you ought to avail yourfelves of thefe advantages for
fortifying and guarding you wherever you lie expofed ?

I have juft named what appears to me your fex's weakeft
fide. To arm you on that I have had opportunities of
offering a variety of precautions I now add, and it fhall be
my laft confideration on this occafion, that Revelation con-
curs with Reafon to furnifh the ftrongeft weapons of defence
againft that adulation, which is fo great an enemy to your
fouls

That your fouls are immortal is probable from reafon
and certain from revelation. But the arguments from
either I hold unneceffary to propofe here To attempt the
conviction of female infidels falls not within my prefent defign Indeed I fear it were a hopelefs undertaking The
prepofterous vanity, together with the open or fecret
profligacy, by which they have been warped into fcep-
ticifm, would in all likehood baffle any endeavours of mine.
If

If they be not however fo far gone in that unhappy fyftem, as to be refolved againft all fober enquiry, I would earneftly recommended to their perufal a few of the many excellent writings, which this age and country have produced in favour of religion both natural and revealed At the fame time I would juft remind them, that the daring and difputatious fpirit of unbelief is utterly repugnant to female foftnefs, and to that fweet docility which, in their fex, is fo peculiarly pleafing to ours . not to mention, that from an infidel partner a man can have no profpect of confolation in thofe hours of diftrefs, when the hopes of futurity can alone adminifter relief —To you, my chriftian hearers, I was going to obferve, that the ftedfaft and ferious belief of immortality as pointed out in your frame, and brought to light by the gofpel, will excite fuch a mighty concern to fecure its grand interefts, fuch a high fenfe of your internal dignity, fuch a predominant ambition of being acceptable in his fight, who can make you happy or wretched for ever, as muft neceffarily leffen in your efteem every external and perifhing advantage.

If you be really poffeffed by thofe principles, he that from fpiritual and everlafting objects would turn your chief regard to fkin-deep and fhort-lived allurements, will furely in a moment of recollection at leaft, be looked upon by you as a tempter to be fhunned That pride of life, which in the eye of folly fwells into fuch importance, will fhrink and fade away into its native littlenefs in her view, whofe thoughts are often entertained with the magnificence and fplendor of eternal things To that young woman who, like her of Bethany, " has chofen the good part," who meekly penfive fits at the feet of Jefus, and with delighted reverence hears his words , the infinuation of the vicious, the impertinence of the vain, in fhort, whatever would rob her of her portion, or obftruct her enjoying it, will

not

no', I think, be over pleafing To her the care of her
falvation 's the one thing needful Compared with that,
even the beft things of this world appear, what in truth
they are, but trifles, in which, becaufe the condition of
mortality makes it unavoidable, fhe fhares with chearfulnefs, but in which fhe fhares with moderation too, becaufe
fhe has bufinefs to mind of infinite moment

" What fhall it profit a man, if he fhall gain the whole
" world, and lofe his own foul?" The queftion was afked
by him, who knew right well the value of both Had he
afked, ' What fhall it profit a woman, if fhe fhall gain the
' whole world, and lofe her own foul?' would the ftate of
the queftion have been altered? You will not fay it
Weighed againft a foul, the empire of the earth were duft
in the balance What then fhall we call thofe things, for
which finners are daily forfeiting their falvation? Tell me,
ye flattered fair ones, what is the worth of praife or admiration from knaves, or from fools, for which fo many of
you are ready to forfeit yours? Ye daughters of Vanity,
tell me what will drefs, or fhow, or gaiety of any kind,
where God and goodnefs are neglected, " profit in the
" day of wrath?" In that day of difcovery and decifion,
what will appearances avail?—Give me back thefe laftfen-
tences I had forgotten Drefs, fhow, gaiety, appearances, will be then no more —But hold, before we look
fo far, let us fee what they can perform now.

They can attract attention, they can allure defire, they
can excite encomium, deceive the unwary, and captivate
the weak, for a little But inform us, ye boafted beauties, who are told every day of your power, what permanent effential good can it procure? Bring it to the proof.
Bid the fun that meafures your days, ftand ftill, command
the current of time that hurries you along, to ftop, fay to
wrinkled age, to fell difeafe, to grim death, Approach me
                                                    not,

not, ye frightful forms. Alas! they are deaf as the adder,
and ftubborn as the rock Try then your influence in
fome fmaller thing Make the experiment on the head-
ach enjoin it to be gone. It goes not But perhaps the
heart-ach may hear, and obey your inward feelings at
leaft fhould be under your controul But you have given
them the rein, nor will they be checked on a fudden.
While you have thought only of conquering other hearts,
you have fuffered headftrong paffions to conquer your own
Summon then your worfhippers, and order them to inter-
pofe, fee if by all their incenfe, and all their zeal, they
can keep you young in fpite of years, or make you glad
in fpite of affliction. They are filent Afk them, if they
will undertake to die for you? They retire Call after
them—' Will you anfwer for us at the judgment-day ?'—
Again that awful period rufhes on the mind. Ah, my
friends, what will ye do then without religion? The
thought is big with horror Then, then it fhall be feen,
with an evidence bright and terrible as the funeral fire of
Nature, that " beauty is deceitful, and favour is vain "—
But what means that univerfal fhout of human and angelic
voices? What words are thofe, which I hear refounding
through the affembly of the univerfe? " A woman that
" feareth the Lord, She fhall be praifed! '

SERMON

SERMON XI.

ON FEMALE PIETY.

1 TIM ii. 10

——Which becometh women professing Godliness.

PROV xxxi 30.

Favour is deceitful, and beauty is vain : but a woman that feareth the Lord, She shall be praised.

IF, from what has been advanced concerning Female Piety, you be satisfied of its importance and necessity; you will naturally attend, while I proceed, without any preface, to shew you, in what manner it may be cultivated with most success.

It is difficult to say whether the instrumental duties of religion, as they are usually termed, have been more misrepresented by superstition and hypocrisy on one hand, or by vicious refinement and vain philosophy on the other. By the former they have been extolled, as if they were the whole of religion, while the latter have decried them as vulgar, unavailing, and insignificant. The real truth is, that they are not only a part of religion, but an essential, and important part of it; essential, as expressing its several affections, and important, as nourishing and maintaining them, essential, as a direct compliance with the divine authority, and important, as rendering such compliance more ready and habitual.

Habits, we all know, are formed by many reiterated acts; and if these be discontinued, those will in time be lost. As good impressions are at first produced by proper
attention

attention, fo, if this be fufpended, they will foon fade from the mind, and the fooner, no doubt, that many of them at leaft were produced there in oppofition to appetite, fafhion, and the maxims of the world Even friendfhip itfelf, which has originally fo powerful a hold of the human heart, is not to be preferved alive, without that interchange of words and actions, if the parties be near; or that commerce of thoughts and wifhes, if they be rot, to which it naturally inclines. What could you expect from him, who fhould profefs to entertain an affection for you, and yet teftify no defire of your company, take no delight in your converfation, or if abfent never enquire after you? Religion is a Divine Friendfhip, to be begun and continued nearly in the fame mannei with that which is human, making allowance ftill for the infinite difparity between the CREATOR and the CREATURE, between the Sovereign Spirit all pure and perfect, and a dependant mind embodied and frail.

In cultivating a friendfhip which you wifhed to be thorough and lafting, you would often ftep afide from the crowd to enjoy the freedom of undifturbed converfe; you would lay open your heart with confidence to the object beloved, liften to each communication with pleafure, enter more and more into the fame conceptions, exchange every poffible mark of efteem, and, in the end, eftablifh an union of interefts and of fouls alike clofe and tender Now here we have fome refemblance of private devotion. It is not my defign to purfue this refemblance through its feveral parts; neither do I pretend to fay, that it holds minutely in every one of them, but the general ground is clear to her who believes in an omniprefent Deity, and knows that between minds there may be an intercourfe independent of the fenfes The application can only be learned by practice, and much practice too.

It

It will not be learned by thofe who have no relifh for retirement. The ALMIGHTY's voice muft be often attended to in the filence of the paffions, and the fecrecy of the
foul. Thofe are yet ftrangers to their MAKER, who cannot endure to think of him, or do not love to turn to him,
when alone Is the reverfe of this, my dear hearers, your
cafe? Are your meditations of GOD fweet? Does your
heart go out after him, as its beft and greateft object? Is
it your joy, to pour it forth into his paternal bofom? Do
you frequently find the exercife fo delightful, as to quit it
with unwillingnefs? Do you generally perceive your fentiments raifed and refined by it, your ideas of your duty
quickened and enlarged, your deteftation of the contrary
confirmed and heightened, your refolutions invigorated of
courfe, your gratitude, humility, meeknefs, refignation,
and good affections of every kind, improved? Then are
you a true worfhipper Thefe are fome of the genuine
workings of piety

I enquire not, whether they be the refult of longer or
fhorter prayers, of ftudied forms or extempore addrefs, of
more or fewer ftated feafons for fuch offices In thefe particulars different minds require a diverfity, or a different
education occafions it. But fhe I fuppofe, will be the
greateft proficient in the Spirit of Prayer, who is at the
greateft pains to be fo, I do not mean in the way of fcience
or art, but in that of earneftnefs and perfeverance.

Befide the regular, invariable, and folemn performance
of your morning and evening devotions, it would be well
if not a daily, efpecially on the day of facred reft, you
took repeated opportunities of entering into your clofet,
fhutting your door, and praying to your FATHER who
fees in fecret according as you found yourfelf in a happier fpot on for fuch employment, or were prompted to
it by fome peculiar occurrence in your fituation, or exi-
gence in your foul And if at certain times of the year,
                                                  pointed

pointed out by religious cuftom, or fixed upon by perfonal choice, you are to confecrate a whole day to holy retreat and devotional exercifes, joined with prudent fafting, you would I am perfuaded, find it as highly beneficial in your own practice, as it comes ftrongly recommended by the experience of the faints.

If you might be advifed by me, you fhould in prayer neither truft wholly to your fingle fund of thought and expreffion, fuppofing it even rich and various, nor confine yourfelf entirely to forms, by whatever man or fet of men compofed, but ufe fometimes one, fometimes the other, and fometimes a mixture of both, juft as the attraction of your mind feems to lead at the moment, or as any of thefe methods may on trial be attended with moft fatisfaction and and advantage. In effect, I am convinced that of thofe who, in this kind of commerce, limit themfelves to their own unaffifted ftock, the greater part will often, particularly in circumftances of bad health or fpiritual drynefs, be reduced to fuch ftraits as muft produce a poverty of devotion which they could not fuffer, did they proceed on a larger foundation   On the other hand, I cannot conceive, that, even amongft thofe who are moft devoted to forms, any fincere worfhipper fhould not by the fwelling of fentiment, and the current of devotion, be frequently carried away into a freer and fuller effufion of the heart.

As to the length of thofe duties, I would only fay, that you muft be governed by your condition both outward and inward, that you are to avoid every thing carelefs, or formal, whether with or without preconceived words; that little intermiffions are often extremely ufeful to relieve the mind, and fit it for a new exertion of its powers, but that on the other fide, by praying in continuity, the foul is often warmed into life and energy, till that exercife which was begun with languor is concluded with affection.

When

When I speak of affection, let me warn you not to mistake the effervescence of fancy for the spirit of devotion. They are two things widely different "By their fruits "ye shall know them" The fluency, tears, and rapture produced by the first, are mechanical, superficial, and ineffective, engendering only the confidence of Enthusiasm, or wasting themselves in the scrupulosity of Superstition. The last, though frequently accompanied with fluency, tears, and rapture, at least in minds of much sensibility, is yet often not so: but when it leaves the heart better, however this may not be discerned immediately. She who sometimes perhaps, like the self-abased publican, is able only to sigh out " Gon be merciful to me a sinner," may in that all-seeing eye be as acceptable as the most eloquent petitioner that ever addressed the throne of heaven. We read of " the spirits helping our infirmities" in this very exercise, " and making intercessions for us with groanings that cannot be uttered."

Mental prayer, and silent ejaculation, I will not now consider. They are the attainments of persons far advanced in devotion By pursuing the track I point out, you may hope to reach them in one degree or another and some experience in them will lead you to more. Those who can abstract and concentrate their minds, so as readily to place themselves in the presence of God, wherever they are, and to converse with him even in a crowd, whether by continued contemplation, or by sudden dartings of pious affection towards him on the point of a vigorous thought, certainly possess a very noble secret, fruitful alike of edification and enjoyment, such too as renders them much less dependant on the accidents of their situation, since let their business or other engagements be what they will, they may be still with God, calm, self-possessed, and happily disposed to " pray always " a state of spiritual life, which there is reason to fear is known by f.

There

There is a kind of middle practice, which is probably less uncommon, as it is certainly more easy. that of praying with a repressed voice, or one not in the least audible to a second person, while yet the words are distinctly and deliberately spoken by the worshipper, who by such means preserves his ideas from dissipation and impresses them more deeply on his own heart   I said deliberately, because, in this as well as in every other method of prayer, hurry and precipitation are utterly incompatible with the spirit of devotion

Of even the strongest and most retired minds it may, I believe, be affirmed, that they never think at all, on whatever occasion, without the secret or internal use of language, although they seldom attend to it   Be that as it may, I am satisfied that vocal prayer, whether more or less articulate, will be found, in general, by far the most proportioned to the human, and particularly to the female faculties   Of the manner last mentioned we have a remarkable example in the mother of Samuel   It is a beautiful passage, strongly expressive of the working of a devout but sorrowful spirit, and at the same time of the power of devotion to turn sorrow and sighing into joy and praise.

One thing we may boldly pronounce, as a maxim which will never fail; that she has worshipped to purpose, in whatever mode she has worshipped, who comes away improved or established in worthy dispositions, whether these be attended with much emotion or with none, with much delight or with little, at the time   This remark I judged peculiarly necessary here, considering how easily you, my young friends, may be misled on this subject by that ardour of passion, and that vivacity of fancy, which are so natural to you, and which, wherever devotion is concerned, are so prone to assume its name, when at the very best they can only aid its flights.

On

On the fame principle, I would caution you not to lofe
yourfelves in generalities, which, however they may
chance to engage the underftanding, or entertain the imagination, feldom touch the confcience, or intereft the heart
In converfing with a virtuous and intimate friend, you
would choofe certainly to dwell on thofe matters that affected you moft nearly, or to throw out thofe reflections that
moft readily occurred   In this higher correfpondence you
fhould do the fame, only with more folemnity, and greater
abftraction from fecular objects

Nothing can be more erroneous than the common opinion, that the feveral parts of prayer, as they are ufually
termed, ought to enter into every longer act of devotion
What is this, but to reduce into a mere trial of fkill, or to
reftrain within the trammels of a fyftem, and thereby degrade to a laborious and jejune piece of formality, that
which ought to be free and unaffected, natural and noble?
—' I am going into the company of a bofom-friend   Let
' me fettle before-hand the whole plan of our converfation;
' that I may be fure to introduce fuch and fuch topics, in
' order to difcufs them feverally one after another, at full
' length, and with due connexion.'—He who fhould talk in
this manner would difcover, methinks, very little acquaintance with the fpirit of friendfhip   In that, my fifters,
and in true devotion, there is nothing believe me, artificial, nicely managed, or elaborately ftudied. Efteem,
fentiment, confidence, a fympathy of foul, and the over-
flowings of the heart, are all in all.   I think not at prefent
of the public offices of religion, where, in thofe who lead
them, more regularity and accuracy are no doubt required

On the whole, when you addrefs the feat of mercy, you
ought to fpeak what you feel moft ftrongly at that particular
feafon, to follow without fcruple the inward attraction before mentioned, to infift on thofe things of a fpiritual
nature,

nature, that are then attended with the greateſt reliſh . to continue your attention to them calmly, but fixedly, while that reliſh remains , then to paſs on, if time and other circumſtances permit, to ſomething elſe, ſtill without any agitation or violent effort , nor deeming it neceſſary to follow out this new track, ſhould another preſent itſelf that ſeems more promiſing, or that lies more parallel to the courſe of your thoughts on the occaſion , chiefly concerned to keep alive a ſenſe of that great preſence in which you are, of thoſe wants and weakneſſes under which you labour, of what you owe to others as well as to yourſelves, and of that divinely efficacious interceſſion, through which alone you wiſh and hope to be heard and accepted

A compoſed, affectionate, and ſteady attention to theſe and ſuch like rules (for I cannot now enter into the full detail) will, if I be not greatly miſtaken, prove one effectual means of cultivating the life and power of religion within you   I need not add, what you have been told times without number, and what your own hearts cannot on the leaſt reflexion fail to repeat , that no prayers can be effectual for this or any one good purpoſe, which are not accompanied with a correſpondent watchfulneſs and faithful diſcharge of every other duty.

But it may be neceſſary to ſubjoin, that the practice of devotion, now recommended, cannot take place without much preparation from time to time · of which one well-known part is the Reading of the ſcriptures   On this a very few obſervations ſhall ſuffice

For acquiring what is generally ſtyled Religious Knowledge, reading the Scriptures throughout, and often large portions at a time, may be perfectly proper   For improving in that which thoſe ſcriptures ſpeak of chiefly under this denomination, I mean a practical and vital ſenſe of things

P   divine

divine and everlasting, a different method, as I conceive, should be followed

Short and select passages from both Testaments, but especially the New, and more particularly from the history and sermons of our Saviour, should be perused and pondered at leisure, first without any commentary at all, and so indeed for the most part, except where there is a manifest difficulty, in doing which, you should with awful reverance and child-like simplicity lay your minds open to the native impressions of the truth, and to the secret teachings of its author When, in this way, you meet with one or more verses, that strike you with peculiar conviction or delight, close the book, revolve them again and again, look up to heaven, and implore the Father of Spirits to write their meaning on your hearts, as " with the point " of a diamond " Read nothing more at that time, nothing at least that has not a near relation to the ideas and affections they excite Give these an easy unstudied vent in prayer The pleasure and the benefit will be unspeakable Only suffer not the tincture thereby left upon you, to be lost in the succeeding scenes Next morning review the same passage, endeavour to recall the same sentiments, and with your pencil mark it for your future benefit.

A young lady formerly of my acquaintance, who is now reading the character and will of her Creator in the light of the beatific vision, used daily to follow this practice Her bible was infinitely prized by her; whatever was most excellent in it, she had thought and weighed all over Its sacred contents were engraven on her soul, or rather her soul was delivered into the mould of it. She lived in innocence, and died in triumph.

Is it necessary, my beloved disciples, that I should urge you to the study of a book which, while it tends to make you wise to salvation, is calculated also to convey the
most

moſt affecting views, and to awaken the ſublimeſt ſenſibilities, on a thouſand topics ? A book it certainly is, full
of entertainment as well as inſtruction, compoſed by a great
diverſity of authors, and all of them divinely taught. I
think I ſee them, one after another, preſenting for your
improvement their reſpective writings, with an aſpect of
dignity and ſweetneſs combined, the dignity of truth, and
the ſweetneſs of benevolence, both derived from him, who
inſpired them to be the teachers of mankind, and who, in
order to gain them the more belief and veneration, inveſt-
ed many of them with a command over Nature, and a
knowledge of Futurity, which none but the God of Nature, and the Spirit of Omniſcience could impart I think
I hear them ſeverally addreſſing you, in the name of God,
with an authority that can only be equalled by their mildneſs, on ſubjects the grandeſt and moſt important, in a
happy variety of ſtyles, amidſt an uniformity of ſentiments,
and an agreement in facts, which, the multiplicity of them
conſidered, muſt ever appear truly admirable ! What ſhall
I ſay more ?—I will not deſire you to read this book called
the Bible, if you can ſhow me another containing ſo much
to inform, and impreſs, and delight reflecting minds, laid
together in a manner ſo extenſively adapted to their various
turns of underſtanding, taſte, and temper ; which people of
different and diſtant countries, through a long ſucceſſion of
ages, have held in ſo much reverence, and read with ſo
much advantage, where it is ſo difficult to determine,
which are moſt diſtinguiſhed, eaſe and ſimplicity, or ſublimity and force, but where all are ſo beautifully united,
where there is ſo little to diſcourage the weakeſt ſpirit if
docile, and ſo much to gratify the ſtrongeſt if candid,
where the fancy and the heart, the intellect and the con-
ſcience, are applied to by turns with ſuch familiarity, and
yet ſuch majeſty, in fine, where the frailties, diſorders, and
diſtreſſes of human nature, are all ſo feelingly laid open,
and the remedies which heaven has provided ſo tenderly applied. But to proceed

Of books in Divinity I do not wish you to read very many. Those in the way of Religious Controversy, as it is called, but which are frequently written in a most irreligious spirit, that is, without any candour or fairness, I do not wish you to read at all. Mere argumentative theology, I have never known to improve the temper, or regulate the conduct, but often to hurt both. Happily for you indeed, the female taste very seldom lies in that way; never, I think, where there is female sweetness. By a good providence you have been taught " the truth " as it is in Jesus." Be it your ambition to practise, not to dispute about it. Enjoy your faith in modest silence, and think well of those who differ from you in opinions, if they agree in morals, but learn to despise the futility, while you discourage the impudence, of such as would pretend to talk you out of your religion. Be assured they are often empty, and always worthless. If they attempt it in the style of banter, they offer you an affront. If they affect to seem in earnest, to be sorry for your prejudices, and solicitous to remove them by conversation, and by books which they are ready to lend you, a hundred to one, but they are actuated by the worst designs. Flee them, my fair pupils, flee them with horror, as tempters and ravagers at the same instant.

By making conscience of sincerely obeying the precepts of the gospel, while you meekly embrace its doctrines, as they appear to you set forth in the scriptures, you will have the witness of its divinity within yourselves. From thence you will be disposed to choose and adhere to those writers of whatever communion, that are calculated to make you most in love with your Saviour and your duty. The formal and frigid you will naturally dislike; the uncharitable and illiberal you will nobly detest; the trifling and superficial you will very easily contemn. Those books, how well soever recommended, that even in your gravest hours

do

do not attract and perfuade you, (I now fuppofe you pious)
ye will readily perceive are not the books for you   Such
as do both in a greater or lefs degree, it is apparent, are
adapted to your caft of mind.   Thofe, in fhort, will be
your favourite authors, whether in verfe or profe, whom
you find moft frequently new and interefting , who prefent
the moft pathetic pictures of this world and the next, who
tell you moft convincingly what you are, and what you
ought to be, who, in a word, feem to addrefs themfelves
with the greateft power to the fpirit of ingenuity, humility,
contrition, felf-denial, folid virtue, and affectionate devotion.

I take it for granted you attend on the Public Inftitutions
of religion.   The fuperior regularity of your fex in this
refpect the men, to fay the truth, fhow very little inclination to difpute   May the women take care to convince
them, that it is fomething more than mere regularity ! In
the mean time I am fure, that they who perform their firft
duties, are much more likely to perform their fecond alfo,
than they who do not.

Let your attendance be more than what the world calls
decent   let it be punctual.   She that becomes deficient in
fuch punctuality, will foon become indifferent about the
whole   Having omitted her duty unneceffarily once, a
fecond, and a third time, fhe will omit it the fourth with
lefs compunction , and ere long will be ready to neglect
it without any.   It is wonderful, how foon a fenfe of futurity dies from the foul.   Have you ever known it to live,
after the Sabbath was grown into contempt ? What multitudes have been forced to date their ruin from that period ?

But not to fpeak of the openly profane, do thofe fanctify
the fabbath to whom it is not a delight, who vifit the
                                                      houfe

houfe of God without preparation, and worfhip there without devotion? What fhall we fay of many a young woman
who paffes for good and pious, although fhe cannot for an
hour together behave with fedatenefs, or compofure, in
the immediate prefence of the Moft High? That mind
muft be volatile indeed, which the folemnities of a chriftian affembly cannot fix for a little Do we wifh you then
to disfigure your faces like the Pharifees, to hang
your heads like a bulrufh, or to practife religious grimace
of any kind? No Is even the graveft look, or moft recollected manner, a certain fign of piety? It is not. and yet
will you fay, that fuch a look and manner are of no importance on fuch an occafion, that they are not naturally
fuited to it, or that the fpirit of piety may very probably
dwell in her heart, whofe countenance and carriage even
on that occafion do not bear the marks of it, who even then
cannot reftrain the rolling eye, forget the confcious air, or
leave the fluttering demeanour?

Believe me, ladies, a different behaviour would appear
much more becoming Men of fenfe and fobriety would
entertain a much better opinion of your principles, nor
would it be any difadvantage to your Perfons Never
perhaps does a fine woman ftrike more deeply, than when
compofed into pious recollection, and poffeffed with the
nobleft confiderations, fhe affumes, without knowing it,
fuperior dignity and new graces, fo that the beauties of
holinefs feems to radiate about her, and the by-ftanders
are almoft induced to fancy her already worfhipping amongft
her kindred angels

But to return to the point immediately before us, I fay,
that the habit of ferioufnefs and devotion in church, will
produce very defirable effects on your temper and conduct
out of it By beginning the week well, you will retain
through the remainder, a certain impreffion of goodnefs,
that

that will follow you every where, at the fame time that, by
fuch avowed teftimonies of refpect for your Maker and Saviour, you will enfure the continuance of the divine be-
nediction and affiftance,

The great advantages arifing from a diligent attention to
the Preaching of the word, and alfo from an early, frequent, and devout participation of the Lord's fupper, I will
not now enter on.   They are abundantly obvious, and
have been frequently enforced   But I cannot quit the fubject of the fabbath without obferving that to thofe, who
join in the public fervices of that day, its utility is often
totally defeated by their refigning in the evening to company and recreation, the general tendency of thefe being
to efface any ferious impreffions made in the preceding
part of it   For fuch a practice, you my fair charge, who
have commonly fo much leifure upon your hands, cannot
plead the leaft excufe.

Very hard it is, if thofe who give fo many other evenings
to amufement, cannot find in their heart to give this or a
part of it to God   But, alas! it is that very paffion for
amufement, which prevents or dulls the tafte for devotion,
To her indeed, who will not be perfuaded to refcue fo
fmall a portion of her time from the gaieties of the world
for the purpofes of her falvation, we cannot hope to fay
any thing that will be of ufe.   She who cannot enjoy the
company of her Creator for an hour or two, remote from
all other company, was never initiated into the myfteries
of divine friendfhip· fhe is yet in her fins, " alienated
" from the life of God, dead while fhe lives," in a fpiritual
fenfe dead, alive only to animal nature and the tumultuous
dreams of a diftempered mind, in fhort, a poor giddy
worthlefs creature, incapable of whatever is wife or happy

" Oh!

" Oh ! loft to virtue, loft to fober thought,
" Loft to the noble fallies of the foul,
" Who think it folitude to be alone,
" Communion fweet ! communion large and high !
" Our reafon, guardian angel, and our God !
' Then neareft thefe, when others moft remote,
' And all ere long fhall be remote but thefe.
" How dreadful then to meet them all alone,
" A ftranger, unacknowl-dg'd, unapprov'd !

I tremble at the thought   Nor will it avail you, in this
cafe, to plead even the utmoft exactnefs and conftancy in
your attendance on the fanctuary   That alone will prove
nothing. Entertainment may ftill be the idol which you
worfhip, and worfhip even in the temple of Jehovah
If you fay it is not, let us bring you to the teft   When
you return home from the houfe of God, can you retire
with pleafure to your clofets, impofe filence on your fancies, command your paffions to be ftill, exclude every
thought of drefs and diverfion, company and admiration,
review what you have been doing, recall what you have
heard, make application if it admit of any (there are few
difcourfes that admit not of fome,) and then cafting yourfelves down at the footftool of the throne of God, pour
out your hearts before him, confefs with fimplicity and
forrow your fins and corruptions, implore the grace of
repentance and remiffion for what is paft, of difcernment
to know your duty for the future, and of fortitude to do it,
forming at the fame time unfeigned refolutions to that purpofe, joining to the whole the adoration of the divine attributes, as they fucceffively or jointly rife to your view,
and finally, throwing yourfelves on the divine mercy through
Chrift Jefus ?—Can you do this ? Is it your favourite and
habitual employment, in the evening of that day which God
has made for himfelf ? To her who can honeftly anfwer
in the affirmative, I will acknowledge freely that, next to
the daily tenor of a conduct uniformly chriftian, fhe gives
one of the beft proofs of fincerity in her religious profeffion,

on, nor is there any thing excellent in that, which I
should not expect from a practise so wise and pious   But
what is to be expected of those who know nothing of this ?
Or what can be said of their intentions in going to church,
who the moment they leave it leave every reflection which
it ought to have imprinted, and resolve to think of religion
that day no more than if they had not heard or mentioned
a syllable relating to it ? St James will inform you whom
they are like   They are " like unto a man beholding his
" natural face in a glass for he beholdeth himself and
" goeth his way, and straightway forgetteth what manner
" of man he was "————Do men then so readily lose the
image of themselves ? No, but the apostle must be understood to speak of some thoughtless creature, who on looking accidentally into a glass, and observing certain spots or
stains in his face, which he ought instantly to wipe off, turns
away in haste without availing himself of the discovery,
and, in the pursuit of other objects, entirely neglects a circumstance that demanded his immediate attention   I leave
you to apply the remark, and only add in general, that the
closet must enforce what the pulpit has suggested, that as
like Lydia, you should attend diligently to the things
which are spoken in the name of God, so like Mary, you
should keep and ponder them in your hearts, and that as
Jesus himself, dismissing the multitudes together with his
disciples, " went up into a mountain apart to pray," so
you, disengaging yourselves from the interruption of a
crowd, and the company even of your most intimate connexions, should step aside, more particularly at the season
in question, to converse with his Father and your Father,
with his God and your God.

   Think not from any thing I have said, that I want to
subject you to the rules of Jewish rigour, under the mild
dispensation of the Gospel   What I propose will render
the Christian sabbath no less pleasant than improving
                                                           Nor

Nor do I mean to preclude on that day the chearful reciprocations of holy friendſh p , which they that have a taſte
for them will eaſily diſtinguiſh from the unſeaſonable paſ-
times and promiſcuous viſitings, in which many fine ladies
of the preſent age paſs their Sunday evenings.

Thus I am brought to ſay ſomething of Religious Converſation　An attempt to diſcuſs ſo important a topic
would carry me too far　To manage religious converſation with propriety and advantage, is for the moſt part an
affair of great delicacy.　In the more retired intercourſe
of congenial minds, well taught and well furniſhed, it may
not be difficult　But ſuch, I fear, are not often found;
and even where ſuch have the happineſs to meet, grave
diſcourſe will require to be frequently varied, relieved,
and ſuſpended, in order to keep up its reliſh.

Much ſentiment is apt to overwhelm　The ſoul quickly ſeeks releaſe on　The bow cannot be long bent without having its elaſticity impaired　In general company, ſubjects of devotion and morality would, as the world goes,
be utterly improper　Good Lord! to what is this generation ſunk, that even amongſt characters otherwiſe decent
a man can ſeldom or ever introduce a ſolemn reflection,
without incurring the imputation of cant or impertinence?
When ſhall it be the mode to converſe like immortal beings?
Where is the faſhionable circle now, in which a ſerious
obſervation can be prudently hazarded, if not ſtolen upon
them with art and inſinuation?　Neither is this a part for
you to take upon yourſelves

Female modeſty is often ſilent, female decorum is
never bold　Both forbid a young woman to lead the converſation, and true religion dreads every thing that might
look oſtentatious　The moſt prudent courſe you can pur-
ſue is to aſſociate, as much as poſſible, with thoſe that
from

from real principle love the fhade With them you may
fafely unbofom yourfelves on the heft fubjects, without
the danger of ridicule, or the fufpicion of affectation. When
the children of Wifdom affemble out of the fight and
din of Folly, 'what improvement and felicity crown the
fcene! How delightfully do they then mingle fouls! Nor
does their parent difdain to fport with her offspring I
mean, that genuine piety knows how to blend recreation
and fmiles with fentiment and gravity.

Having mentioned Sentiment fo often, I will now once
for all offer you a caution, on which I lay a particular ftrefs.
It is this, not to miftake the capacity of thinking juftly,
or of talking well, for the fame thing with a difpofition to
act wifely The truth is, that people are not wife in confequence either of profound knowledge, or vaft learning, or
beautiful notions, or the moft cultivated tafte, or the greateft ability in difplaying thefe, but by virtue of a few plain
notions fettled into principles of conduct, even as people
are not healthy by feafting on rich dainties, or indulging
to a nice palate, but by living on fimpler fare, where temperance does not wifh for much variety, and where hunger
does not want it

Neverthelefs, there is not perhaps any thing that flatters
the human mind more than depth or fluency of remark,
than compafs or facility of converfation. In effect, they
are talents not often poffeffed, and fuch as confer a fuperiority felt by all, however it may be acknowledged by few.
When it is acknowledged, fuch praife tranfports, and
thofe who receive it fet themfelves down for every thing
that is great and accomplifhed. Alas! they forget, that
thefe are ftill at beft but in the fecond clafs of excellence;
that in a moral view they are of no value; and that fine
difcourfe and a fine character are things totally diftinct

In

In reality your beſt talkers are very ſeldom your beſt livers From their encomiums on virtue, and their declamations againſt vice, they often receive ſuch high pleaſure as with them paſſes for love for the one, and abhorrence of the other, when it is only perhaps a vain complacence in their own powers, joined to that natural ſenſe of right and wrong, which is common to them with all others In this they reſt, well ſatisfied to leave to others the leſs ſhowy and more troubleſome part, which belongs to practiſe To that alſo ſpeculation is frequently an enemy, in the ſame manner as familiarity is to reſpect.

Religion, beloved, is a majeſtic form always to be treated with reverence, with affection too, I confeſs, as being likewiſe an amiable form But this affection reſembles that which a wiſe ſubject would ſhow for his prince, into whoſe friendſhip he found himſelf graciouſly admitted. Such a man would never forget his own ſubordination ſo far, as to drop the reverence due to royalty. If his prince condeſcended to treat him with the openneſs of confidence and the careſs of joy, yet ſtill would he bear in mind, that he was only a ſubject, and every freedom on his ſide would be tempered with reſpectful modeſty.

Perhaps there is nothing ſo uncommon as to ſpeak of divine objects with the proper veneration. How have I been ſhocked to hear the ſanctimonious, yet audacious, prate of ſome pretenders to religion Thoſe that have the ſtrongeſt perceptions of t, will be moſt ſtruck by its ſublimity, and moſt conſcious how far they fall ſhort of ſo high a ſtandard By conſequence they will profeſs it with the greateſt modeſty, and mention it with the utmoſt caution Thoſe that are moſt intimately acquainted with God and themſelves, will be moſt deeply impreſſed with his grandeur and their own littleneſs, will moſt clearly perceive the difference between knowing his will
and

and performing it, will feel moft fenfibly how much easier it is to defcant on all his perfections than to copy one of them

In conclufion; let me befeech you, beyond all things, to converfe much with your Maker and yourfelves; to ftudy his character and your own, to trace his attributes wherever difplayed, to learn his counfels however revealed, to examine your confciences, chiefly by the written word, to canvas your paft actions, prefent purfuits, and prevailing views; to approve or condemn, as under his eye, to afcertain your intereft in the friendfhip of your Divine Sovereign, and cherifh an unalterable faith in his Spirit and Providence, as ever ready to affift your honeft though feeble efforts, together with a joyful affurance, that, if you are not wilfully wanting to yourfelves, you fhall at laft attain immortal excellence and glory, through JESUS CHRIST our LORD.

SERMON

S E R M O N XII

On Good Works.

1 TIM. ii. 8, 9, 10

I will—that women adorn themselves in modest apparel, with shamefacedness and sobriety; not with broidered hair, or gold, or pearls, or costly array, but (which becometh women professing godliness) with Good Works.

YOU have seen a venerable matron encircled with a race of lovely daughters, all different from one another, yet all marked with an air of mutual resemblance, and taking jointly after their honoured parent, to whom from time to time they direct their looks with dutiful attention; while she smiles on each by turns, superintends their behaviour, prescribes their several occupations, encourages them in every thing praise-worthy, and, with a proper regard to their respective talents and dispositions, trains them to growing excellence. In her, my fair ones, you beheld an emblem of Religion. Thus is that most dignified of all forms surrounded by the Virtues, her beautiful offspring, thus do they bear the lineaments of their common descent, and near affinity, and thus——But I leave you to trace the particulars of the similitude. The general truth on which it is founded, seems plainly intimated in our text, where Godliness is assumed as the leading principle of all that the apostle inculcates on women. As women professing Christianity he addresses them, and whatever a consistency with that profession demands, he would be understood to enjoin. He mentions particularly modest apparel, shamefacedness, sobriety, and Good Works. It now remains to enforce the last of these, together with those Kind affections which they presuppose, and to touch as we go along on

their

their Connexion with the Religious Principles which give them birth

But before we proceed, truth requires one mortifying obfervation. It is this, that amongft the many women profeffing godlinefs, the number of thofe that practife it, is comparatively fmall   In all profeffions the mere pretenders will ever be numerous   They will be more fo, in thofe that are at once reputable and difficult.   That of religion, as was formerly remarked, is approved of in your fex even by fuch as laugh at it in ours.   At the fame time it is certain, that when the habits of piety have not been very early acquired, and very happily directed, by means of a wife education, the rareft as well as the greateft of bleffings, the forming of them afterwards will always prove a tafk too arduous, and painful, for the generality of thofe who are bred to diffipation and pleafure

But then, on the other hand, where this divine principle is cultivated with care and judgment, it is no lefs certain, that we may expect from it the moft valuable fruits   And firft, I fay, that a young woman profeffing godlinefs with underftanding, and from choice, will never be wanting in the great article of Filial Duty. On this fubject, as on many others, the fubtilty of fpeculation has put cafes, which there is little probability of happening in life   But where cafuiftry is not neceffary, it is apt to be hurtful, by involving the mind in perplexity and diftrefs, if not warping the heart from that rectitude and fimplicity, which, next to the immediate illumination of heaven, are the fureft guides to a worthy conduct

Of filial duty in all its branches fhe will naturally acquit herfelf beft, who has the deepeft fenfe of religion   " Keep " thy father's commandments, and forfake not the law of " thy mother. Bind them continually upon thy heart,

" and

" and tie them about thy neck When thou goeft, it fhall
" lead thee, when thou fleepeft, it fhall keep thee, and
" when thou wakeft it fhall talk with thee Whofo reji-
" leth his father or his mother, his lamp fhall be put out
" in obfcure darknefs The eye that mocketh at his fa-
" tner, and defpifeth to obey his mother, the ravens of the
" valley fhall pick it out, and the young eagles fhall eat it "
Jefus was fubject unto his parents " Children obey your
" parents in the Lord, for this is right Honour thy fa-
" ther and mother (which is the firft commandment with
" promife) that it may be well with thee, and thou may-
" eft live long on the earth," All this a chriftian daughter
has read with attention, and reflects upon with awe It
correfponds, in fubftance, with the inftinct of nature,
which it contributes at once to corroborate and exalt She
who truly reverences her parent in heaven, would tremble at the thought of difhonouring his reprefentatives on
earth From their authority fhe has acquired the idea of
his, and this laft, including all that can be conceived of
great and good, is the commanding idea of her life. If
your parents be indeed pious, and you have profited by
their inftruction and example, how will your natural refpect of them be heightened by religious gratitude ! You
will think of them with fecret rapture, as the inftruments
of a happy and immortal exiftence, your devouteft prayers
for their prefervation and comfort will daily afcend to the
throne of God Thofe prayers will, at the fame inftant, cherifh the affections by which they are prompted,
and ftrengthen your refolutions never, for any confideration, to tranfgrefs the laws of filial piety. For how could
they bear to be the wilful authors of pain to thofe, for
whofe felicity they are led by every motive to prefent every day the moft fervent fupplications ?

But many of you have not the happinefs of fuch parents
as I have fuppofed I am heartily forry for it But the
want

want of principle in your parents will not diffolve the ties of
duty, however it may affect the fentiments of efteem, and
if you think rightly, it will only excite your endeavours,
by every winning refpectful way, to promote their reformation, for which you will at the fame time offer up, from
the depth of retirement, your fighs and vows to him who
has the hearts of all in his hand In truth, I am inclined
to believe, that if there be any one thing more likely than
another to draw down the grace of converfion on a parent,
it is fuch a conduct in a child Ah, my young friends,
what honour and joy would in this cafe be yours! What a
noble fuperiority to thofe unfeeling creatures of your fex,
who fhow no folicitude with regard to their parents, but
how to obtain from them fome new article of drefs, or
other gratifications, on which they have fixed their foolifh
fancies!

But fome of you complain, that your parents are cruel
and tyrannical. I fympathize with you yet more if your
complaint be juft. But what do you mean by Cruel and
Tyrannical? That they will not indulge your extravagant
vanity, or that they choofe to reftrain you from purfuits,
which they are apprehenfive would be hurtful? It is a wife
and kind feverity, if feverity it muft be termed. How much
are you indebted to them for preventing by a little temporary mortification, real and permanent infelicity! Not to
fay, that a fmall degree of delicacy and confideration would
teach you to fpare them in points, where your ftations
and their circumftances concur, it may be, to render your
requefts particularly improper

But I will fuppofe the worft, that they are really hard
hearted, and unnaturally rigid. It is a mighty trial. To
bear it well will require all the fortitude of faith. Here
then is an opportunity for difplaying your principles in
their utmoft power. You are called forth to the conflict,

Q

as into a field of battle, where even your fex may reap
immortal laurels She is a heroine indeed, whofe regard
for her parents no unkindnefs of theirs can conquer

But they would force you to facrifice your happinefs to
a man whom you cannot love There your fubmiffion
muft ftop No rules of duty can oblige you to involve yourfelves in mifery and temptation, by entering into engagements to love and to honour, where your hearts withold
their confent —Barbarous wretches, and bafe, to offer thus
to difpofe of your children, as you would of your cattle, to
to the higheft bidder , to attempt, againft every maxim of
Nature and Religion, to drag the reluctant victims to the
altar, and compel them there in the moft folemn manner
to profefs what the do not mean, and to vow what they
cannot perform!

I am willing however to believe, that fuch compulfion is
ufed but feldom The greateft danger is left you, my unexperienced friends, fhould be tempted to form the moft important of all connexions, without the approbation of your
parents What fhall we fay in fuch a cafe? Where the
refolution is once formed, he that fhould undertake, by any
methods of diffuafion, to prevent its being executed, might
as well propofe to check a torrent rufhing from the top of
a mountain But we would addrefs you while in your
fober fenfes, before your imagination is perverted and inflamed Affure yourfelves, my young hearers, the ftep in
queftion is very feldom taken but it is fincerely repented,
with this bitter addition, that fuch repentance can do no
good The paffion that guided and hurried the parties is
quickly abated There is nothing fo tranfient, as the enthufiafm of mere youthful lovers after marriage And now
that reflexion takes place, and, confequences begin to prefs ,
a thoufand improprieties, fears, and difquietudes, unthought
of before, rife up to view, and quite difenchant our romantic
                                        adventurers.

adventurers. It is indeed wonderful, what appearances of firmnefs and fatisfaction a woman in fuch a fituation will wear before the world, in order to juftify her choice But furely unhappinefs is not leffened by being devoured in fecret, and in public difguifed. Perpetual reftraint is perpetual wretchednefs —Allow me to repeat it. Under the the immediate impulfe of a violent attachment, I fhould hardly give you or myfelf the trouble to argue ' but while you are difengaged and calm, it may not be amifs to remind you, that a parent, generally fpeaking, is much more likely to judge with fondnefs for a daughter, than fhe is for herfelf, that Fancy alone is too faguine a counfellor to be a prudent one, that proteftations of eternal fidelity, of uninterrupted affection, made in the heat of blood, have no folid bafis, in a word, that the deliberate advice, which is dictated alike by length of days, knowledge of the world, and earneft folicitude for a child's welfare, ought to be relied upon, rather than the hafty conclufions of juvenile defire

After all, it is certain, that the wifeft parents may be miftaken about the man with whom they wifh a daughter to be connected But fhe that marries with the fanction of their countenance, will from that, and from their continued or even augmented kindnefs, derive in the cafe of difappointment a confolation which fhe could not enioy, had fhe brought it on herfelf by her own indifcretion and obftinacy.

One thing here muft not be forgotten, that the reflexion of having acted undutifully, in this or any other inftance of importance, to thofe who gave you birth, were alone fufficient to poifon the whole pleafure of life, that is, if you be not loft to every ingenuous impreffion, but efpecially fhould their death put it for ever out of your power to make atonement The horrors of guilt, that in fuch a circum-

Q 2

ſtance are apt to haunt and diſtract the mind, more particularly if the parents were uncommonly worthy, I have had
repeated opportunities of obſerving, but have no adequate
language to expreſs ; ſo profound is the conviction implanted by nature of the ſacredneſs of filial piety !————Need
I add, that this extends ſo far as to demand ſubmiſſion in
every caſe, where your duty to God or your peace of mind
does not interfere ?

But it is not ſubmiſſion alone that is demanded ; nor will
ſhe prove in any relation an aimable character, who does
not ſhow herſelf an affectionate daughter On the other
hand, when a young woman behaves to her parents in a
manner particularly tender and reſpectful, I mean from
principle as well as nature, there is nothing good or gentle that may not be expected from her, in whatever condition ſhe is placed Of this I am ſo thoroughly perſuaded,
that were I to adviſe any friend of mine as to his choice of a
wife, I know not whether my very firſt counſel would not
be, "Look out for one diſtinguiſhed by her attention
and ſweetneſs to her parents" The fund of worth and
affection indicated by ſuch a behaviour, joined to the habits
of duty and conſideration thereby contracted, being transferred to the married ſtate, will not fail to render her a mild
and obliging companion

Your ſituation in life, which keeps you more at home
than ſons, together with the turn of your education, and the
ſoftneſs of your frame, that fit you for a thouſand little
ſoothing offices, as well as domeſtic ſervices, which they
cannot properly perform, ſeems to point out to you a peculiar ſphere of filial excellence————And here I pleaſe myſelf with the thought, that ſome of your boſoms are at this
moment throbbing with tenderneſs towards a ſick or aged
parent, whom heaven, willing to furniſh a field for the exerciſe of all your gratitude and zeal, has at laſt thrown
upon

upon your care. I think I fee you, my charming friend, like fome guardian angel tending day and night the bed of an honoured father, who has loft your mother, and who is worn out with toil, and years, and pain. I fee you liftening in deepeft filence, to catch the leaft intimation of his wifhes. I fee you watching eagerly every look to learn his wants before he fpeaks them, now gently raifing his languid head, to fmooth the pillow, or minifter fome reviving cordial, and then wiping from his reverend face the cold fweats, that begin perhaps to announce the approach of his end. His groans anfwered by fighs ftealing from you, but fuddenly fuppreffed, for fear of adding to his anxiety on your account. To be the inftrument of imparting to him a minute's comfort, a minute's eafe, is rapture. Mean while the good old man's eyes are now turned to you with all the unutterable fondnefs of paternal love, melted by thofe marks of duty, anon they are lifted to heaven in thankfgiving for fuch a child, and fupplication for everlafting bleffings on your head —Great God! what muft a mind like yours experience in this conjuncture? Where is the daughter of Difobedience or Folly, that ever felt in the gayeft hour a fatisfaction, a tranfport to be compared with that, which confcious piety diffufes through your bleeding heart? Nor will thefe exalted fenfations be at all diminifhed, if (Providence having denied the fupplies which affluence gives) your virtue has prompted you by your labour or ingenuity, or, it may be, by parting with fome admired ornament worn in your better days, to procure for a parent in thofe circumftances neceffary fupport, or feafonable refrefhment.

Let me next fay fomewhat concerning Sifterly affection. "Behold how good and how pleafant it is for brethren," and fifters, "do dwell together in unity!" Precious ointment is not more grateful to the fmell, nor morning dew more refrefhing to the fight, than domeftic love is to the

foul Reprefent to yourfelves a numerous young family
free from care and animofity, full of reverence for their
Maker and their parents, ambitious to pleafe and to excel,
in a word, pious, dutiful, friendly, happy; where the
good humour and good fenfe of each contribute to the eafe
and entertainment of all; while thofe agreeable diverfities
of temper and underftanding that take place amongft them
ferve, like difcords in mufic, to carry on the intellectual
harmony Who would not wifh to be acquainted in fuch
a houfe, who would not confider it as the abode of felicity,
I hope, I paint no unufual fcene

Where the members are but few, felicity perhaps is not
fo often found, unlefs it be in the more fhady walks of
life, where love and innocence delight to frequent And
why is it not? When I fee two fifters, both of them pleafing and both efteemed, living together without jealoufy
or envy, yielding to one and other without affectation,
and generoufly contending who fhall do moft to advance
the confequence and happinefs of her friend, I am highly
delighted dare I add, the more highly, that fuch characters are not very common? And why are they not? The
love of a fifter for her brothers is much more ufual. Whence
does this too proceed? Examine your own hearts on thefe
feveral points Poffibly they can explain to you the difference, fo obfervable where there is a competition, and
where there is none, or where any tendencies towards it
are happily loft in the involutions of a larger number.

Martha of Bethany was on the whole a worthy woman
She certainly loved her Saviour with fincere devotion.
Her folicitude to entertain him in the beft manner fhe
could devife, was the refult of her refpect. But it was carried to an extreme, and her fifter's conduct fhould have
taught her wifdom Inftead of this, fhe grows peevifh,
and complains of that fifter She is admonifhed of her
fault,

fault, while Mary is commended for her better behaviour.
" Martha, Martha, thou art careful and troubled about
" many things · but one thing is needful ; and Mary hath
" chosen that good part which shall not be taken away
" from her " What pity that any tincture of ill humour
under whatever disguise, should have place in any breast
where Jesus is revered ! Surely there is nothing more beautiful in a christian woman, than good temper and kind
affection upon all occasions.

I was once acquainted with a lady, who seemed to be
held up by Providence, as an example of the joint power
of these and of divine principle She lost her father early.
Her mother's want of health made it necessary for her to
exert herself with double assiduity and attention, in a family by no means small, of which she was the eldest child
She was naturally active to a degree very uncommon in one
of her disposition, which was the softest and meekest that
can be conceived. She had imbibed from her infancy the
deepest sense of devotion, that I have ever known It was
a devotion of that kind, which meeting with a heart originally
upright produces uniform excellence. Such excellence was
hers When, in the course of a few years, her extraordinary
character recommended her to the choice of a man of singular worth, and good fortune, she did not, with the selfishness common on such occasions, forget her mother or
the family she had left behind her, but continued, with
the entire approbation and cordial concurrence of her hufband, to manifest her filial and sisterly regards in the most
effectual manner. She was none of those narrow-souled
women, who no sooner step into houses of their own,
than they seem to have all their affections and ideas abfor-
bed in their new condition ; relinquishing at once the best
companions of their youth, dropping the pen of friendly
correspondence, and shrinking up into a little wretched
circle of anxieties, that exclude every liberal sentiment,
and

and every enlarged connexion. When the mother of this
lady died, which happened not long after, she became a
mother to the helpless orphans, superintended their education, watched over their deportment, promoted their fet-
tlement in the world, and sympathized with them in all
their diftreffes. When they also spread out into families,
she acted like a parent to their children —To her own, of
whom she had many, bleffed Lord, what a parent! Was
it poffible for them not to love one another, with such a
pattern before them, and with such inftructions as she
gave them? For they too were deprived of their father,
while the greater part were very young Her inftructions
were pious and wife but it was her example, it was that
ineffable charm of humble worth and modeft dignity, of maternal complacence and mildnefs almoft unparalleled,
which render them irrefiftible, and diffufed among all about
her the spirit of amity, and the fmile of happinefs You
will not be furprifed if I fubjoin, that there were many
other families who fhared in her labours of love, and among
the reft a very large one, the Poor, whofe bleffings attended her through life, and whofe tears followed her to the
grave: for, when fhe died, they also had loft a mother
It is hard to fay upon the whole, whether fhe was moft
beloved, or venerated, by thofe who knew her But I
ufed to think that, wherever fhe appeared, her prefence
infpired fenfations fomewhat like thofe we fhould probably
feel, if we beheld a good angel.

And thus I come naturally to fpeak of Good Works in
a comprehenfive view, that is thofe which proceed from
kindnefs and compaffion in general When such difpofitions predominate, let it be obferved, in the firft place,
that they are ingenious to difcover, and diligent to improve
thofe ways and means of beneficence, which pafs unregarded by the giddy and unfeeling Many of you, my honoured audience, have it not in your power, through the
obfcurity

obfcurity of your fituation, and the ftraitnefs of your circumftances, to indulge the generous propenfions of your
nature. While thoufands of your fex are inflamed with
the emulation of beauty, or agitated by the conflict of rivalfhip, or miferable becaufe they cannot be gratified with
fuch an article of fhow, or admitted into fuch a party of
pleafure, you are fighing, becaufe not able more exten-
fively to fuccour indigence, or more effectually to comfort
forrow Your fighs, beloved, are heard in heaven, your
wifhes are regiftered there under the head of Virtues; the
willing mind is accepted now, and fhall be recompenfed
at the refurrection of the juft, your leaft good deed fhall
not be forgotten by him, who marked and applauded the
widow's mite "Whofoever fhall give to drink" unto a
follower of Jefus, "a cup of cold water only, in the name
"of a difciple, verily I fay unto you, he fhall in no wife
"lofe his reward" You fhall be eftimated by the largenefs
of your hearts, not by the fize of your fortunes. "The
"liberal foul, that devifeth liberal things," that executes
what it can, and ftops only where it muft, or rather goes
on panting and praying for that happinefs to the human
race, which it cannot have the joy of imparting,—how
honourable in the fight of God!

Let me remind you farther of what ought alfo to folace
you amidft all your kind cares. Human happinefs is made
up of many little ingredients, with a few principal ones;
and next to religion, thofe in reality contribute to it moft
largely, who give the greateft confolation by their fympathy, and the greateft pleafure by their friendfhip Friendfhip and fympathy, when thoroughly awake, are conftantly employed in numberlefs pleafing fervices, and amiable
attentions, to which language cannot appropriate names,
but which the heart of the perfon obliged feels, and which
rebounds with redoubled delight on the heart of the perfon
obliging. I go farther, and fay, that the very idea of
                                                  your

your being difpofed to oblige is obligation ; becaufe it is in itfelf agreeable, and we are indebted to every one that fupplies us with an agreeable idea.

Who has not likewife remarked, that in doing benevolent things there is, both as to the time and the manner, a propriety which gives ineftimable value even to the leaft ? The manner, in particular, is of marvellous effect A charitable action gracefully done is twice done. To fome people one would be willing to owe almoft every thing, fo handfomely do they confer a kindnefs , while from others a favour, for the oppofite reafon, is a load But who fo capable of delighting by the manner, yet more than by the deed itfelf, as a lovely young woman, whofe words, and fmiles, and foftnefs, are, to the laft of thefe, what a beautiful fymphony and judicious accompanyment in mufic are to a well managed voice ?

But, in truth, the advantages which your fex and age afford you in this divine employment of doing good, are not to be expreffed Would to God your zeal were but in proportion to it !—Forgive me, Proteftants, if on this occafion I remark with concern, how far many of you are outdone by multitudes in the Church of Rome, efpecially amongft her female votaries Their frequent vifits to the abodes of misfortune and pain, of poverty and ficknefs, their gentle miniftrations to the fufferers, their ftooping fo meekly to the meaneft offices of compaffion, offices of which the moft diftant thought would fhock the falfe refinement of a gay lady, have to me, I muft own, notwithftanding all the errors of their faith, ftill placed them in a point of light highly refpectable and engaging Who can help me to a reafon, why a practice fo Chrift-like is not adopted in this country, where the gofpel is profeffed with fo much purity ? Are we afraid of being thought to embrace the doctrine of Merit by good words, entertained in that church? It cannot be, amongst those who have learnt the truth as it is in Jesus None surely was ever more self-denied on this head than St Paul yet St Paul was a flame of charity In his doctrine, and in his conduct grace and virtue, faith and good works, went hand in hand, inseparable and triumphant.

Ah, ye fair ones of Britain, who doat on the parade of public affemblies, and fail along in the full blown pride of fashionable attire, of which the least appendage or circumstance must not be discomposed; thoughtless of human woe; insensible to modest worth at that moment pining in many a solitary residence of want—ye gaudy flutterers, " with " hard hearts under soft raiment ," how much more brilliant and beautiful would you appear in the eye of saints and angels, were ye now and then to exchange those scenes of selfish splendour for the gloomy dwellings of wretchedness, in order to light them up by your pity and beneficence? I blush for many of my country women, possessed of fortune, who have never yet learnt its noblest and happiest use; in whose ears the circulated whisper of a well-dressed crow'd admiring their appearance, is a more grateful sound than the praise of widows and orphans sharing their bounty, who prefer the empty breath of adulation to the blessings of them that were ready to perish.

God be thanked, there are exceptions. Among the rest I recollect, with peculiar pleasure, one lady of rank, whose name is never mentioned by those who knew her without calling up the image of Charity, who, having no family of her own, has adopted the indigent and deserving, whose whole life, not a short one, has been devoted to munificence, who, in a word, feems to regard her wealth merely as a fund deposited in her hands by the Almighty, to be laid out with the strictest faithfulness for the god-like purpose of making thousands happy. Exalted creature! how

how honourable, independant of thy birth; how bleſſed,
to underſtand ſo well the deſtination of riches! A rare,
and as it ſhould ſeem from this circumſtance, a difficult
ſcience! Juſtly might the poet exclaim,

> ' The rich muſt labour to poſſeſs their own,
> " To feel their great abundance, and requeſt
> " Their humble friends to help them to be bleſt;
> " To fee their treaſure, hear their glory told,
> ' And aid the wretched impotence of gold."

He adds indeed,

> " But ſome, great ſouls! and touch'd with warmth divine,
> " Give gold a price, and teach its beams to ſhine.
> " All hoarded treaſures they repute a load,
> " Nor think their wealth their own, till well beſtow'd "

Amongſt the properties of the Virtuous Woman, in that
celebrated paſſage formerly ſurveyed, it is ſaid, " She
" ſtretcheth forth her hand to the poor, and reacheth her
' hand to the needy." On which it has been remarked,
that after her induſtry for the acquiring of wealth is deſcri-
bed, her liberality is next mentioned, as being the principle uſe ſhe made of it, and precedes her providing ſcarlet
for her houſhold, or fine linen and purple for herſelf
What ſhall we call thoſe women, who either never think
of the poor at all, or never till they have firſt ſacrificed to
ſuperfluity and pride

Where are thoſe female penitents of this land, that, like
her of Judea, convert the inſtruments of their former folly
and extravagance into matter of humiliation and piety,
that conſecrate, ſo to ſpeak, the ſpoils of Vice, by offering
them at the feet of their Saviour, while they proſtrate
themſelves there in deep contrition?——The poor you
have always with you, and by ſhewing mercy to them,
you may at once ſhow your reſpect for him, and help to
enſure mercy for yourſelves

It

It is worthy your obfervation, that in the lift of female names recorded in fcripture with renown, that of Tabitha ftands marked with a particular note of approbation, as " a difciple who was full of Good Works, and alms which " fhe did " What a glorious memorial! And what additional honour does it receive from the account immediately following! This excellent woman dies. An apoftle is in the neighbourhood He is fent for in hafte, he arrives, he is conducted to the chamber of the deceafed Her female friends ftand by him " weeping and fhewing him " the coats and garments which fhe had made" for the poor How natural a circumftance, and how eloquent! He felt it, " kneeled down and prayed, and turning him to the body," faid with a voice of power, " Tabitha, arife," working a miracle to reftore a life fo ufeful From this amiable perfon's being denominated in the hiftory a Difciple, I would only remark, that in thofe days, a Chriftian was known and characterized by real excellence whereas every thing now is a Chriftian, not excepting her who never, but when forced, went into the houfe of mourning, never knew the joy of giving purely for the love of God, without expecting any thing again ; let me add, never denied herfelf one trapping of Vanity to clothe the naked, nor one indulgence of Luxury to feed the hungry ——— Alas! my poor friend, what wilt thou fay for thyfelf at the tribunal of Jefus? I leave with thee that queftion. anfwer it to thy confcience, as in the prefence of thy judge You have read the procefs which he will obferve, nor can you have forgot it

On thefe points it were eafy to enlarge at great length and with exact method I am willing however to hope that, by the grace of God, a few hints thus thrown out with plainnefs and affection, may fuffice to every mind that is open to the fentiments of humanity, but efpecially to every heart that is impreffed with the principles of religion.

gion. It is these principles, my honoured hearers, that serve beyond every thing else to enlarge and inspire those sentiments. It is the love of God, the faith of Jesus, and the hope of immortality, that chiefly expand affection, and animate zeal The divine character is the sovereign standard of benevolence, the christian institution its brightest display, and a happy futurity its highest reward. Can you worship the Universal Father, and not feel for his family ? Can you believe in the Common Saviour, and not live to those for whom he died? Can you contemplate yonder world of friendship, and not anticipate its joys, and not cherish an ambition that your works of charity may praise you in the gates of heaven ?

SERMON

SERMON XIII.

ON FEMALE MEEKNESS

1 PET III 3, 4

Whose adorning, let it not be that outward adorning of plaiting the hair, and of wearing of gold, or of putting on of apparel but let it be the hidden man of the heart, in that which is not corruptible, even the ornament of a Meek and Quiet Spirit, which is in the fight of God of great price.

THE apostle of the Circumcision, like him of the Gentiles, seems to have been no stranger to female nature, or to what becomes it   Both were sufficiently aware, that ornament was a favourite object with women, and both were too well acquainted with the arts of persuasion, to think of combating the general idea.   It was their business to make the best use of such a handle.   Accordingly, their converts of that sex might continue to study embellishment as much as ever; only those inspired teachers wished them to direct it right, by turning their chief care to that which was of greatest value and longest duration, namely, " the hidden man of the heart "   The doctrine of St Paul on this point we have examined very fully.   That of St Peter, now read, we propose for the ground-work of our concluding discourse, with a view to complete the plan which we have prosecuted thus far   We have reserved it for this place, as believing, that Meekness, cultivated on Christian principles, is the proper consummation, and highest finishing, of female excellence   The subject being so important, may we not hope to be still honoured with your attention ?

I begin with observing, that the virtue in question has

its

its Foundation in the Softer Compofition of the fex. That
there is a fex in minds was hinted before This original
diftinction has never, I think, been better underftood than
by our great epic poet As in his admired work of Paradife
Loft he has with equal judgment and delicacy marked,
throughout, the feperate characters of the Firft Pair, fo,
in two l nes, he has happily expreffed the principal object
of their refpective deftinations,

> " For contemplation He, and valour form'd;
> " For fo nefs She, and fweet attractive grace "

The virtue of meeknefs, it is true, our religion requires
of all without exception. Mofes is celebrated for it in an
eminent degree, and our Saviour characterizes himfelf by
the epithets Meek and Lowly The difpofition, in general, may be confidered as Charity's firft-born, appearing
in all the mildeft attitudes of forbearance, gentlenefs, and
peace But ftill in men, it may be often found connected,
with the greateft boldnefs, and moft undaunted magnanimity Much for the honour of true courage, it has been
obferved, that the braveft minds are commonly the moft
humane, generous, and forgiving Thefe feveral qualities
are beautifully blended in many parts of the hiftory of that
Man of God juft now mentioned Nor can you have forgotten the calm heroifm of our divine Deliverer, together
with that dignity of goodnefs, which dwelt about him, in
circumftances of the deepeft humiliation and forrow.

As for you, my fair pupils, we no doubt wifh you to
poffefs fuch fortitude as implies refolution, wherever your
virtue, duty, or reputation is concerned But along with
that we expect to find, on other fubjects, a timidity peculiar to your fex, and alfo a degree of complacence, yield-
ingnefs, and fweetnefs, beyond what we look for in men
Nor r owe, fo far as I know, ever rank amongft feminine qualities Valour, ftrictly fo called A woman head-
                                                ing

ing an army, rufhing into the thickeft of the foe, fpreading flaughter and death around her, or returning from the
field of battle covered with duft and blood, would furely to
a civilized nature fuggeft fhocking ideas.

Your beft emblems, beloved, is the fmiling form of
Peace, robed in white, and bearing a branch of olive.
Like the apoftles and firft chriftians, your higheft glory is
to conquer by benignity, and triumph by patience.   Roughnefs, and even ferocioufnefs, in a man, we often overlook,
and are fometimes diverted with   In a woman, we are always hurt by them.   A loud voice, a bold gefture, a daring countenance, every mark of bravery, fhall pleafe in
the former, when his courage is particularly called forth:
but in a female we wifh nothing to reign but love and tendernefs, and where they do reign, they will produce very different effects

No, my friends, you were not made for fcenes of danger and oppofition   I repeat it again   fearfulnefs to a certain degree becomes you, not that cowardice, which many of you fhow, and fome of you affect, on every trifling
occafion, and frequently without any occafion at all   Such
behaviour is in you childifh, and to us uninterefting, if not
an object of contempt.   But a worthy woman, fhrinking
from manifeft hazard, or threatened violence, we are always
forward and proud to protect ; while, on the other hand, an
intrepid female feems to renounce our aid, and in fome
refpect to invade our province.   We turn away and leave
her to herfelf.

Let it be likewife obferved, that in your fex manly exercifes are never graceful ; that in them a tone and figure,
as well as an air and deportment, of the mafculine kind,
are always forbidding ; and that men of fenfibility defire
in every woman foft features, and a flowing voice, a form

R   not

not robuft, and a demeanour delicate and gentle Thefe
are confidered as alike requifite and natural , I mean, where
there is any tafte for elegance   I am even inclined to believe that, fuppofing other circumftances equal, the coar-
feft clown would be better pleafed with them than with
their oppofites

Yet farther, the aptitude obfervable, in all the better
kind of women, to commiferate and comfort, to melt into tears at the fight or hearing of diftrefs, to take the care
of children, to play and prattle with thofe pretty innocents,
to mingle in all the mild fympathies and tender charities of
life the wonderful dexterity with which they difarm fierce-
nefs, and appeafe wrath; the powerful eloquence they
difplay in affuaging the cares, and calming the forrows of
thofe men with whom they are connected; their ftrong
propenfity to an union of hearts, and their unutterable
fondnefs where it takes place ,——thefe lovely peculiarities
in their temperament, thefe finer turnings of their minds,
feem additional proofs, that foftnefs is your proper attri-
bute Womanifh Softnefs, as it is ftyled, has never been
imputed to any man by way of reproach, without a tacit
acknowledgment of this truth in your favour. In the
male compofition, it is certainly a blemifh wherever found;
in the female, a beauty.

From thefe remarks, I think it appears that the bafis of
the virtue we now recommend is laid in the original make,
or fpecific character of the fex. The fuperftructure which
Chriftianity raifes upon it, or, in other words, the improvements it receives from religious principle, fhall be our
next confideration

The gofpel is, in truth, the religion of human nature;
building charity and all virtue on whatever is kind, ingenuous, or praife-worthy in that ; correcting its diforders,
                                                    mitigating

mitigating its diftreffes, fupporting its weaknefles, and from each educing good, by turning them into matter of humility and circumfpection, of faith and refignation, of docility and meeknefs. Thefe are all connected together, but the firft and laft are nearly allied   They are twin-fifters. Humility is ever difpofed to ferve, and fhe affords the other fingular affiftance

They that have a juft fenfe of their own infirmities and failings, will be naturally of an unpretending, a forbearing, and a forgiving temper   The reverfe of this is the genuine offspring of Pride   A proud character was never a meek one, whereas there is no act of kindnefs, no inftance of condefcenfion, which the felf-diffident are not ready to perform   They enter thoroughly into the fpirit of thofe precepts that require Chriftians to " be courteous, to con-" defcend to men of low eftate, and in honour to prefer " one another.

Picture in your own minds a young lady, lively, agreeable, careffed, as yet unacquainted with her Maker, with herfelf and with the claims which fociety has on every reafonable being that is fent into life   The magic power of Fancy, fet to work by vanity, ambition and hope, creates a kind of world within, to which fhe fondly refers that without as always fubordinate, and chiefly fubfervient   In this little empire " fhe fits as a queen, and faith in her heart " I fhall fee no forrow," and dreams of conqueft and triumph, of fplendid houfes and fhining equipages, of paffionate lovers and difappointed rivals, with namelefs enchanting vifions more, which may never be realized, but which fhe regards as the moft certain realities, fo certain, that he who fhould attempt to undeceive her would run the rifk of being hated as her greateft enemy. This world of phantoms, it is true, is always fluctuating   the gay and the gloomy fucceed by turns   But in each our conceited fair one is ftill

the

the principal figure, and the value of every thing is meaſured, according as it contributes to her importance and
elevation   Hence innumerable illuſions, and ungoverned
paſſions , the ſwelling of ſelf-ſufficiency, and the ſtatelineſs
of diſdain , violent reſentment, or ſullen diſcontent, if not
treated with the reſpect ſhe ſuppoſes to be her due , in fine,
a total inattention to the expectations of others, and abſo-
lute inſenſibility to whatever is beautiful in an unaſſuming,
or noble in a diſintereſted behaviour   Now what is it that
can diſpel this viſionary ſcene, and diſabuſe the much deluded ſorcereſs ? Nothing ſo effectual as Chriſtianity.

If it ſhould pleaſe the Almighty to impreſs upon her
heart its ſacred doctrines, they will ſhow her, in the moſt
affecting lights, her own littleneſs, the degeneracy and miſery of corrupted nature, the emptineſs of temporal and
the reality of eternal things, the duty ſhe owes to her Maker, her Redeemer, and her fellow-creatures ; with the
neceſſity of ſecuring the divine favour by a life of faith, contrition, and charity   By ſuch views, the fantaſtic ſtructures
of Pride will be preſently brought down , on their ruins
the plain and modeſt, but pleaſing and graceful fabric of
Meekneſs, will be eaſily raiſed.   To ſpeak without a metaphor   She will be delivered from the chief cauſes of ill humour ſuch, for inſtance, as the obſtinacy of ſelf-will, the
exorbitance of ſelf-love, a paſſion for thoſe gratifications
that at once diſappoint and enervate, and, finally, the
expectation of too much homage, and too many compli-
ances   The ſalvation of her ſoul, and the ſpirit of her
Saviour, will become her principal objects: every virtue
connected with theſe, will be her habitual ſtudy ; and
among the reſt " peace, long ſuffering, gentleneſs, good-
' neſs, meekneſs "   With ſuch a temper ſhe will not be
apt to think herſelf affronted , that revengeful diſpoſition,
of which your ſex have been accuſed even to a proverb,
will be her abhorrence, ſhe will not dare, for a moment,
                                                        to

to with-hold from others that forgiveness, which she is conscious of wanting from the great God to herself, and as for her behaviour in general to those about her, it will breathe that winning mildness, which seems to me the most distinguishing lineament in the image of Jesus.

He, my sisters, was the perfect model of kindness and courtesy. The Friend of Man was his characteristic. He conversed with those whom the world despised, he stood still to hear the cries, and relieve the miseries of the wretched, he even stooped (astonishing goodness!) to wash the feet of his own disciples, "the son of man came not to be ministred unto, but to minister" The greatness of humility, and the beauty of compassion, he exemplified on all occasions. He showed by his own practice, that there is nothing more becoming than the tear of generous sorrow, nothing so soothing as the language of a benovolent heart Jesus weeping over the grave of Lazarus, consoling his mournful sisters, and instructing the solemn circle in the ideas of immortality, with the means of attaining it, is surely an object by infinite degrees more interesting and glorious than all the conquerors of the earth crowned with laurels, and riding on the car of triumph, with numberless captives in their train

His institution is of a piece with his character It includes the grand principles of universal humanity. Every wall of partition between the nations it throws down, abolishing the narrow distinction of Jews and Gentiles, and exploding the illiberal opposition of Greeks to Barbarians The spirit of conquest for the sake of power it discourages, while it proclaims, enforces, and inspires " peace on earth, and good will towards men," whom it teaches to consider and love as brethren, forming one great family under one common parent, held together by charity as the bond of perfection, and of such account with the supreme that he gave his only begotten son to save them.

Need

Need I labour to prove how fweetly fuch difcoveries as thefe coincide with the difpofitions to modefty, fympathy, generofity, the defire of pleafing, the dread of violence, the horror at barbarity, the promptnefs to cherifh tender fentiments, and form endearing connexions, which are all fo natural to the worthieft part of your fex?

The virtues of a Roman Matron, in the better times of that republic, appear on fome accounts to have been greatly refpectable   They were fuch as might be looked for from her education amongft a people where ideas of prowefs, patriotifm, and glory ran high, where, in effect, thefe things were regarded as the fummit of human excel- lence and felicity   But not to infift on the national pride and ungenerous prepoffeffions, on which thofe ideas were founded, it is manifeft to me, that whatever force or grandeur the female mind might in other views derive from them, fuch advantage was far over-balanced by the lofs or the diminution of that gentlenefs and foftnefs which ever were, and ever will be, the fovereign charm of the female character   Nor do I wifh the women of Great Britain, who profefs a fyftem fo much more juft, amiable, and happy, to adopt for the regulation of their temper any ftandard different from that in my text

Some of the moft agreeable and important Confequences of a meek and quiet fpirit in your fex, let us now proceed to furvey. Where nature has beftowed any kind of perfonal beauty, be it ever fo inconfiderable, how early is it known, and at what pains are the generality of the too confcious poffeffors to difplay it, on all occafions, to the utmoft ad- vantage! But Nature has endowed the greater part of the fex with a conftitutional Softnefs, which, under right di- rection, would render them unfpeakably more pleafing than any poffible attraction that is purely external   Yet how few of you feem acquainted with its proper ufe, fo as to turn it to any valuable account! What efteem might you not procure, and what happinefs communicate, if inftead of employing this foftnefs, merely to fofter paffion in yourfelves or others, you made it fubfervient to all the amiable purpofes of a mild and obliging behaviour! How prepofterous to think of any allurement, rather than that which fhould chiefly adorn you as Women!

The gift I fpeak of is imparted in different degrees, and with various mixtures · nor will any culture prevent a diverfity from appearing in individuals, with regard to this as well as other features of the female mind neither indeed ought it. Such diverfity is not only beautiful in itfelf, but agreeably adapted to the various and different taftes of men But ftill fome portion of the quality under confideration is abfolutely effential to feminine excellence Like every other one, no doubt, it requires the guard of Virtue and the guidance of Difcretion. The truth is, that any good difpofition you can name, how laudable or how eminent foever, if you could fuppofe it to be found alone, would conftitute a character extremely imperfect, and produce effects fufficiently hurtful. Where an eafinefs of temper is particularly prevalent, and the heart uncommonly fufceptible of warm emotions in the way of love and friendfhip, there, without queftion, a peculiar ftrain of prudence and fortitude is required, to prevent a young perfon's being betrayed into great inconveniencies, and dangerous tendernefles But while I confider Meeknefs as the crowning grace of a woman, it will be naturally underftood, that fome fhare of the virtues and accomplifhments before recommended is prefuppofed

A cultivated mind and delicate fpirit, together with ftrict principles of conduct, will teach you to make the neceffary diftinctions amongft thofe you converfe with, to join caution with freedom, and, while with a graceful eafe

you give to others what their characters claim, with a modeft firmnefs to fupport your own   There are few things
perhaps, more contemptible than an undiftinguifhing female, who can fmile alike upon all, who feems prepared
for every addrefs, who looks as if the freeft would not be
unwelcome, who fcatters herfelf amongft promifcuous objects, who, if I may be indulged the expreffion, proftitutes
to every vagrant eye, and every new comer, any mental
charms fhe may poffefs, inftead of preferving them for the
intimacies of virtuous love, or of facred friendfhip   You
will readily conceive, that the deportment I would enforce
is fomething widely different.

In effect, were religious and moral confiderations fet afide
fuch women would not be very pleafing on the footing
of female foftnefs alone   Coquettes have commonly but
little fenfibility   Their natural graces, if any they had,
are loft in levity and affectation. While they court the regards of all, they have none to beftow upon any. Let
what was faid long ago be here remembered, that a forward
appearance, and light demeanour, immediately difguft a
man of the leaft delicacy; who if he be weak enough to
love the courtfhip, has commonly however fo much perception as not to approve of her who offers it. But good nature, under the government of good fenfe and real worth
will engage our efteem without flattering our folly, and
reach that juft ftandard of the female character, which
confift in a fine compofition, of gentlenefs and dignity, of
fweet complacence and virtuous referve, the happy medium
fo hard to hit between Prudery and its oppofite extreme

As the former of thefe is moft directly repugnant to that
lovely quality which we are now confidering, I will proceed to offer a few remarks upon it, willing to rectify the
notions were it but of one of your fex, on a fubject which

in

in the prefent age, may be reckoned, by fevere judges, leaft of all neceffary in difcourfing to young women.

That a prudifh behaviour is never fincere, I will not take upon me to affirm   It may arife fometimes from an original frigidity, or ftrange infenfibility of make   I fpeak not of the diflikes that women conceive to particular men, while from others they are by no means unfufceptible of kind impreffions.   Neither do I fpeak of thofe females whofe firft addrefs is frequently forbidding, occafioned by a peculiar refervednefs of manner rather than temper, not at all incompatible with good affection, fince it evidently wears off in a little time, and that exceffive bafhfulnefs gives place on proper encouragement, to a carriage equally courteous and modeft   But where a woman bears amongft candid fpirits the character of a prude, there I muft confefs myfelf tempted to doubt both her honefty and her underftanding.

This we are fure of, that it is very common for people to affect moft the appearance of thofe virtues which they leaft poffefs   What they want in reality they would fain fupply in fhow, afraid of fufpicion, where they are confcious of guilt, whereas thofe that are found at heart, are feldom apprehenfive of being fufpected.   " A good man " fhall be fatisfied from himfelf," and generally leaves others to collect his principles from his practice   An honeft confidence in the rectitude of his own intentions begets a fimplicity of manners, that defpifes oftentation in all cafes, and fupercedes profeffion in moft.   I do not mean Religious Profeffion, which a good man will never think unneceffary, though he will always make it with modefty.   In fhort, true virtue, whether male or female, is like the fun, beft feen in its own light.

Of a defect of fenfe I look on prudery as an indifputable proof

proof It never succeeds in its attempts to impose A woman of this character is considered by our sex as a hypocrite, by yours as a hypocrite and a spy at the same time. Both are incited to a keener inspection into her conduct,

On the least failure, both are provoked to sharper reproach, and should the ungracious dissembler at last drop her disguise altogether, the triumph over her is universal, nor does the world forget a miscarriage which was preceded by pretensions to superior strictness In any case she is a disagreeable creature, whom none can love, and whom most will shun How just the words of an elegant writer on this subject!

"Virtue is amiable, mild, serene!
"Without all beauty, and all peace within:
"The honour of a Prude is rage and storm,
"'Tis ugliness in its most frightful form,

Should such a woman live to grow old in the single state she will be regarded with a mixture of hatred and contempt. When I say this, every one will recollect the imputation which has been so frequently brought against Unmarried females at that age It is an unpleasant idea? The inference is plain Let it be your care to lay in now such a store of good humour and christian meekness, as mingling with other agreeable acquisitions, may prevent the advance of life from spoiling your chearfulness, or robbing you of that benignity which communicates a grace to every condition, and of that consequence which youth and beauty alone cannot preserve. Establish it betimes as a certain maxim, that to be married is neither the one, nor the chief thing needful Are all in that state happy? Or must she be necessarily unhappy, who is not in that state? May not a single woman be wife and virtuous? and if wise and virtuous, will she not be contented? and if contented, is she not happy in the best sense, as much so as

can

can be expected in the mixed and variable lot of mortals?
Is there any thing wrong in this reasoning? If it be right
now, will it not be right ten, fifteen, twenty years hence?
And in the mean while do you not fee women in the situation suppofed, who, from the goodnefs of their temper,
breeding, and underftanding, are objects of tender regard;
a regard fo much the more valuable, that it is entertained
by the worthieft of their acquaintance, that it is no longer
a tribute levied by the power of beauty, or aided by the
influence of cuftom, but the pure reward of genuine merit,
a merit tried by time, and matured by reflection?

But do you imagine, that thofe only are difregarded and
avoided who are peevifh, fretful, or fufpicious from age?
Depend upon it, that fuch difpofitions are always difgufting; were fhe that indulges them blooming as the fpring,
or beautiful as the day. No heart was ever won by difdain,
no lover was ever kept by coldnefs A man, whom the
extravagance of his paffion has weakened, may fubmit
for a while to the petulent airs, and even infolent treatment
of a female that is handfome and young Nay, fuch is
the debility fometimes produced by this paffion in men of
little fpirit or low underftanding, that bad ufage, blended
with fits of kindnefs, fhall actually make them doat the more
But what fhall we fay of that woman, who finding a man
in her power fports with his heart, and to fhow her dominion plays the tyrant? Alas! fhe knows not that true
greatnefs confifts in generofity, that a graceful compliance
is inexpreffibly pleafing, and that a man of worth may be
for ever obliged by a noble franknefs She forgets too how
foon an immoderate fondnefs is cured by connubial familiarity, and what referve revenge may be taken after marriage by him whom fhe treated ill before it, were he difpofed to retaliate

But you want to maintain your dignity, and why not?
Would

Would you co it in the most effectual manner? Worth
and understanding are the proper means. Haughtiness is
always little, violence impotent, and peevishness the infirmity of a child. Worth and understanding confer a consequence that is seldom in danger of being despised. She
who shows a just sense of what belongs to her as a Woman,
and as a Christian, will engage respect without seeking to
command it. From her a word, a look expressive of virtuous disdain or pious indignation, will dash the boldest offender, if not uncommonly obdurate indeed. Nor can she
probably be often obliged to bear the company of a wretch,
who is proof against the lightning of excellence provoked.
Be assured, on the other side, that good nature well placed
will never lessen your value.

Look up my fair ones, to the First Lady of this Land,
and learn affability: learn to know, that however grandeur
may secure external reverence, it is goodness only that inspires heartfelt esteem, that Royalty itself derives lustre
from meekness, and that the highest prerogative of rank is
the power of imparting felicity more largely. Happy
Prince! thus to have found a companion, by whose chearful temper and gentle manners the cares of government are
softened, and that satisfaction is enjoyed at home, which
the splendour of a crown cannot confer. Illustrious pair!
live long blessed in each other and in your children, bright
examples of superior sanctity, parental affection, and domestic joy.—The personage I speak of seems so thoroughly
good, so naturally obliging, that I cannot doubt but she
would have proved such in any station. But certain it is,
that from those who are placed in the higher walks of life, a
little condescension, a little favour, gives great delight. Is
it not wonderful that women of birth and fortune should
not please more generally, when they might please at so
cheap a rate?

But

But not to dwell on thefe accidental diftinctions , what man is not charmed with an amiable courteoufnefs in any young woman, efpecially if otherwife attractive? Even common civility is grateful   But would you be refiftlefs? Acquire a habit of fixed attention   It is a fort of filent flattery truly exquifite, and withal perfectly innocent   To the moft attentive perfon in company you may obferve the converfation almoft always directed, while by interruption, liftlefsnefs, or a vacant look in thofe that are prefent, every creature that offers to fpeak is fure to be mortified   As a fmall degree of knowledge entertains in a woman, fo from a woman, though for a different reafon, a fmall expreffion of kindnefs delights, particularly if fhe have beauty.   But, in truth, without uttering a word, fhe has it in her power by this fingle mark of good breeding to captivate more than I can tell.   In fhort, liftening to the perfon who fpeaks, with a recollected, mild, and fteady afpect, which nothing frivolous can divert, is perhaps the moft valuable fecret in the wnole fcience of genuine politenefs   From an agreeable young woman to an intelligent man it is incredibly foothing.

If to your natural foftnefs we join that chriftian meeknefs, which I now preach, both together will not fail, with the affiftance of proper reflection and friendly advice, to accomplifh you in the beft and trueft kind of breeding   You will not be in danger of putting yourfelves forward in company, of contradicting bluntly, of afferting pofitively, of debating obftinately, of affecting a fuperiority to any prefent, of engroffing the difcourfe, of liftening to yourfelves with apparent fatisfaction, of neglecting what is advanced by others, or of interrupting them without neceffity

When thefe are not the effects of mere youthful folly, and even when they are difpleafing, it is plain, they proceed chiefly from pride and vanity.   But we faid before
that

that meekness is nearly allied to humility, and mightily
assisted by it If you be truly humble, you will manifest
a noble forgetfulness of yourselves, with a becoming respect
for others, a diffidence of your own sentiments, with a deference to theirs in doubtful points, or in such as they are
entitled to know better ; a readiness to learn of every one,
with a disposition to give each an opportunity of appearing
to advantage, and thus to make all happy in their turn.
Where the prevailing modes happen to be innocent, you
will not affect to display the refinement of your taste, or
the strictness of your principles, by a scrupulous singulari-
ty, or a saucy contempt of the opinions and manners of
others Nor will those contests and differences about pre-
cedency, form, and fashion, which inflame so many of
your sex, interest minds that have learnt the dignity of
yielding, and that despise the littleness of pride In a
a word, the most important branches of christian breeding
you will practise with ease and pleasure, from an internal
principle. A meek deportment is the natural and spontane-
ous growth of a lowly mind Politeness in you will be the
offspring of the heart. How much preferable to that species, but hollow complaisance, studied by the fashionable
and the false, which consist in an artful disguising of their
own passions, and a flattering application to those of others,
in a supple framing of the face to all occasions, in professing the greatest respect without feeling the least, and in
having very often the worst designs under the smile of familiarity, and the shew of friendship!

I used the phrase Christian Breeding, that kind of courtesy, which I point out, being expressly enjoined by one of
the writers of the New Testament Perhaps you think of
St Paul, that accomplished apostle, who himself became
all things to all men, that he might gain some. Such a
precept might have been easily suggested by his early education in a seat of learning, and would have come very naturally

turally from the hand that drew fo divine a picture of charity, the parent of Meeknefs But the fact is, that it fell
from the pen of an illiterate man, bred to the rougheft of
all employments It was St Peter, the infpired fiherman,
man, that faid, " Be courteous "———to intimate that the
religion which he had learned from the meek and lowly Jefus, was able to foften the keeneft, and fubdue the hotteft
temper, and even give gentlenefs to one trained amongft
winds and waves.

What ftrangers to the fpirit of the gofpel are thofe women
who have never controuled their own humours, whofe
looks are contempt, and whofe words are arrogance ; whofe
general demeanour, unlefs when they are propitiated by
adulation, or foothed by fubmiffion, is big with infolence
and fcorn ! How fhall we exprefs our horror at thofe female furies that, loft to decency and every mild feeling of
their fex, can abandon themfelves to " all bitternefs, and
" wrath, and anger, and clamour, and evil fpeaking, and
" all malice !" " It is better," fays Solomon, " to dwell in
" a corner of the houfe top, than with a brawling woman
" in a wide houfe ," he might have added, or in a magnificent palace. In fo doing, he would have probably fpoken from experience , fince it may be prefumed that fome
of thofe eaftern ladies, who had by their beauty enflaved
the unhapyy monarch, were willing now and then by their
tongues to convince him of their prerogative. The faying
of the Son of Sirach, on the fame fubject, is yet ftronger,
as well as more ironical   " A loud crying woman," fays
he, " and a fcold, fhall be fought out to drive away the
" enemy " That fpirited writer fatirizes the female vices
in general, with great freedom , but there is fcarce any of
them, which he more frequently or more feverely expofes,
than this of unquietnefs and ill-temper

When a woman of fuch difpofitions enters into the nuptial

tial ftate, what wretchednefs can equal him to whofe lot
fhe falls? To be tied for life to a being, whom neither
reafon can convince, nor patience win, nor any thing
conquer but main force a domeftic plague, a bofom fiend,
from whom only her death or his own can deliver him
——myfterious Providence! who can unfold the reafons of
thy procedure, when fuch is the portion of a good man,
who, mild himfelf and amiable, would have given and received peculiar felicity, had be been connected with fome
gentle female?

But let it be remembered, that violence is not neceffary to conftitute ill temper Obftinacy alone will do it.
Let me conjure you, by all that is dear and lovely, to
guard againft that Be affured there is not a man living,
whofe affection it does not chill, let him be otherwife ever
fo warm an admirer There may be thofe who, during
the fhort reign of Beauty, will fupport it. But that being
over, and the fafcination of appetite diffolved, a difputatious, perverfe, and ftubborn female, will always offend,
and, where there is any manhood left, will often provoke
to a dangerous degree In the mean time, every one who
is not in love will be difgufted, nor can any charm of en-
derftanding, or of perfon, compenfate in a woman the
want of foft compliance, and meek fubmiffion Thefe the
men are taught by nature, by education, and by cuftom,
to confider as your duty, and their right neither will they
be eafily brought to difpenfe with it Some of them you
may fubdue, but you can perfuade none of them into a
different fyftem If yet, after all, you will place your
glory in defpotic rule inftead of kind attraction, choofing
rather to tyrannize over daftardly flaves under the form
of hufbands, than to influence thofe hufbands as tender
friends, what can we fay, but that we pity them much
and you more? For the idea of a little paltry power af-

fumed

fumed without title, and exercifed without difcretion, to give up the worthieft triumphs of your fex, how mean and how miferable! "Tell it not in Gath, "publifh it not in the ftreets of Afkelon; left the "daughters of the Philiftines rejoice; left the daugh- "ters of the uncircumcifed triumph."

§

SERMON

SERMON XIV.

ON FEMALE MEEKNESS.

1 PET iii 3, 4

Whose adorning, let it not be that outward adorning of plaiting the hair, and of wearing of gold, or of putting on of apparel but let it be the hidden man of the heart, in that which is not corruptible, even the ornament of a Meek and Quiet Spirit, which is in the sight of God of great price.

As a friend to your sex, I cannot forbear lamenting, that so many of them should lose their consequence, by building it on qualities insufficient to support it Dress and show will never long captivate any but superficial minds The reign of youth and beauty are necessarily short Mere vivacity may amuse in a girl, but in a woman cannot give lasting delight; and trifling accomplishments are all too feeble to fix the heart Yet such things, I am sorry to say it, are the only sources from whence the generality of young women at present seek to derive their power In this pursuit, the unmeaning applause, or momentary admiration of a few, is supposed to found a superior and permanent importance with all What are the effects ? From that moment, female softness is forgotten, christian condescension is held mean, Humility, the parent of almost every excellence, is utterly despised, and hence a perpetual aim at proud dominion, instead of that obsequious majesty ascribed by the poet to innocent Eve—an aim, indeed, frequently thwarted in these her daughters, and, when successful, productive of a triumph always disgusting to us her sons—Hence to an unnatural compound of conceited allurement and affected prudery, in place of those genuine attractions which are attendant on

modesty

modefty and fweetnefs, hence, to fay no more, rivalfhip in figure, and quarrels for conqueft, without end. How often, alas, have we feen thefe things difgrace the fingle ftate! Nor need we wonder, that from habit they are often carried into the conjugal, with this difference, that the folly and prefumption, before diffufed and practifed on all, are now, perhaps, concentered and turned upon the hufband Would you, my dear charge, avoid a conduct fo indecent and unhappy? Would you fecure, in both conditions, an influence equally juft and amiable? To all other virtues and attainments befitting your fex, learn to join Meeknefs Meeknefs is followed with every honour, while fhe arrogates none. Female Meeknefs the better part of mankind have always confpired to crown with never fading wreaths of love and of praife It is thine thou fair form, to command by obeying, and by yielding to conquer In the family of Religion, " many daughters have " done virtuoufly, but thou excelleft them all "

The merits of this moft lovely grace I have engaged to difplay Its importance in the married ftate I mentioned in the clofe of my laft difcourfe Let me prefs that confideration, and then proceed.

In the paffage from which we have taken our text, the apoftle exhorts chriftian women to be in fubjection to their own hufbands, adding as a motive which deferved their regard, " that if any obey not the word, they alfo with- " out the word may be won by the converfation of the " wives, while they behold your chafte converfation cou- " pled with fear ," and fo he goes on to recommend that meek and quiet fpirit, which ought to be their principal ornament With relation to the particular cafe by him fuppofed, his meaning evidently is, that thofe his female difciples might, by a pious and exact deportment, full of fweetnefs and moderation, gain their hufbands over to a

religion

religion which they had not yet embraced, but which they
would be no longer able to refift, when they beheld and
experienced its happy effects on the tempers and manners
of their wives   To every excellent woman, that in this
way has been inftrumental to fave a foul from death, we
may addrefs, though in a lower fenfe, thofe words which
were fpoken by Gabriel to the Virgin Mary on a great occafion, " Hail, thou that art highly favoured, the Lord
" is with thee   bleffed art thou among women."

I cannot do juftice to this part of my argument without
remarking, that there is reafon to fear much of the worthleffnefs of many married men, as well as much of the unhappinefs both of them and their partners, muft be imputed to the Turbulent Paffions or Uncomplying humours
of the latter. Such is the famenefs of the matrimonial
ftate on one hand, fuch its cares on the other, and, it is
but fair to add, fuch the indifpofition of numbers of men
to be long delighted ; that, to preferve the attachment of
a hufband unimpaired, the utmoft attention and the mildeft complacence are commonly requifite on the fide of the
woman

 " E'en in the happieft choice, where fav'ring heav'n
 " Has equal love and eafy fortune giv'n,
 " Think not, the hufband gain'd, that all is done
 " The prize of happinefs muft ftill be won;
 " And oft, the carelefs find it to their coft,
 " The lover in the hufband may be loft ,
 " The GRACES might alone his heart allure ;
 ' Then and the VIRTUES meeting muft fecure 't

I am aftonifhed at the folly of many women, who are
ftill reproaching their hufbands for leaving them alone, for
preferring this or that company to theirs, for treating
them with this and the other mark of difregard or indifference , when, to fpeak the truth, they have themfelves
in a great meafure to blame   Not that I would juftify the
men

men in any thing wrong on their part. But had you behaved to them with a more refpectful obfervance, and a
more equal tendernefs, ftudying their humours, overlooking their miftakes, fubmitting to their opinions, in
matters indifferent, paffing by little inftances of unevenefs,
caprice, or paffion, giving foft anfwers to hafty words,
complaining as feldom as poffible, and making it your
daily care to relieve their anxieties, and prevent their
wifhes, to enliven the hour of dulnefs, and call up the ideas
of felicity· had you purfued this conduct, I doubt not but
you would have maintained and even encreafed their efteem,
fo far as to have fecured every degree of influence that
could conduce to their virtue, or your mutual fatisfaction;
and your houfe might at this day have been the abode of
domeftic blifs.

There may, it is true, be fome hufbands whom no
goodnefs can imprefs. We owned it before; but ftill we
have ground to believe, that of men who would have turned out better, had they met with difcreet and obliging women, multitudes have been loft by the inattention and neglect, as well as not a few by the impertinence and per-
verfenefs of their wives. Little do many of you think how
eafily the heart may be alienated. A generous readinefs to
make every kind allowance for what may be amifs in others,
is perhaps the rareft quality in the world; it is however
one of the moft neceffary, in the feveral connexions of fociety, but efpecially in the neareft of all connexions. And
yet how few hufbands, comparatively fpeaking, have the
good nature to exercife it towards the companions of their
life! How foon after marriage does it often happen, that
every error is magnified into a fault, every fault into a vice,
and often a fingle look is conftrued into I know not what
enormity! One great fource of this mifery is, that moft
men expect too much from the women they marry, expect
to be always received with fmiles, and cherifhed by endearments,

dearments; forgetting that they do not always deserve
them, that those women are like themselves imperfect, that
even the best temper will be hurt by circumstances, and that
the brightest sky cannot for ever remain unclouded But notwithstanding all this, it continues true, that women might
often do much more to please   Their dropping to the husband, as we have frequently seen, those engaging manners
which they practised on the lover, is impiety and distracti-
on at the same instant, as if the solemn vows they made at
the altar were words of course, and their only concern was
to be married, not to be happy, or to gain a heart, not
to keep it   They are apt also to forget in their turn, that
the complacence and obsequiousness of courtship seldom extend into wedlock, that the raptures of a common passion
are necessarily short, that an attachment without tenderness,
or at most an affection without delicacy, is as much as can
be hoped from the ordinary run of husbands, and that to
preserve even this requires both vigilance and gentleness.

But that vigilance which is forced will be frequently sus-
pended, and that gentleness which is put on will always
be precarious   Therefore we wish you to acquire early
the habits of self-controul, and to cultivate from principle a
meek and quiet spirit.   This you will do with success, if
imploring and depending on the grace of God, you make
conscience of curbing betimes the irascible passions of nature,
of submitting calmly to the daily mortifications of life, of
generously yielding to those about you, and particularly of
condescending to persons of low estate

I have never seen a woman eminent for the last of these
qualities, who was not excellent in many other ways Respect to superiors may be enforced by fear, or prompted by
interest, and is therefore no demonstrative proof of a good
heart. But habitual mildness to those of inferior rank, is
one

one of its fureſt indications. That young lady cannot have
a bad mind, who readily enters into the diſtreſſes, and af-
fectionately contributes to the felicity, of thoſe whom Providence has placed beneath her In reality, there is no ſuch
diſcovery of your tempers as your treatment of domeſtics
She is always the worthieſt character who behaves beſt at
home, and is moſt liked by the ſervants. They are the
trueſt judges of a woman's diſpoſitions, becauſe to them diſguiſe is laid aſide, and they fee her in all lights An unaffected propenſion to uſe them well, without partiality
and without caprice, argues a confirmed benevolence.
Thoſe who uſe them otherwiſe, will urge indeed their mercenary ſpirit, their want of gratitude, their want of worth,
and ſuch complaints may in many inſtances be too well
founded But Humanity is noble, and will riſe above little conſiderations; Chriſtianity is divine, and will not be
overcome of evil, but will overcome evil with good. A
faithful ſervant is a treaſure, entitled to every mark of regard, and ſome ſuch there certainly are in this country.
But it muſt be confeſſed, the generality of that claſs are often highly provoking, they are ever ready to corrupt one
another, and there can be little attachment where there is
no principle. Nevertheleſs, I am perſuaded, that treating
them with tenderneſs when ſick, and with gentleneſs at
other times, without making them confidents, would,
joined to a wiſe and pious example, go far to gain and reform many of them At any rate, condeſcenſion and generoſity to thoſe of a lower ſtation, will always give ſatiſ-
faction to the mind in which there is real ſuperiority

Your behaving hanſomely to your friends, and courte-
ouſly to all with whom you converſe, though not ſo certainly characteriſtic of the virtue I paint, will yet be a natural and agreeable effect of it. Meekneſs is like the light,
which ſpreads itſelf every where: though like the light too,
it pleaſes moſt where it is leaſt looked for. To carry on
the

the refemblance ; like that it will be fometimes obfcured, but like that alfo, we cannot bear its being long abfent. Starts of petulance may be forgiven to profperity, fits of fretfulnefs are natural to affliction : but what can be pleaded for harbouring a Paffionate or a Peevifh Temper, eafily provoked and hardly pacified?

When I have feen a woman in a rage, I have always wifhed for a mirror at hand, to fhow her to herfelf. How would fhe have ftarted back from her own image, if not an abfolute Dæmon! To thofe of fuch a ftamp I have nothing to fay but this, that a place awaits them where their rage will have its full fcope for ever. But fome are of a calmer ftrain, four, fplenetic, and fullen; not lefs unchriftian, or lefs unfemale than the others, and on one account much worfe. In thofe the ftorm breaks and clears ; in thefe all is fettled gloom, that admits no funfhine, that prefents no profpect of the chearful kind. For vulgar and unenlightened fpirits, thus continually overcaft, there may be fome excufe, from the want of better inftruction, that might have helped to correct their natural infelicity of temper. But what fhall be faid for habitual rancour, deep refentment, and cool malignity in thofe women who, together with underftandings originally good (for fome fuch there are) have enjoyed the advantages of books and converfation, of elegant breeding and knowledge of the world ? In truth their heads feemed to have ftarved their hearts , and the talents they poffefs ferve only to render them completer fiends.

It is a ftrange miftake of many who think, that provided they do not indulge to one particular paffion, they may give a loofe to all the reft · as if a woman could offend only by incontinence ; or as if her not committing a fin to which perhaps from the coldnefs of her complexion fhe has no propenfity, or from which fhe is reftrained by the dread of
immediate

immediate infamy and ruin, would atone for the commiſſi-
on of others without number ; for vanity and arrogance,
for ſelfiſhneſs and envy, for ſuſpicion and revenge, for unbounded cenſoriouſneſs, or the blackeſt malice.   I am ſufficiently aware that Pride may not comprehend the remark,
and that Uncharitableneſs may not forgive it but no candid hearer will miſtake me when I ſay, that, however ſcan-
dalous and however deſtructive the luſts of the fleſh may
be, thoſe of the mind are yet more heinous, being the
proper and peculiar image of the worſt and wickedeſt
being in the univerſe; in one word, they are infernal.

Our Maſter underſtood the diſtinction well, and was not
afraid to ſhow that he underſtood it.   In the capacity of a
teacher he converſed freely with publicans and ſinners , he
treated them tenderly . he came not, as be himſelf ſaid, "to
"call the righteous but ſinners to repentance" What
gentleneſs did he not diſplay to the poor creature taken in
adultery ! What forgiveneſs of the well-known female pe-
nitent, who but a little before had been plunged in diſ-
order and ſhame ! Such he declared ſhould enter into the
kingdom of heaven more readily than the Scribes and
Phariſees, in ſpite of all their ablutions and prayers, their
frequent faſtings, and ſpecious demeanour ; a proud,
ſelf-juſtifying, and moſt unmerciful ſet of men, whom
he ſcrupled not for theſe reaſons to pronounce "the chil-
"dren of the devil" Let me perſuade you, from the
example of your Saviour, to learn Pity towards ſuch as
have gone aſtray.   How ungracious in women not to ſhow
mercy to women ! Let me prevail with you never to expreſs a ſupercilious contempt, or unforgiving ſeverity, on
the ſubject of thoſe hapleſs beings whoſe miſery pleads for
commiſeration yet louder than their crimes call for cenſure.   Which of you can be ſure that you would not have
yielded to the ſame temptations which overcame them ?
Where

Where are thoſe perfect characters that can anſwer for
their own ſtability? Who made you to differ from the
wretchedeſt of human kind? Believe me, chriſtians, the
moſt genuine virtue is always the moſt humble, and the moſt
charitable ——Merciful heaven, may the beſt gifts of thy
providence, and the ſweeteſt influence of thy grace, deſcend
evermore on that bleſſed eſtabliſhment, which has opened a
ſanctuary for wretched females weary of vice and willing to
reform. May all its benefactors obtain mercy in the day of
the Lord What ſuperior honour does ſuch an eſtabliſhment,
with its ſiſter inſtitution, that happy Aſylum for the help-
leſs young creatures of your ſex who are yet uncorrupted reflect on this nation! They are truly the moſt diſtinguiſh-
ing glory of Britain, the faireſt flowers, if I may ſo ſay, in
all the garland of Engliſh Humanity.

But let me recommend to you Candour with regard to
your ſex in general, as well as compaſſion towards the unhappy part of it. Ah, my fair clients, what ſhall we ſay
in your behalf to thoſe men who are always telling us of
your ill-natured remarks, or illiberal inſinuations to the diſ-
advantage of one another? Such as reſign themſelves
without controul, to this accurſed paſſion, we give up at
once with indignation and abhorrence. Thoſe wilful and
delib rate deſtroyers of reputation are of their " father the
" devil, who was an accuſer and a murderer from the be-
" ginning;' nor, while they do his works will it avail them
aught, though like him you could in other reſpects " tranſ-
form yourſelves into angels of light." No luſtre of beauty,
no brilliancy of underſtanding, can, even among the warmeſt friends of the ſex, make compenſation for the ſpirit of
cenſoriouſneſs in a female. For my own part, I conſider
good nature and candid ſentiments as ſo peculiarly indiſpen-
ſable in every woman, that when I want to eſtimate the
character of any young lady, I take the firſt opportunity
of commending higly ſome perſon of her own ſex, and
                                        about

about her own age, but rather younger, whom fhe knows, and who is defervedly a favourite with the men   If without hefitation, referve, or a fingle But, if with apparent pleafure and cordiality fhe joins in the praife ; I am willing from that moment to form a favourable opinion of her heart   I may be miftaken   it may be all artifice · but for the moft part, I think not   If on the contrary——— But I need not exprefs the reft   Inform us, ye ftudents of human nature, what it is in the female mind that, without the reftraints of fuperior worth, inclines it fo ftrongly to the love of fcandal ? I am difpofed to hope that, befide the competitions formerly explained, it may be often owing to the acrimony produced by difappointment, and often to the habits contracted by affociating with thofe who, having no fund of entertainment in themfelves, are forced to feek it at the expence of others. Be it owing however to what it will, one thing is certain, that a pronefs to indulge it is always deteftable; as, on the other hand, fhe who has the generofity to approve moft, will have always the fatisfaction of being moft approved ; and for the beft of qualities, an amiable temper —No, my fair ones, nothing can make amends for the want of that   It is like wifdom , " It cannot be " valued with the gold of Ophir, with the precious onyx " or the faphire.   The gold and the chryftal cannot equal " it, and the exchange of it fhall not be for jewels " of fine gold   No mention fhall be made of coral or " of pearls · for the price of it is above rubies   The " topaz of Ethiopia fhall not equal it " Preferve it dearly beloved, and cherifh it for ever.

Let " the law of kindnefs" be in your tongue.   " A forward mouth and perverfe lips put far from you."   Guard againft every word, againft every hint that would give pain unnecelfarily to any creature   Beware of miftaking pertnefs for vivacity, or petulance for fpirit.   Tremble at the

thought

thought of facrificing friendfhip to a jeft. Indulge in no
cafe a propenfity to contradiction, or the itch of criticifm.
Be not hafty to draw characters, in general companies efpecially. Whenever you do, be fure to touch on what is
praife-worthy fomething praife-worthy there is in every
character. Over what is culpable throw the veil of charity as often as you can. As well in this as in other refpects,
" charity fhall hide a multitude of fins " When the abfent
are condemned, juftify their conduct, if poffible, extenuate it, if not fome circumftance of extenuation may be
almoft always found If in your judgment of human actions you muft frequently err, let it be ever on the favourable fide, and remember, that one of a noble nature had
much rather be thought humane than witty, fimple than
fevere Show yourfelves pleafed, as often as you really are
fo, and you will feldom fail of pleafing. Join to all the
reft the magnanimity of applauding freely in other women
that beauty, and thofe accomplifhments, which you yourfelves may chance not to poffefs, or to poffefs only in an
inferior degree ——— How lovely and great will you appear
by an unaffected attention to fuch maxims! the fparkling
of wit, or the fplendour of fortune in others, may amufe
and dazzle for a time; but you fhall fecure folid and lafting
efteem Your fociety will be fought, as eafy and fafe,
your friendfhip will be prized as fincere and affectionate,
in your tender bofoms your acquaintance will long to re-
pofe their hearts, and from your fympathetic manner of
entering into their concerns, they will receive confolation

But is there no danger of finking into infipidity, by fuch
a behaviour? Not the leaft, if it be accompanied with thofe
other qualities which women ought to cultivate. And
what fhould hinder the fofteft fpirit of your fex from acquiring, iffhe will, any one virtue or accomplifhment propor-
tionate to her capacity? It is poffible indeed, that fuch a
caft of mind may be attended with lefs refolution in difficulties,

ties, with lefs endurance of affliction, with lefs acutenefs
of wit, or lefs force of underftanding; but by due pains
taken with herfelf, a woman of this fort will, I apprehend,
beyond all others, improve into that form of character
which we would willingly convince you is the moft beautiful
in a female   There are, I will acknowledge, now and
then in fome of a different mould, certain little caprices, or
lively fallies and ftarts of humour, that are not unpleafing
on particular occafions.   But then they require to be bounded by decency, and blended with fenfe; nor muft the
great principles of good affection be ever forgotten.

Amongft the many other advantages refulting from female meeknefs, I muft not omit to mention how much it
will conduce to Perfonal Attraction.   As it commonly implies calm paffions, fo it naturally produces, or happily
promotes, that ferene manner which is always engaging,
(a flutter never is) and which, meeting a fentimental mind
refines very readily into a gracefulnefs of mien, more real
than any that is acquired in gay affemblies, and to an ob-
fervant eye much more alluring.   Imagine a circle of handfome young women, where one is diftinguifhed above the
reft by a flowing yet compofed affability? by a meek look
and modeft carriage, in which there appears no confcioufnefs of beauty, no return upon herfelf, no ftudy to become
the object of the company, no vifible attention to her
drefs or perfon, but a recollected air, and fteady regard to
thofe about her; what fuperior pleafure and refpect will
her prefence neceffarily infpire! Suppofe her, if you will,
entirely filent, from a difpofition to give place to others
who may feem more defirous of talking, will not her very
filence intereft? But when, on finding room left her to fhare
in the difcourfe, fhe delivers herfelf with that fweetnefs of
voice which often accompanies mild affections, expreffing
in gentle unftudied accents fuch fentiments as are worthy
of

of her character; I leave you to guess the effect on every
susceptible by-stander. Alas! my friends, what is all the
momentary lustre you are continually labouring to give
those lips, compared with the permanent beauties of a
lovely mind, breathing from them in agreeable conversation? Let me add, where the grace of meekness has the
soul in full possession, it will be often seen beaming in the
eyes with a bland sensibility, and sporting on the countenance in placid smiles, more soft than the softest glow of
a summer evening, especially, when the mind is at any
time exalted into livelier emotions of benignity and joy.
Or once more let us suppose, that affliction has given to
such a face a cast of solemnity and languor, it will still
retain a kind of sober charm that is inexpressibly affecting
In truth, beauty never touches the heart so deeply, as
when with a sweet unreluctant surrender it seems ready to
faint under the shock of misfortune, or the load of sorrow.
But to proceed.

I would take the liberty to observe, that christian meekness will be of particular use to prevent the Artful Behaviour so frequently complained of in women, and in many
instances so justly   The complaint, I confess, comes
with an ill grace from those men, whose daily study it is, in
one shape or another, to impose on the sex, nor can I
doubt but many of the latter would have more sincerity, if
the others had less design   They probably think themselves
justified in baffling art by art, and from the science of defence and resistance, they are too apt to pass to that of stra-
tagem and attack   It is marvellous indeed to what lengths
many of them carry it, till they become mere compositi-
ons of hypocrisy, where ingenuous feeling is lost, and every
word, look, motion, and minute proceeding, is a lye Whether it be that Nature has given them more subtilty, or
that education has taught them more disguise, or that their
conduct affords them greater leisure to think of such things,
                                        or

or that they are willing to make up in wiles what they want in ſtrength; whether it be owing to one, or to all of theſe cauſes, I know not; but the fact is this, that there are very few men able to contend with a cunning woman in her own way

Nevertheleſs, I muſt inform ſuch diſſemblers, that cunning is not true ability; it is at beſt but left-handed wiſdom; it carries with it an obliquity, and an impotence, that a noble mind will, and that a capable one ought to deſpiſe. I need not ſay, that it is diametrically oppoſite to the ſimplicity of the goſpel, which admits our being " wiſe as ſerpents," only ſo far as is conſiſtent with our being " harm-" leſs as doves." The maxims of a virtuous prudence are comprehenſive, and ſhe who has learnt, with an humble reliance on heaven's direction, to apply them as occaſion requires, will never want the aſſiſtance of artifice. In ſhort, artifice is very often a feeble auxiliary, and almoſt conſtantly betraying thoſe that truſt to it Fond prepoſſeſſion, or unſuſpecting candour, may no doubt be eaſily deceived by female diſguiſe, but it is difficult to act a part long. Diſſimulation will ſometimes let fall the maſk; and he has not the-ſpirit of a man, who does not abhor and ſcorn the detected impoſtor. Mean while, what a laborious taſk is hers! How anxious, ignoble and wretched! From this, my fair diſciples, native goodneſs and chriſtian meekneſs will ſave you By being what you ought to appear, you will be under no temptation of appearing what you are not. An obliging converſation, and ſoft deportment, will proceed from you freely as from a living fountain. Having no bad paſſions to conceal, your thoughts and manners will be tranſparent Truth will be your prompter, while Diſcretion is your guard. In you virtue will wear her mildeſt aſpect, without conſtraint and without ſtudy The baſeneſs and barbarity of inviting and encouraging addreſſes which you mean not in the end to accept, you will avoid

and

and deteſt A proffered heart you will refuſe with civility
and gratitude, where you cannot return your own; or
where you can and ought, you will accept with generoſity
and affeſtion Let me add upon the whole, that as every
mode of diſſimulation is equally injudicious and unbecoming, ſo ſhe will always be the moſt attractive, while ſhe is
the only honourable character, who cultivates genuine worth
inſtead of artificial forms, and practiſes undiſſembled ſweetneſs inſtead of fictitious courteſy.

Such a one was Iſabella, the darling all who knew her.
It is true, ſhe lived where virtue was not eclipſed by fortune, and where depravity of manners did not prevent the
admiration of excellence. Her mind was very early accompliſhed, it was that of a woman, when ſhe was yet but
a child It ſhone in her face with a generous warmth,
and at the ſame time a calm intelligence, ſeldom ſeen in a
countenance ſo young; it produced in her whole deportment a mixture of ſoftneſs and dignity; which ſhe alone
did not perceive In company, the merits of others, not
her own, engaged all her attention. She was never pert.
Her diffidence kept her too frequently ſilent; when ſhe
ſpoke, it was with ſweet ſimplicity and ſmiling reſpeſt.
Her voice was melody itſelf, without that frivolous whine
which is often occaſioned by diſſembling, and often by af
feſtation Amongſt her intimate companions ſhe wa
ſprightly and playful: for then ſhe felt the enthuſiaſm o
friendſhip Her pen flowed in a ſtream of ſentiment alike
tender and exalted; it was the interpreter of the heart.
Every duty becoming her ſtation, and conſiſtent with her
years, ſhe fulfilled from inſtinct ſanctified by piety; a piety, in which meekneſs ſtill preſided Heaven beheld ſo
gentle a ſpirit with complacence, and took her away from
the evil to come, took her to itſelf, in all the purity of un-
tainted virtue She was ſeized on a ſudden · I then ſaw
her ſhe was no way alarmed. Young and beautiful,
admired

admired and happy, ſhe ſurrendered her ſoul with a placid
reſignation, ſhe ſmiled in her laſt moments, the ſmile
remained on her clay-cold viſage for ſome time after the
informing mind was fled   She was lovely and pleaſant in
her life, and in her death an object of univerſal and affectionate lamentation   Her little ſtory furniſhes a proof, that
ſentiment and meekneſs conjoined, are ſuperior to all other
allurements; and that diſpoſitions at once mild and virtuous require neither diſguiſe nor heightening.

I preſume you know, that the language of inſpiration
repreſents the internal character under the notion of a perſon or living form.   Which it ſtyles the Old or the New
Man, according as the principles of ſin or of holineſs have
the aſcendant.   By the ſame figure of ſpeech, the inward
graces and decorations of a chriſtian are here termed " the
" hidden man of the heart, in that which is not corrupti-
" ble," to contraſt them with that corporeal beauty and
thoſe external embelliſhments, which are immediately
palpable to the ſenſes, and like them ſubject to decay and
corruption.   Thus it is that St Peter would call off your
too anxious attention from inferior, outſide, and ſhort-
lived attractions, whether original or aſſumed, to ſuch as
are of ſupreme value, being in their nature ſpiritual and
immortal.   Nor does he ſimply reſt there, but farther re-
commends the latter as highly Acceptable to your Maker,
" even the ornament of a meek and quiet ſpirit, which is
" in the ſight of God of great price."

Such a ſpirit, indeed, bears a near reſemblance to his
own moſt merciful and bleſſed attributes, to his well beloved Son, and our divinely benevolent Saviour, to thoſe
good and happy creatures that conſtitute the angelic world,
and to all the excellent ones of human kind, both on earth
and in heaven, that belongs to the ſame great family of
love.   Such a ſpirit proceeds directly from the common

T   parent,

parent, and cannot but be pleafing to its author   What
fays St James? " The wifdom that is from above is firft
" pure, then peaceable, gentle, and eafy to be intreated,
" full of mercy and good fruits "   Such is the temper of
chriftianity, and fuch are its effects

To cherifh them in yourfelves let all the preceding
confiderations incite you; but above them all, be engaged by the divine ambition of being approved by the fovereign Judge and rewarder of excellence.   What can be
added to fuch an argument; or what can we offer upon it,
that will be any way anfwerable to its dignity? To appear
beautiful in the eye of God, to be beloved by the monarch
of the univerfe, to be admitted, if I may ufe the phrafe,
as fo many fair and fhining pillars into his temple below,
while he contemplates each with a pleafing afpect, and
purpofes to remove them in due time to his fanctuary on
high, where they fhall remain his everlafting delight, as
well as the never ceafing admiration of furrounding cheru-
bim:—great Creator, what can equal fuch exaltation and
felicity? and can any of you, my hearers, be fo deftitute
of every noble fentiment as not to afpire after privileges
like thefe? Unmoved by fuch ideas, can you turn away
with patience, and run to fcenes of drefs and fhow with
like inglorious paffions as before; preferring to the approbation of the Eternal the flighteft regards from the fillieft
mortals? Go, thou fenfelefs creature, and boaft of being
admired by the butterflies of the day. See what they will
do for thee, when he whofe favour thou neglecteft, and
for fuch things, fhall caufe thy " beauty to confume like
" a moth," and thy heart to fink within thee like a ftone
Imagination fhudders at the thought of that day, when thou
fhalt enter trembling, forfaken, and forlorn, thofe difmal
regions which the voice of adulation cannot reach, where
nothing fhall be heard but founds of reproach, and blafphe-
my and woe, where ftript of every ornament that now
                                                      decks

decks thy body, and ſtript of that body itſelf, thy mind
muſt appear without ſhelter or covering, all deformed and
ghaſtly, mangled with the wounds of deſpairing guilt, and
diſtorted by the violence of envenomed paſſions, while de-
mons ſhall mock at thy miſtery   Save us, almighty Redeemer, ſave theſe young people from a doom ſo dreadful!

Would you concur to prevent it ? Begin with reſtraining
the love of ornament, or rather, turn that dangerous affection into a higher channel, and let it flow   it will then
become ſafe, uſeful, noble   Here you will have ſcope
for the largeſt fancy   To the adorning of your characters
we wiſh you to ſet no bounds   In dreſſing the ſoul for company of ſaints, of angels, of God himſelf, you cannot employ too much time or thought   In ſtudying and cultivating " the hidden man of the heart," you will every day
diſcover new charms, that will improve with age, bloom
in ſickneſs, live in death, ſurvive the deſolation of the
grave, aſcend triumphant to the world of perfect beauty,
and continue to brighten under the ſmile of heaven for
ever. In a word, all the beſt beings in the creation, together with the Creator himſelf, concur in loving and ho-
nouring a beauteous mind

Nor is this a diſtinction, for which you muſt contend
with too many competitors   Carry the paſſion for dreſs almoſt ever ſo high, you will ſtill have the mortification to
find ſome one or other outſhine you in taſte, or in magnificence ; but the palm of wiſdom you may bear away from
the greater part unenvied, if you will only allow them the
ſuperiority of faſhion   Oh! that I knew how to awaken
on this ſubject the ſpirit of ambition in thoſe who are ſo
prone to indulge it on a thouſand others Happy preacher,
couldſt thou behold thy hearers filled with emulation to ex-

cel

cel one another, in all the modeſt graces and mild accompliſhments that can adorn their ſex! Happy Britain, were
this the era, in which religion, with her whole train of
Virtues, might riſe into repute amongſt thy children; in
which thy ſons might be " as plants grown up in their
" youth," and thy " daughters as corner-ſtones poliſhed
" after the ſimilitudes of a palace!"

CONCLUSION

CONCLUSION

THE preacher can readily suppose, that many things advanced on the subject of Women in the course of these Sermons, will be deemed by the generality of his own sex too soothing, while by the majority of yours many will be judged too severe, such is the force of prejudice on both sides. That he himself is quite impartial, it is impossible for him to be certain. He can only say, that he has honestly endeavoured, according to the best of his capacity, to hold the balance even. Throughout the whole, he had but one single point to study; which was, to advance what he believed to be true, and what he hoped at the same time might be useful. He knew, and considered, that he is accountable at a higher tribunal than any upon earth. If he has wished to please, it was from a solicitude "for your good to edification." If he has happened to offend, it was without malignity or design. He should be sorry to be counted your enemy, for telling you the truth. But his concern in that case would be for you, not for himself; he is ambitious of your approbation, but he is much more so for his own.

His happiest days having been chiefly past in the conversation of women of worth and understanding, it is certain, that for such he has entertained a peculiar esteem. He pretends not indeed, that even amongst them he has found any jewel without a flaw. But notwithstanding their imperfections, justice exacts from him this testimony, that when they have in any tolerable degree approached to the standard of what we have so often styled Female excellence, they have appeared to him, with a few exceptions in favour of the other sex, by far the devoutest worshippers, the

warmest

warmeſt friends, and the moſt ſentimental as well as entertaining companions What he has principally to lament
is his meeting with ſo ſmall a number, who have had elevation enough to practiſe an entire ſimplicity of manners,
ſenſe enough wholly to forget their perſons in the company
of men, and meeknefs enough to be quite content when
not the objects of immediate attention

If the preacher has endeavoured upon the principles of
candour, to account for ſome paſſions in the ſex that ſeem
at firſt ſight leſs innocent, or leſs excuſable, it was under
the ſanction and impreſſion of that great evangelical law,
" Judge not, that ye be not judged For with what judg-
" ment ye judge, ye ſhall be judged, and with what mea-
" ſure ye mete, it ſhall be meaſured to you again" If
he has addreſſed thoſe young perſons who formed his audience, in a ſtyle of peculiar tenderneſs, the reaſon, in plain
terms, was becauſe he felt it, nor does he think, that either as a man, or as a preacher, he ought to ſuppreſs, if
he could, an affection which nature has implanted, and
which, kept within proper bounds, Religion does not prohibit

If he has attempted to inſinuate inſtruction under the
ſmiles of complacence, or to enforce admonition with the
fervours of friendſhip, ſay, ye cenſors of the age, is he
really to blame? Is an auſtere countenance the proper
face of zeal, or a diſtant formality the genuine mark of holineſs? To diſguſt by rudeneſs, or to diſcourage by rigour
——is that the way to win ſouls? Was it the way of the
Apoſtles, or of their Maſter? Merciful Saviour! what
words can paint thy benignity, into whoſe lips grace was
poured, who didſt " not break the bruiſed reed, nor quench
' the ſmoaking flax," whoſe character was like that of
thy Father, love? I touched before on the ſpirit that
breathed in his teaching, let me juſt add here that his pa-
rables,

rables, which made fo great a part of it, were pointed to
the imagination no lefs than to the heart, prefenting the
ftrongeft pictures of life and nature, at the fame time that
by thefe very means they impreffed the nobleft leffons of
piety and truth. To fpeak in general, will any one fay,
that the feverity of cenfure muft never be foftened, nor
the awfulnefs of folemnity tempered, not even when the
preacher has the Youthful and the Gay for his hearers?
Thofe furely are ftrangers to true Wifdom who fuppofe
her monitions incompatible with chearful images or joyful ideas, furely thofe are unacquainted with the human
mind, who hope to reform its errors without conciliating
its affections, or think tnat the tutoring of terror alone
will produce the love of goodnefs.

In fome fentiments which I have offered to your confideration, I fhould not be furprifed if I have been taxed
with idle refinement. We live in an age when whatever
is held by the Few moft folid and valuable, is by the Many
derided as vifionary, or decried as infignificant In the
prefent age an accomplifhed female is apt to be fhunned
under the notion of a Learned Lady, and the Virtuous
Woman of the Proverbs would be in danger of being ridiculed as a compofition of affectation. In this age the fubject of drefs and ornament, I am ready to acknowledge, is
better underftood than formerly, but in thefe how often
are modefty, frugality, and fimple elegance, given up to
levity or fafhion, to vain competition or miftaken appearance! In this age the ftrictnefs of female decorum, and
the retirings of female referve, muft expect to be conftrued
into ignorance of the world, if not into hypocritical airs of
female fanctity In this polite age, I had almoft afked,
where is the man that believes any woman to be modeft
at heart, and where is the woman that dares to be fuperior to the follies of her fex? A paffion exalted by generofity, and refined by fentiment, in which the man, not the

equipage

equipage, was regarded, in which the highest gratifications
of sense were the lowest objects of affection—such a passion
is now considered by the generality as romance. Such lovers might exist in the days of old, or possibly may be yet
found in the obscurity of retreat, but in the gay world,
where all is tainted with sensuality, and sacrificed to show,
they would appear too ungenteel to be respectable, and
too insipid to be happy Here, alas, how few have the
fortitude to live to their own hearts, the worth to cultivate
the joys of friendship, or the soul to seek conjugal felicity
in conjugal esteem! Amidst the hurry and dissipation of
diversions, the profligacy or insignificance of play, the futility or frivolousness of formal visiting, what regard or
what room is left for self-possession or mutual confidence,
for rational conversation or improving study, for the pleasing cares of a family, or that amiable mixture of minds
without which social life is modish disguise or mean indulgence? Is it necessary to add, how scanty a portion of time
is now given to private devotion, how little the sabbath is
made a day of rest from the toil of pleasure, or the tumult
of passion, and to what banter from the licentious of both
sexes she is exposed, who would fill up the duties of that
day with seriousness, reverence, and constancy? Let me
only subjoin, that the modes of breeding now established
for young women are such, that composure and softness are
hardly deemed consistent, that a demeanour perfectly attentive is in hazard of passing for want of vivacity, and a
temper thoroughly meek for want of spirit

But what are you to infer from all this? "That you must
"follow a multitude to do evil," or relinquish Wisdom,
because she is renounced by fools? No She still continues
to be " justified of her children;" and be assured, my dear
auditory, that those very fools shall be forced one day to
acknowledge her worth A few short years rolled away
and this gaudy scene will disappear Where are now many
                                                          of

of the miferable flutterers, that we have feen fret their
hour on the ftage of Vanity? Doctrine like this They too
once defpifed as idle refinement, or difrelifhed as naufeous
dulnefs. Do ye imagine they are of the fame mind ftill?
How, think ye, will it appear to yourfelves in the decrepi-
tude of age, and on the bed of death? By what ftandard
fhall you then wifh to have regulated yourfelves; by that
of reafonable women and virtuous believers, or by the
manners and maxims of a diftracted and degenerate age?

Againft the latter let me warn you, by every thing that
is prudent and good, by all that can promote the importance of your fex, the reformation of ours, and the happinefs of both; let me warn you, in the name of your
country, in the name of your pofterity, in the name of
God! Suffer not Folly to deceive or Flattery to abufe you.
The time cannot be very diftant, at which beauty fhall
fade as a flower, by the courfe of nature; the period may
be near at hand, when it fhall fhrink at once, under the
violence of difeafe. However you may try to forget it,
life is all uncertain and when thofe eyes, now full of lucid
fpirit, fhall fink in darknefs, when that complexion, now
bright and blooming, fhall die away into a livid hue, and
men fhall turn with horror from thofe features which they
behold at prefent with delight, what will the world avail
you, or the world's applaufe? Death, my dear hearers,
Death is no courtier, he will fhow you to yourfelves as
you really are, divefted of every external decoration and
fkin-deep allurement. If deftitute of mental acquifitions
and moral graces, the unfading luftre of an enlightened
foul, " the hidden and incorruptible man of the heart,"
what will it avail you that you are now fair and flattered?
The reputation of wit, the popularity of politenefs, the
profeffion of piety itfelf, will in that conjuncture be alike
ineffectual. It is only the retrofpect of capacity well employed, the confcioufnefs of benevolence worthily exerted,

ted, and the principles of faith and hope poffeffing the mind that will then fupport and gladden it,

Where there is nothing but a picture of virtue, or a few fhadowy qualities that may fubfift without any real excellence, death will hide them for ever in the night of defpair The blackness of darkness will clofe upon the naked and wandering ghoft, while its loathfome remains are configned to oblivion and putrefaction in the prifon of the grave, with the profpects of a worfe doom hereafter But where there is a living image of true goodnefs begun in this ftate, death will deliver it with fafety into the finifhing hand of Eternity, to be produced with every mark of honour in the open view of heaven, where its now mortal partner, refcued from the difhonours of the duft, and brightened into the graces of eternal youth, fhall rejoin it in triumph to fuffer the pang of feparation no more —Everlafting Jehovah, what a crown of joy will it confer upon the preacher in that day, fhould this little fervice be rewarded with the reflexion of having contributed to the falvation or improvement of any of thefe young perfons whom he now addreffes ! If ever thine ear was open to my cry, hear me, O Lord, hear me, in their behalf. What cannot thy fpirit perform, perform by the weakeft hand? May that fpirit " feal them unto the day of redemption !"——At that glorious period may I meet you all amongft " the redeemed of the Lord ," happy to fee you fhining with immortal fplendor, in " the " general affembly and church of the firft-born," tranfported to think, that I fhall live with you for ever, and joining in the gratulations of your fellow angels round the throne of God, when he fhall in the fight of all " clothe you " with the garments of falvation, and cover you with the " robe of righteoufnefs, as a bridegroom is decked with " ornaments, and as a bride is adorned with her jewel. " Amen

 F I N I S

Printed in the USA
CPSIA information can be obtained
at www.ICGtesting.com
LVHW012350051023
759999LV00005B/387